Educating Nurses for Leadership

Harriet R. Feldman, PhD, RN, FAAN, is dean and professor at the Lienhard School of Nursing and co-chair of the Institutional Review Board at Pace University. She is editor of the journal *Nursing Leadership Forum.* Dr. Feldman has authored more than 60 articles, book chapters, and editorials, and is coauthor of *Nurses in the Political Arena: The Public Face of Nursing.* She is editor of *Strategies for Nursing Leadership; Nursing Leaders Speak Out: Issues and Opinions;* and *The Nursing Shortage: Strategies for Recruitment and Retention in Clinical Practice and Education.* She has served in leadership roles in a number of professional organizations, including the New York State Nurses Association, the American Association of Colleges of Nursing, Sigma Theta Tau International, and Nurses Educational Fund, and on the board of the Commission on Collegiate Nursing Education and the New York State Board for Nursing.

Martha J. Greenberg, PhD, RN, is an associate professor at the Lienhard School of Nursing at Pace University. She has served in leadership roles as chairperson of the 4-year Baccalaureate Nursing Program from 1995 to 2000, as a member of the NCLEX-RN Success Team of Lienhard, and as faculty advisor to the Student Nurses at Pace (SNAP) organization. She teaches didactic and clinical nursing leadership and alternative theories management courses in the 4-year Baccalaureate and Combined Degree (BSN/MS) nursing programs, and maintains a clinical practice. Her areas of research interest are humor and complementary health and healing. Dr. Greenberg serves on a variety of community boards and task forces in Westchester County, New York.

Educating Nurses for Leadership

Harriet R. Feldman, PhD, RN, FAAN
Martha J. Greenberg, PhD, RN
Editors

 Springer Publishing Company

Springer Publishing Company, Inc.
11 West 42nd Street
New York, NY 10036-8002

Acquisitions Editor: Ruth Chasek
Production Editor: Sally Ahearn
Cover design by Joanne Honigman

05 06 07 08 09 / 5 4 3 2 1

Library of Congress Publication Data

Educating nurses for leadership / [edited by] Harriet R. Feldman,
   Martha J. Greenberg.
      p. ; cm.
   Includes bibliographical references.
   ISBN 0-8261-2664-2
   1. Nursing services—Administration—Study and teaching.
   2. Nurse administrators—Education. 3. Leadership. [DNLM:
   1. Education, Nursing—methods. 2. Leadership. 3. Models,
   Educational. 4. Models, Nursing. 5. Teaching—methods WY
   18 E236 2005] I. Feldman, Harriet R. II. Greenberg, Martha J.
RT89.E34   2005
362.17'3'068—dc22   2004027279

Printed in the United States of America by IBT Global.

Contents

Part III: Leadership Education in the Clinical Setting

Contributors

Jane Aroian, EdD, RN
Associate Professor
Northeastern University, Bouvè
    College of Health Sciences,
    School of Nursing
Boston, MA

Julia W. Aucoin, DNS, RN, BC
Assistant Professor
University of North Carolina at
    Greensboro
Greensboro, NC

Sandra Bunkers, PhD, RN, FAAN
Associate Professor
Marquette University College of
    Nursing
Milwaukee, WI

Laura D'Alisera, MPA
Associate Director, Institute of
    Government
University of North Florida
Jacksonville, FL

**Jacqueline A. Dienemann, PhD,
    RN, CNAA, FAAN**
Visiting Professor and Interim
    Chair, Adult Health Nursing

University of North Carolina,
    Charlotte
Charlotte, NC

**Lesley Downes, BS (Hons), Dip
    HE, RGN**
Associate Director of Nursing
University Hospital of North
    Staffordshire
Staffordshire, England

Joellen B. Edwards, PhD, RN
Dean and Professor
East Tennessee State University,
    College of Nursing
Johnson City, TN

**Patricia A. Edwards, EdD, RN,
    CNAA**
Director of Nursing Research
Excelsior College
Albany, NY

Betsy Frank, PhD, RN
Professor
Indiana State University School of
    Nursing
Terre Haute, IN

John W. Frank, EdD
Executive Consultant
  DiaComVentures
Jacksonville, FL

Deborah R. Garrison, PhD, RN
Associate Professor and Chair of
  the School of Nursing
John and Nevils Wilson School of
  Nursing at Midwestern State
  University
Wichita Falls, TX

Nelda S. Godfrey, PhD, RN, CS
Associate Professor and Chairperson
William Jewell College,
  Department of Nursing
Liberty, MO

**Helen Green, MEd, DMS, BS
  (Hons), RGN, Cert Ed**
Assistant Director of Nursing
University Hospital of North
  Staffordshire
Staffordshire, England

Sheila Grossman, PhD, APRN, BC
Professor
Fairfield University School of
  Nursing
Fairfield, CT

Patricia M. Haynor, DNSc, RN
Associate Professor
Villanova University, College of
  Nursing
Villanova, PA

Jewett G. Johnson, RN, MS
Assistant Professor
John and Nevils Wilson School of
  Nursing at Midwestern State
  University
Wichita Falls, TX

Janice M. Jones, PhD, RN, CS
Clinical Associate Professor
University at Buffalo, State
  University of New York, School
  of Nursing
Buffalo, NY

Judith A. Lemire, RN, DNsc, CNAA
Associate Professor
Purdue University-Fort Wayne
  Campus
Fort Wayne, IN

Susan Letvak, PhD, RN
Assistant Professor
University of North Carolina at
  Greensboro
Greensboro, NC

**Sandra B. Lewenson, EdD, RN,
  FAAN**
Professor and Associate Dean
Pace University, Lienhard School
  of Nursing
Pleasantville, NY

Debra A. Morgan, RN, MSN, EdD
Assistant Professor
John and Nevils Wilson School of
  Nursing at Midwestern State
  University
Wichita Falls, TX

Margaret M. Patton, MEd, MSN
Lecturer
University of North Carolina,
  Charlotte
Charlotte, NC

Sandra L. Ramey, PhD, RN
Assistant Professor
Marquette University College of
  Nursing
Milwaukee, WI

Deborah A. Rastinehad, PhD, RN, CWCN, COCN
Graduate Nursing Faculty
Excelsior College
Albany, NY

Jane Romm, BA
Blind Brook Middle School
Fiber Artist/Home and Careers
  Teacher
Rye Brook, NY

Kay Sackett, EdD, RN
Assistant Clinical Professor
University at Buffalo, State
  University of New York
Buffalo, NY

Paula Scharf, PhD, RN
Associate Professor
Pace University, Lienhard School
  of Nursing
Pleasantville, NY

Mary S. Tilbury, EdD, RN, CNAA, BC
Assistant Professor
University of Maryland, School of
  Nursing
Baltimore, MD

Lucy B. Trice, PhD, ARNP, BC
Associate Dean
University of North Florida,
  College of Health
Jacksonville, FL

Connie Vance, EdD, RN, FAAN
Professor
College of New Rochelle
New Rochelle, NY

Joy E. Wachs, PhD, APRN, BC, FAAOHN
Professor
East Tennessee State University
Johnson City, TN

Linda D. Wagner, EdD, RN
Associate Professor
Southern Connecticut State
  University
New Haven, CT

Angela Northrup Wantroba, BS, RN
Staff Nurse
Memorial Sloan-Kettering Cancer
  Center
New York, NY

Sharon M. Weinstein, MS, CRNI, FAAN
President, Global Education
  Development Institute
President, Core Consulting Group
  LLC
Lake Forest, IL

Bev Williams, PhD, RN
Assistant Professor, Faculty of
  Nursing
University of Alberta
Edmonton, Canada

Connie Wilson, EdD, RN
Associate Professor
University of Indianapolis
Indianapolis, IN

Preface

The need for effective leadership is critical. "Nothing is more important perhaps than preparing future leaders. They are our hope—hope for our profession, hope for health care, hope for our nation" (Feldman, 2002). All nurses are leaders. Nurses lead patients, families, groups, communities, committees, organizations—all highly challenging and demanding in our complex health care environment. Although there seems little time for leadership development, essential leadership skills are in great demand.

The Leadership Education Model (LEM), the outgrowth of a 2-year grant from the Helene Fuld Health Trust, was developed by six nurse educators who saw the importance of bringing focus to developing leaders. Key components of the LEM are (a) integration for application of leadership knowledge and skills; (b) progressive learning to higher level modeling and decision making; (c) the evolving nature of leadership learning; and (d) general systems theory as a conceptual framework. Part I of *Educating for Leadership* describes the LEM and details the six modules that have been developed; that is, leader as achiever, communicator, critical thinker, expert, mentor, and visionary. The model and six modules were first published in 2002 as an issue of the journal, *Nursing Leadership Forum*.

Parts II and III are the result of a call for strategies used to teach nursing students and those in clinical practice how to lead. Some of the strategies relate directly to the LEM, for example, chapter 22, and the remainder represents strategies grounded not only in theories and models, but also in ingenuity, invention, and creativity. Part II specifically identifies strategies with an academic focus, for example, classroom and related course exercises. Part III describes strategies with a clinical focus, including clinical experiences that are part of nursing education programs and some for nurses working in practice settings.

Searching the literature in preparation for this book, we were struck by the absence of references in nursing that solely addressed the preparation of future leaders. The annotated bibliography at the conclusion of the book describes a number of articles on leadership development strategies, but this is the only text of its kind that provides strategies that educators, clinicians, and administrators alike can use for leadership development. We are in an information age that requires our attention and understanding, and our ability to demonstrate leadership behaviors to navigate diversity and chaos. Furthermore, the environments where nurses work demand that they have well-defined leadership roles, are self-directed, self-reflecting, and internally motivated, think critically, multitask effectively, and have excellent interpersonal skills. *Educating for Leadership* provides tools to prepare nurses to be effective leaders so that they may advance practice and the profession.

We hope that you find the book useful as teachers and learners.

HARRIET R. FELDMAN AND MARTHA J. GREENBERG
EDITORS

Feldman, H. R. (2002). Preparing future leaders. *Nursing Leadership Forum, 7,* 46.

Acknowledgments

We would like to thank Springer Publishing Company for seeing and responding to the need for the publication of this seminal text. We strongly believe that *Educating Nurses for Leadership* fills a void not previously addressed in nursing education, administration and practice. Our sincerest appreciation goes out to our many contributing chapter authors, whose expertise, creativity, dedication, and hard work make this a worthy text. We would also like to acknowledge the many outstanding leaders in our professional and personal lives who have inspired, guided and mentored us, as well as our colleagues and our students who have supported our learning about how to educate and lead the next generation of nurses. Last, we would like to acknowledge our families, whose love, patience, and support mean so much for us. They have played a significant role, as well, in our development as leaders.

PART ONE

A Model for Educating Future Leaders

CHAPTER ONE

Preparing Nurse Leaders: A Leadership Education Model

Judith A. Lemire

Nursing continues to struggle with the development of the leadership knowledge, skills, and attributes that will contribute to the stability, growth, and effectiveness of the profession. With the role of all nurses expanding, and the potential impact of the advanced practice role on the delivery of health care, it seems imperative that nurses at all levels acquire the leadership skills necessary to influence this dynamic and uncertain environment (Ferguson, 1998). Considering the powerful relationship between leadership and influence, leadership development should be a priority for the profession.

To enhance leadership development efforts, a first step would be to focus on redefining the traditional caregiver role to include critical thinking, leadership attributes, and professional expertise. The major responsibility for leadership development lies within nursing education. A well-defined leadership profile could help to advance this shift to endure through a tumultuous health care future. Further, the profile could provide the framework for a leadership education model to guide the learning process.

The Helene Fuld Health Trust funded the study to strengthen the leadership capabilities of nurses through the integration of a leadership education model into the curriculum of RN to BSN and graduate

Editor's Note: This article was originally printed in *Nursing Leadership Forum, 6*(2).

nursing programs. A national Task Force of six nurse educators with leadership expertise developed a data-based leadership education model. The model was designed to assist faculty to integrate leadership constructs into the curriculum. This article presents the descriptive study that identified leadership skills and knowledge and the subsequent development of the leadership education model (LEM).

There is uncertainty within the nursing profession as to not only what leadership is but what knowledge and skills are necessary for nursing to influence health care (Antrobus, 1997; Wilson & Porter-O'Grady, 1999; Wright, 1996). Leadership behaviors have not been adequately developed because undergraduate educational programs have not emphasized leadership skill development. This is particularly evident in associate degree graduates whose programs, bulging with curricula, have created a large population of nurses with very little, if any, leadership learning.

In reviewing the Health Care Forum study of leadership practices and values in health service organizations, Shortell and Kaluzny (1997) found a significant disparity between current competencies and values and those required to effectively lead in today's health care organizations. This disparity may have been fostered by inadequate, traditional methods for teaching leadership (Washburn, 1998; Wilson & Porter-O'Grady, 1999; Wright, 1996) that have included outdated knowledge concerning what constitutes a leader and lack of a well-defined practicum. An innovative leadership education model is crucial in guiding the development of a progressive and innovative leadership curriculum that will facilitate the acquisition of new leadership behaviors within the profession.

When designing an effective model for leadership development one should avoid treating only the symptoms of inadequate leadership, designing quick fixes, and promoting a few strong leaders in a few high profile roles. Instead, a model should focus on continuous learning associated with leadership development and an integrated and progressive learning and teaching process.

REVIEW OF THE LITERATURE

Leadership is a widely researched and explored construct with thousands of books and articles having appeared in the literature over the last 25 years. The aspects of leadership addressed in the literature are so varied that a comparison of results is often difficult, and conclusions, therefore, are inconsistent. Much of the literature rehashes leadership issues with little progress toward developing a model for education and development. In over half of the articles reviewed for the study, a specific definition of leadership was not presented. Those that defined leadership offered assorted definitions that most often addressed leadership skills, knowledge, and behaviors. Wilson and Porter-O'Grady (1999) offer a visionary and practical definition of the role of leadership pertinent to nursing as "to facilitate, integrate, and coordinate the complex structures and processes necessary for progress" (p. xiii). There is substantial agreement, however, on the fact that traditional leadership beliefs, practices, education, skills, and behaviors are inadequate for success in today's complex environments (Aroian, Meservey, & Crockett, 1996; Ashby, 1999; Barker, 1997; Wilson & Porter-O'Grady, 1999; Wright, 1996). Not surprising is the consensus on the need for redefining effective leadership attributes and functions as well as education about and development of leadership skills and behaviors. Although a complete review of the leadership literature is beyond the scope of this article, the support for academic and experiential leadership learning that evolves from a data-based leadership education model is abundant in the literature. Leadership development continues to be a complicated process that occurs over time and in different settings.

Although nurses agree that effective leadership is crucial to the advancement of nursing practice, many believe that the state of leadership in nursing is so poor that immediate attention is needed (American -Association of Colleges of Nursing, 1996; Andrews-Evans, 1997; Antrobus, 1997; Corcoran, 1999). Leadership development with the associated skills and behaviors is important at all levels of the organization, which creates a need for leadership education for nurses in all roles and at all levels (Fralic, 1999; Grossman & Valiga, 2000; Krejci & Malin, 1997; Tilbury, 1998). Recognizing this need, there is increased support for some of this learning to occur in the classroom and to develop data-based leadership education models (Fralic, 1999; Schwartz, Axtman, & Freeman, 1998; Washbush, 1998; Wilson & Porter-O'Grady, 1999).

Some of this discussion focuses on process and content learning using varied teaching methodologies, calling for an integrated approach in both the classroom and the health care setting with an emphasis on experiential learning in a practicum or clinical setting

(Aroian, Meservey, & Crockett, 1996; Collins, 2000; Fritz & Brown, 1998). The application of leadership learning is enhanced through case method, using real life case studies in the classroom and clinical settings (Ashby, 1999; Wilson & Porter-O'Grady, 1999). This complex and progressive learning is a continuous process that occurs throughout one's career (Aroian, Meservey, & Crockett, 1996; Grossman & Valiga, 2000; Wilson & Porter-O'Grady, 1999).

INSTRUMENT DEVELOPMENT AND SURVEY ANALYSIS

A national survey was conducted to determine consensus on the most important leadership attributes in a leadership education model for nursing education. This process began with the development of a questionnaire comprised of 31 items denoting leadership constructs. After a review of the literature the items were identified by the six-member Task Force with the following members: Judith A. Lemire, DNSc, RN, CNAA; Jane Aroian, EdD, RN; Jacqueline Dienemann, PhD, RN, CNAA, FAAN; Patricia Haynor, DNSc, RN; Connie Vance, EdD, RN, FAAN; and Betsy Frank, PhD, RN. The objective of the survey was to determine if the identified knowledge and skill constructs of leadership development would be perceived as important to those sampled. A descriptive survey was mailed to nurse administrators, nurse educators, and nursing students. The Leadership Education Model Needs Assessment (LEMNA) was designed with three sections. The first section contained nine leadership principle and development items; the second section contained nine basic leadership knowledge and skill items; and the third section contained 13 advanced leadership knowledge and skill items, for a total of 31 items.

Each item was categorized according to similarity into one of six modules in preparation for model development. The seven leadership constructs labeled as modules were chosen by the Task Force for their close association and similar description with three or more of the 31 knowledge, skills, and attribute items. The modules are leader as communicator (6 items), leader as visionary (7 items), leader as achiever (3 items), leader as critical thinker (4 items), leader as expert (5 items), and leader as mentor (6 items). The items on the LEMNA were rated on a 4-point Likert Scale with the indicators:

1. Very important,
2. Important,
3. Somewhat important, and
4. Not important.

There was also a "not applicable" option. Cronbach's alpha coefficient was used to calculate internal consistency. The alpha coefficient for the LEMNA is very strong at .8840. With the exception of leader as expert at .6147, the alpha coefficients for the individual subscales (modules) were also strong, with communicator .7204, visionary .6978, achiever .7177, critical thinker .7691, and mentor .7288.

The LEMNA was sent to 1,371 members of the American Organization of Nurse Executives (n = 1000), the Council of Graduate Education for Administration in Nursing (n = 124), and students who were currently enrolled in RN to BSN and graduate programs in nursing (n = 247). Participants were asked to rate the importance of each item according to their perception of leadership development. The questionnaire was completed by 521 registered nurses (return rate of 38%). Respondents self-selected their present roles as faculty, nursing administrator/manager, staff educator, student or other. Since only five selected staff educator as their role, this category was collapsed into the category of Other with the following results: nurse administrator/manager 270 (51.8%), RN to BSN and graduate student 98 (18.8%), faculty 87 (16.7%), and other 66 (12.7%). Six nurse executives did not see themselves as nurse administrators/managers and self-selected themselves to the category of "other."

A comparison of group means, standard deviations, and minimum and maximum scores for the 31-item questionnaire is presented for the entire sample and the four subgroups (Table 1.1). These computations show a high level of agreement on the importance of the 31 items as well as a high level of consistency for this agreement between the groups. The same statistics are provided (Table 1.2) for the total sample and the six leadership modules (subscales). These tables identify the degree of agreement on the importance of the items in the subscales of communicator, visionary, achiever, critical thinker, mentor, and expert. The actual range of scores and variability in responses was greatest in the areas of leader as visionary, mentor, and expert, indicating less agreement than the other subscales. Leader as critical thinker and achiever had the smallest actual range of scores and least

TABLE 1.1. Total Group and Four Sub-Groups on All Items

Group	n	M	SD	Minimum	Maximum
Total Sample	521	43.96	8.42	25	74
Faculty (Group 1)	87	44.00	8.84	30	67
Nurse Administrator and Managers (Group 2)	270	43.47	7.73	25	67
Students (Group 4)	98	44.81	9.95	30	74
Other (Group 5)	66	44.67	8.16	31	64

variability in responses, indicating high agreement. The minimum scores in Table 1.1 and Table 1.2 that are below the minimum of the range of scores for that area indicate that some respondents did not rate all 31 items or rated some as not applicable.

A one-way analysis of variance (Scheffe's test) determined that there was no significant difference between groups on the LEMNA. A difference between groups was found, however, on two subscales: critical thinker and mentor. Analysis also revealed that nursing administrators/managers perceived the critical thinking and mentoring items as more important to leadership development than nursing students. In addition, the standard deviations showed that the nursing student group responses had the greatest amount of variability while the nursing administrator/manager group had the least amount of variability.

To better understand the ranking of items on a survey with high levels of agreement, the 10 items with the lowest means (M) and the 10 items with the highest means were identified. The 10 most important leadership constructs with the lowest means are listed in Table 1.3. The 10 least important leadership constructs with the highest means are listed in Table 1.4. Although there was a high level of agreement on the importance of the 31 items on the questionnaire, the lowest 10 items are of concern. Experience has shown that a single course or seminar is inadequate for leadership development and will not create nursing leaders (Barker, 1997; Fitz & Brown, 1998). Thus the following questions emerge:

- Is there an understanding and appreciation for the leadership constructs and theory from which leadership skills, behaviors, and attributes evolve?

TABLE 1.2. Total Group for All Modules

Leadership Module	*M*	*SD*
Communicator	7.71	1.19
Visionary	11.64	2.78
Achiever	4.35	1.41
Critical Thinker	4.66	1.24
Mentor	7.86	2.05
Expert	7.74	2.19

$N = 521$. Range of mean scores: Communicator = 6–24; Visionary = 7–28; Achiever = 3–12; Critical Thinker = 4–16; Mentor = 6–24; Expert = 5–20.

- If the items pertaining to (a) leadership development involve learning in the academic setting, (b) a leadership development involve learning in the health care setting, (c) a leadership practicum with a preceptor, and (d) a leadership practicum with a master's prepared preceptor are all included in the 10 least important items, then where and how does the profession see this development occurring?

- Are the responses to this survey influenced by the respondents' perceived quality of a leadership learning experience related to their experience in academia, the health care setting, and with preceptors?

A qualitative analysis was performed on the 168 comments in the section of the questionnaire entitled "Other knowledge, skills, and behaviors important to a leadership education model." The responses included several leadership traits. The analysis concluded that the respondents confused the terms leadership and management (Dienemann, 2000a), supporting the consensus in the literature about the confusion between management and leadership (Andrews-Evan, 1997; Barker, 1997; Grossman & Valiga, 2000; Washbush, 1998).

DEVELOPMENT OF THE MODEL

The Leadership Education Model (LEM) is based on the leadership profile that emerged from the above survey. The leadership modules

TABLE 1.3. Ten Most Important Constructs With the Lowest Means

Leadership Construct	M
Critical Thinking	1.12
Systematic Problem Solving	1.19
Advanced Critical Thinking Skills	1.19
Complex Problem Solving	1.19
Two-Way Communication	1.21
Leadership Involves the Capacity to Develop, Inspire, and Nurture Others Through Role Modeling and Mentoring	1.22
The Integration of Critical Thinking Skills and Professional Ethics Provides a Foundation for Leadership of Development	1.23
Team Building	1.23
Multifaceted Communication Skills	1.23
Influencing Others	1.26

TABLE 1.4. Ten Least Important Leadership Constructs With the Highest Means

Leadership Construct	M
Leadership Development Involves Integrated and Progressive Learning in an Academic Setting	2.20
Synthesizing Leadership Knowledge Changes the Attributes and Behaviors of the Total Person	1.88
Leadership Practicum With a Master's-Prepared Preceptor	1.79
Leadership Development Involves Integrated and Progressive Learning in the Health Care Setting	1.74
Leadership Theory	1.74
An Organization Framework Should Guide Leadership Development	1.64
Leadership and Goal Attainment	1.57
Understanding That Management and Leadership are Different but Related Concepts	1.55
Effecting Cost Containment	1.53

of communicator, visionary, achiever, expert, mentor, and critical thinker are the major components of the model that was -designed to guide the learning process. The following components are basic to this learning process.

Integration. Teaching strategies should integrate the elements of the six modules to emulate the application of leadership knowledge and skills in real life. Leadership education should be integrated into the total curriculum.

Progressive. Leadership learning is progressive, beginning with leadership theory and basic knowledge and skills, and progressing to a higher level of modeling and complex decision making.

Evolving. Leadership learning is a process that constitutes continuous growth and development. The formal learning process begins in academia and evolves through experiential learning in the clinical practicum, the health care setting, professional endeavors, and the eventual mentoring of others.

General Systems Theory. General systems theory provides the conceptual framework from which leadership characteristics evolve. General systems thinking creates the opportunity to see the larger picture and have a better understanding of issues.

The following summarizes the leadership modules that were developed by the Task Force.

Leader as Visionary. Great leadership demands the ability to create and communicate a personal vision that points the way for others. The power of such a vision stems directly from its use as a vehicle for elucidating an underlying and often intangible organizational purpose. Inspired organizations are deeply purposeful. A vision that is inspiring, compelling, and continually recited can guide change toward the vision in a clear visible way (Manthey, 1998). A workable captivating vision serves as both a vehicle for people to discover an underlying purpose and as a source of power around which they can align. Effective leaders catalyze alignment through sharing their personal vision and enabling others to do likewise (Aroian, 2000).

Leader as Expert. An expert has profound knowledge and is skillful in using this knowledge. If we combine all that is encompassed in the conceptual meaning of leader and expert, we could say that the leader as expert is the person or persons who have the depth of knowledge and know how to use it in such a way as to move a group or an organization to a greater level of functioning and to achieve the mission as identified by that group or organization. That depth of knowledge includes expertise in all the ways of knowing—the empirical, aesthetic, ethical, and personal (Carper, 1978). While the emphasis in knowledge acquisition is often on the empirical, the other ways of knowing are important if one is to develop the system's perspectives needed to lead in a rapidly changing health care delivery environment (Frank, 2000).

Leader as Achiever. A leader's singular job is to get results (Goldman, 2000). First, he needs to identify a vision or desired future for his scope of responsibility. Results demonstrate the leader's ability to invigorate others to work in collaboration to achieve a mutually desired future. Without a supportive environment that challenges everyone to contribute to progress, obstacles arise that are insurmountable. Thus, leadership is not charisma or following a certain style or set of process; it is the degree to which a leader facilitates the achievement of desired outcomes (Warden, 1999). The evidence of leadership is achievements; organizational achievements are the evidence of effective and efficient processes. . . . The shift from measuring quality from the perspective of professional process to financial efficiency and patient focused outcomes has been revolutionary in health care (Dienemann, 2000).

Leader as Critical Thinker. Leader as critical thinker evolves from the constructs of critical thinking and problem solving. A leader should possess the knowledge and skills to think critically and problem solve in a systematic and timely manner. Thinking critically involves the acquisition of knowledge, reasoning and rational appraisal skills, analytic problem solving behaviors, and reflective thinking. Critical thinking is the theoretical construct from which effective problem solving evolves. These skills are especially important to the administrative and advanced practice roles in contemporary and futuristic organizations. With the emergence of nursing's advanced practice role and the continuous advancement in scientific and technological patient care, it is imperative that nurses utilize complex critical thinking and problem-solving processes that provide the foundation for the evaluation of and reflection on one's thinking. Critical thinking involves a complex thinking order, metacognition, and problem solving (Lemire, 2000).

Leader as Communicator. Communication is the process that enables leaders to give voice to their role as visionary, critical thinker, achiever, mentor, and expert. . . . Effective leaders are skilled communicators who are versatile in all modes of communication whether to individuals or groups. They use judgment in each situation to ascertain the most appropriate mode to send a message and continually evaluate the effectiveness through feedback. These communicators cultivate language patterns that deliver clear and concise messages; develop meaningful interpersonal relationships; and support the development and mainte- nance of a culture conducive to open communication. In establishing rapport with individuals and groups, the leader encourages communi- cation that focuses on the topic at hand and the goals of the organiza- tion. Leaders use communication to influence others to see the common vision and to reach for it (Haynor, 2000).

Leader as Mentor. The leader as mentor plays an essential developmen- tal role in professional socialization and in the personal and career devel- opment of others. In the older, more established professions and in busi- ness, it has been widely recognized that the careful nurturing and coach- ing of aspiring professionals through a mentor relationship is essential in ensuring the highest levels of achievement, success, and satisfaction. Assuming responsibility for assisting future generations of nurses and nursing leaders should be the norm, not the exception (Olson & Vance, 1999). The recruitment and retention of talent, as well as the continuing support of potential, will require the adoption of formal mentor pro- grams and expansion of mentor connections throughout the profession. Leaders grow leaders. Mentoring and coaching by leaders will develop future leaders who will in turn leave their legacy of contribution to the profession and the improvement of health care (Vance, 2000).

The six leadership modules described by the Task Force members constitute the infrastructure for the LEM. The LEM (Figure 1.1) por- trays an educational paradigm depicting continuous leadership devel- opment through progressive, integrated learning. The model allows for variant teaching strategies, promotes innovation, and illustrates the evolving aspect of leadership education.

FIGURE 1.1.

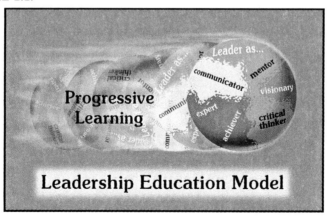

PROGRESS AND NEXT STEPS

The leadership profile for professional nurses developed through the LEMNA consists of concepts found in the literature and supported by over 500 nurse administrators, educators, and students. This profile provided the foundation for the Leadership Education Model and the associated six leadership modules. Seminars have been presented at three universities to introduce regional nursing faculty to the essential knowledge for implementing the newly designed LEM. The ultimate goal is to encourage RN to BSN and graduate programs to integrate the LEM into the curriculum on a progressive learning continuum with a well-defined practicum. The degree to which faculty integrate the LEM into their curriculum and the associated outcomes will be measured at 6 months and 1 year.

The continuing work of the Task Force includes:

1. Further development of the modules to include teaching methodologies and systems for evaluating learning;
2. Additional seminars to introduce nursing faculty to the LEM and integrate it into the nursing curriculum;
3. Consultation in curriculum development;
4. Evaluation of the LEM developmental process; and
5. Outcome measurement.

Two recommendations of the Task Force are to conduct further research on the six leadership modules to determine the degree of agreement on the categorization of the questionnaire items and to better understand the 10 least important items that are inconsistent with the literature. For the latter, a second survey should be considered, with a redesign of these items to focus more on the learning process and goals.

The LEM project has demonstrated the complexity and intensity of leadership learning and the professional challenge to identify a paradigm for leadership development for nurses. This challenge involves nurses in all settings and at all levels of practice. Effective leadership will provide the means for nursing to influence the future of health care.

REFERENCES

American Association of Colleges of Nursing. (1996). *Position paper on vision of baccalaureate and graduate nursing education: The next decade* (p. 6). Washington, DC: Author.

Andrews-Evan, M. (1997). The leadership challenge in nursing. *Nursing Management, 4*(5), 8–11.

Antrobus, S. (1997). Leading from the front. *Nursing Standard, 11*(37), 22–23.

Aroian, J. (2000). *Leader as visionary.* Unpublished manuscript.

Aroian, J., Maguire Meservey, P., & Gilbert Crockett, J. (1996). Developing nurse leaders for today and tomorrow: Part 1. *Journal of Nursing Administration, 26*(9), 18–25.

Ashby, F. (Ed.). (1999). *Effective leadership programs.* Alexandria, VA: American Society for Training & Development.

Barker, R. (1997). How can we train leaders if we do not know what leadership is? *Human Relations, 50*(4), 343–362.

Collins, P. (2000). Leadership clinical activities for baccalaureate nursing students. *Journal of the New York State Nurses Association, 31*(1), 4–8.

Corcoran, R. (1999, February). Letter from the National League of Nursing CEO. *National League of Nursing Update, 2*(4), 1–2.

Dienemann, J. (2000a). *Qualitative analysis of leadership education model needs assessment.* Unpublished report.

Dienemann, J. (2000b). *Leader as achiever.* Unpublished manuscript.

Ferguson, S. (1998). Academy, Foundation Launch Program to enhance nurses' leadership capacity. *The American Nurse, 30*(4), 10.

Fralic, M. (1999). Nursing leadership for the new millennium: Essential knowledge and skills. *Nursing and Health Care Perspectives, 20*(5), 260–265.

Frank, B. (2000). *Leader as expert.* Unpublished manuscript.

Grossman, S., & Valiga, T. (2000). *The new leadership challenge: Creating the future of nursing.* Philadelphia: F. A. Davis.

Haynor, P. (2000). *Leader as communicator.* Unpublished manuscript.

Krejci, J., & Malin, S. (1997). Impact of leadership development on competencies. *Nursing Economics, 15*(5), 235–241.

Lemire, J. (2000). *Leader as critical thinker.* Unpublished manuscript.

Rocchiccioli, J., & Tilbury, M. (1998). *Clinical Leadership in Nursing.* Philadelphia: W. B. Saunders.

Schwartz, M., Axtman, K., & Freeman, F. (Eds.). (1998). *Leadership Education* (7th ed.). Greensboro, NC: Center for Creative Leadership.

Shortell, S., & Kaluzny, A. (1997). *Essentials of health care management.* Albany, NY: Delmar.

Vance, C. (2000). *Leader as mentor.* Unpublished manuscript.

Washbush, J. (1998). From where will the leaders come? Revisited. *Journal of Education for Business, 73*(4), 251–253.

Wilson, C., & Porter-O'Grady, T. (1999). *Leading the Revolution in Health Care.* Gaithersburg, MD: Aspen.

Wright, S. (1996). Unlock the leadership potential. *Nursing Management, 3*(2), 8–10.

CHAPTER TWO

Leader As Visionary

Jane Aroian

Great leadership demands the ability to create and communicate a personal vision that points the way for others. The power of such a vision stems directly from its use as a vehicle for elucidating an underlying, often intangible organizational purpose. Inspired organizations are deeply purposeful. A vision that is inspiring, compelling, and continually recited can guide change toward the vision in a clear, visible way (Manthey, 1997). A workable captivating vision serves as both a vehicle for people to discover an underlying purpose and as a source of power around which they can align. Effective leaders catalyze alignment through sharing their personal vision and enabling others to do likewise.

Communication is a key element if visionary leaders are to enable others. Bennis and Nanus (1985) noted that success requires the capacity to relate a compelling image of a desired state of affairs. Such a compelling image is thought to instill enthusiasm and commitment in others. As a social architect, the leader's role is to communicate a vision. This means that the vision will be shaping values and norms in a way that binds and bonds individuals and groups and motivates them to act to create the vision. Visions are communicated by managing meaning and creating understanding, commitment, and ownership of a vision. Shared ownership of a vision builds trust that glues leaders and followers together.

LEADERSHIP THEORIES AND VISIONARY LEADERSHIP

The work of Senge (1990) and colleagues on systems thinking contains a focus on visionary leadership. They explain visionary leadership by suggesting four core competencies identified as (a) personal mastery, (b) intuition and reason, (c) shared visions, and (d) team learning.

PERSONAL MASTERY

Personal Mastery is the ability to produce intended results of service. It requires the intuition and wisdom to work with forces rather than against them while never losing sight of one's vision (Senge, 1990). Personal mastery relates to individual vision and dedication. It is a private, passionate commitment to lifelong acquisition of new skills and improvement of old ones through learning (Warsh, 1999).

Great leaders naturally inspire others by their unyielding commitment to a vision and to their own high standards of excellence and performance. They also create environments in which other people's abilities emerge and develop naturally in the course of getting the job done. This ability to empower others transcends management style and personality, and is grounded in the experience of inherent greatness.

INTUITION AND REASON

Leadership requires balance between intuition and rational analysis. No rules exist for creating a vision that inspires people—visioning is a deeply intuitive process. Intuition alone is insufficient beacause leaders must also be able to examine and clarify complex organizational dynamics and analyze often ill-defined issues. Great leaders develop a unique interplay between intuition and reason. They use intuition to guide their analysis and they continually subject the intuitive insights to rational examination (Senge, 1990).

SHARED VISION

Shared vision occurs through interactions. Often, shared vision may emerge as a leader and other individuals communicate their personal goals and common underlying purpose. The shared purpose acts as a widely held mental model and binds individuals to a common purpose in an organization. It may be extrinsic (for example, "I was taught to hate the Russians, Yale, and The Hopkins Way," says a Massachusetts General Hospital surgeon), or intrinsic, (that is, ordinary people empowered by computers was the shared vision of the founders of Apple Computer). A shared purpose that is captured in a leader's vision will bind and bond others to work for its attainment.

Team Learning

Team learning is the fourth competency. It builds on personal mastery and shared vision and extends into the realm of improvisation, says Senge, "The great jazz ensemble has talent and a shared vision (even if they don't discuss it), but what really matters is that the musicians know how to play together" (Warsh, 1999). This leads to evaluation of the shared vision as it is implemented in a certain context.

Integration of these four competencies leads to systems thinking, of seeing independent wholes and fathoming their logic. From this the visionary leader affirms or evaluates the vision as a guide to action.

Nanus (1992) developed a formula for implementing visionary leadership using Senge's work as a foundation. He offers the following ingredients of vision:

> Vision is composed of one part foresight, one part insight, plenty of imagination and judgment and often a healthy dose of chutzpah. It occurs to a well informed open mind, a mind prepared by a lifetime of learning and experience, one sharply attuned to emerging trends and developments in the world outside the organization. Creativity certainly plays an important part, but it is creativity rooted in reality of the organization and it possibilities. (p. 39)

His formula is Vision + Communication = Shared Purpose + Empowered People + Appropriate Organizational Changes + Strategic Thinking = Successful Visionary Leadership (Nanus, 1992). This can be used as a guide for readiness of a work team for successful collaboration with a visionary leader.

A second leadership theory that highlights visionary leadership is Transformational Leadership. According to Bass (1990) transformational leaders motivate others to do more . . . more than they thought possible. They set more challenging expectations and typically achieve higher performances. A transformational leader identifies and communicates vision and values. The vision and values can come from many sources. The transformational leader asks the work group to commit to these values and empowers the work group to implement the vision (Bass & Avalio, 1994). This balancing act requires transformational leaders to be grounded in their personal values, live a balanced life, and continuously learn (Dixon, 1999).

RESEARCH-RELATED VISIONARY LEADERSHIP

Support for visionary leadership can be found in the research literature in health care administration, nursing, and business. As early as 1991, the Healthcare Leadership Gap study identified five priority leadership needs for 21st century health care organizations: (a) visionary leadership, based on systems thinking, and a shared vision; (b) a redefinition of health that focuses on healing, changing lifestyle and the holistic interplay of mind/body/spirit; (c) social missions that weld health care organizations objectives; (d) actions with community service that leadership is coupled with; and (e) a never-satisfied attitude that supports continuous quality improvement (Bezold & Mayer, 1996).

Another study by Blake and Guare (1997) indicates that ethical principles may be one source of visionary leadership. The investigators documented moral/ethical situations described by nurses in acute care hospitals. Findings revealed evidence of a shared vision of caring, connectedness, and context to guide moral decision making. Decisions often demonstrated compromise between perceived ideal action and realistic action. This study also demonstrated the value of ethical reflection for nurses. The authors concluded that the dreams and visions of leaders could be realized if their actions reflect the guiding principles of ethical practice, as they acknowledge practice guidelines, rules and regulations of governmental and other accrediting agencies, and professional codes.

Dunham-Taylor and Klafehn (1996) reviewed research over the last decade and found nurse executives who are transformational leaders are more effective achievers with more satisfied staff than those who are transactional leaders. Dunham-Taylor (2000) provides a possible profile of a highly transformational nurse executive. She concludes that many nurse executives who are transformational lack a forum to share and communicate what they do. These findings should encourage peers to become more transformational by creating environments in which learning in action is both acknowledged and valued (Dixon, 1999).

EDUCATION FOR VISIONARY LEADERSHIP

The research of Conger (1996) provides guidance to those interested in teaching visionary leadership. He interviewed more than 150 participants in leadership development programs over a 2-year period to identify the necessary components of an ideal leadership course. His analysis identified three major areas that need to be addressed: shaping strategic vision, aligning the organization, and mobilizing the troops.

Embedded in each of these areas are skill sets necessary for effective leadership. The shaping strategic vision skill set includes a future orientation, role modeling, developing a leadership philosophy based on ethical principles, and persuasion skills. Teaching strategies to assist learners to gain this skill set might include assignments to write a personal philosophy, list ethical principles they use in leadership with specific examples, or give a persuasive talk on their vision in class.

A second skill set suggested by Lachman (1998) creates the capability to develop scenarios that involve others in explicating a shared vision. Visioning is only one side of the leadership coin; the back side of visioning is scenario development. Scenarios assist group members to develop strategies to achieve the vision. One mechanism for scenario development is story telling to get people talking about the effects and consequences of espoused visions. Stories about the future need to include what could happen, might happen, or is likely to happen or what people want to happen. Lachman describes this skill set as aligning the organization or political savvy. In includes coalition forming, bargaining, lobbying, posturing, and increasing visibility. Teaching strategies for this skill set are strategic planning, simulations, and gaming techniques.

From a business perspective, Bradford and Cohen (1984/1997) provide us with guidance on goal setting and visionary leadership based on their experiences as consultants in leadership training. To measure training effectiveness they have developed the Bradford and Cohen Leadership Style questionnaire. As consultants they have worked with more than 250 competent leaders from some of America's premier organizations. One of the key components for these leaders to achieve excellence is the ability to establish a tangential vision or overarching goal for their unit that gives coherence, excitement, and meaning to the department's work. The overarching goal acts as a shared vision to motivate, provide direction, and guide for change in their departments. The effective overarching goal has the following four essential characteristics:

1. reflection of the core purpose of the department,
2. feasibility,
3. challenge to the work team, and
4. larger significance over time.

These characteristics help to transcend the merely adequate performance that occurs when goals are short-term financial targets or nebulous platitudes.

Bradford and Cohen (1984/1997) suggest the following sequence in training leaders to develop an appropriate tangential vision/overarching goal. First, have them identify what the department does for its clients, the total organization, the community and society at large. Second, assess their own skills, interests, and areas of commitment, as well as the department's internal resources. Third, ask them to describe what kind of match can be made between external service needs and internal capacities. Fourth, have them set the goal and formulate a plan to sell it by talking first about what it does for the larger good, then for the organization, for clients, for staff and/or colleagues, and themselves. In general, it is often best to "start small" by identifying a goal component and then clarifying how all interested constituents will benefit.

One goal in developing continuing educational programs to build skill sets for visionary leadership is to provide teaching methods that accelerate learning time. I have found that when learners reflect on past experiences with visionary leadership and examine case studies in seminar discussions, it helps speed learning. Another technique is asking learners to share their reflections and jointly identify skills through case studies. Sharing leadership narratives is particularly important to disseminate practical knowledge among the peer group. By reflecting on experience and by having paradigm cases to build an experiential repertoire, the random nature of learning can be minimized. These methods promote overall integration of formal and experiential learning to assist learners to recognize the benefit of each approach (Horvath, et al., 1997).

CONCLUSION

Visioning is a powerful process that assists us in creating a picture of an ideal future. A vision may be a dream, personally created, of how we would like our world to be. In sharing our personal visions we can find common ground to develop a shared organizational vision and a sense of connection. Today, in an unprecedented way nurses at all levels are expected to exhibit leadership in setting direction for nursing practice. It is evident that visionary leadership is vital because it requires looking ahead and anticipating the future (Pesut, 2000). Visioning is for leaders who can imagine a new and better future and who want to achieve beyond what they currently experience. A vision is not just a direction; it also has a destination (Holland, 1996; Schumaker, 1998). The role of faculty is to facilitate nurses to gain the skills to create and share their vision of the future. Facilitation of student leadership development is an act of empowerment and an expression of caring (Tyrrell, 1994). Faculty that embody this practice demonstrate transformational leadership. Faculty have the opportunity to help the leaders of today and tomorrow find their destination and that of the discipline of nursing in the 21st century.

REFERENCES

Bass, B. (1990). Transformational leadership: Industry, military, and educational impact. Mahwah, NJ: Lawrence Erlbaum.

Bass, B., & Avalio, B. (1994). Improving organizational effectiveness through transformational leadership. Thousand Oaks, CA: Sage.

Bennis, W., & Nanus, B. (1985). Visionary leadership: Creating a compelling sense of direction for your organization. San Francisco: Jossey Bass.

Bezold, C., & Mayer, E. (Eds.). (1996). Future care: Responding to the demand for change. New York: Faulkner & Gray.

Blake, C., & Guare, R. (1997). Nurse reflections on ethical decision making: Implications for leaders. Journal of New York State Nurses Association, 28(4), 12–16.

Bradford, D., & Cohen, A. (1997). Managing for excellence. New York: Wiley. (Original work published 1984)

Conger, J. (1996, Winter). Can we really train leadership? Strategy and Business.

Dixon, D. (1999). Achieving results through transformational leadership. Journal of Nursing Administration, 29(12), 17–21.

Dunham-Taylor J. (2000). Nurse Executive transformational leadership found in participative organizations. Journal of Nursing Administration, 30(5), 241–250.

Dunham-Taylor J., & Klafehn, K. (1996). Transformational leadership and the nurseexecutive. Journal of Nursing Administration, 20(4), 28–34.

Gregory, C. (1995). Creating a vision for a nursing unit. Nursing Management, 26(1), 38–41.

Holland, T. (1996). How to build a more effective board (p. 26). Washington, DC: National Center for Nonprofit Boards.

Horvath, K., Aroian, J., Alpert, H., Costa, M., Powers, M. J., Secatore, J., & Stengrevics, J. (1997). Vision for a treasured resource: Part 2, Nurse manager learning needs. Journal of Nursing Administration, 27(4), 27–31.

Lachman, V. (1998). Care of the self for the nurse entrepreneur. Nursing Administration Quarterly, 22(2), 48–59.

Lemire, J. (2001). Preparing nurse leaders: A leadership education model. Nursing Leadership Forum, 6(2), 39–44.

Manthey, M. (1997). Leading an empowered organization workbook. In D. Miller & D. Wright (Eds.). Creative Healthcare Management. Minneapolis, MN: CHCM.

Nanus, B. (1992). Visionary leadership. San Francisco: Jossey-Bass.

Pesut, D. (2000). Looking forward, being, and becoming a futurist. In Fay Bower (Ed.), Nurses taking the lead (chap. 3, pp. 39–63). Philadelphia: W. B. Saunders.

Senge, P. (1990). The fifth discipline: The art and practice of learning organizations. New York: Doubleday.

Schumaker, R. (1998). Leadership identifies new solutions to tough choices. Association of PeriOperative Registered Nurses Journal, 68(2), 164–165.

Tyrrell, R. (1994). Visioning: An important management tool. Nursing Economic$, 12(2), 93–95.

Warsh, D. (1999, June 6). What is the fifth discipline? The Boston Globe. pp. F1–3, 23.

CHAPTER THREE

Leader As Expert

Betsy Frank

What is a leader? What is an expert? Knowing what these two concepts mean is just the beginning of an understanding of what it means when we say "The Leader as Expert." One has to understand more than simple definitions; one has to go beyond and look at the multiple ways of knowing that leaders engage in when using their expertise to guide organizations in achieving their missions.

What is a leader? As noted by Lemire (2001) countless articles and books have been written on the subject. In one university library alone there are more than 700 book entries on the topic. Despite this voluminous literature, Bender (1997) said that leadership is hard to define, but we know it when we see it. Hodgkinson (1982) suggested that it is the "incantation for the bewitchment of the led" (p. 217). And, Mary Ann Fralic (1999) quoted Grayce Sills who says that leadership is a function, not a position.

Much of what is written seems to confuse or combine leadership with management. Sparrow (1998), for example, talked about management and management by perceptions. Management by perceptions seems akin to what others call leadership. One author, however, seems particularly useful in clarifying the differences between leadership and management. Shotgren (1999) stated that management deals with the day to day affairs, keeps things going, relies on rules and policies, uses the chain of command, and pays close attention to detail, which results in getting things done right. Leaders on the other hand envision what is possible for the future, start the organization in a new direction, lead by example, listen carefully, inspire others to do their best, build teams, encourage risk taking, and welcome ambiguity and disorder, which result in doing what is right. He also notes that charisma is not essential and that leadership can be learned.

What, then, is an expert? A variety of dictionaries and a thesaurus give multiple definitions for an expert. One common theme in all the definitions is that the expert is skillful. An expert has profound knowledge and is competent in using this knowledge. If one combines all that is encompassed in the conceptual meaning of leader and expert, one could say that the leader as expert is the person who has the depth of knowledge and knows how to use it in such a way as to move a group or an organization to a greater level of functioning and to achieve the mission as identified by that group or organization.

LEADER AS EXPERT KNOWLEDGE WORKER

The leader as expert knowledge worker is one who uses multiple ways of knowing for gathering information. Barbara Carper's (1978) classic article gives a framework for looking atall the components of knowledge acquisition. Though the focus of knowledge is often on the empirical, the personal, ethical, and aesthetic ways of knowing are just as important. By using all the ways of knowing in curricular designs, nurse educators will be able to prepare nurse leaders to meet the challenges of an often chaotic health care delivery arena.

EMPIRICAL KNOWING

Getting a grasp of the empirical is the center of the majority of the coursework that students engage in as they prepare for leadership roles. As knowledge grows exponentially, faculties are challenged to achieve the right balance between what to include versus what to exclude in their curricula. Preparation for nursing leadership seems at times to be a particularly daunting task. A nursing leader mustknow the "business of leadership," health care delivery in its largest sense, and must also be an expert in nursing itself. If one is to be a clinical leader, one has to know what the clinical one is leading (Fralic, 1999).

A laundry list of topics to include in course work could be developed. At a minimum, categories of topics include organizational culture and politics, health policy and law, environmental scanning and politics, nursing expertise, and business and technical expertise including informatics, economics, and fiscal accountability. Course work is not the only way one can gain the knowledge needed to be a successful leader. Preceptorships and mentoring relationships are essential for leadership development (Vance, Chapter 7).

Environmental scanning is also essential for leaders. At times it may seem like there is so much information coming from the environment that instead of scanning information, leaders drown in it! Despite the risk of information overload, one thing that leadership educators can do is to show students how to scan efficiently. Regularly reading a few good publications such as the Wall Street Journal, Nursing Economics, and journals from professional associations will help the busy leader keep apprised of the coming trends and develop proactive stances in response to the trends (Garone, 1999). Scanning a few pertinent listservs and websites also keeps one in touch with timely information. Miller (2000) suggested that other strategies for environmental scanning include asking questions, listening, and synthesizing the information received. He goes on to say that without the synthesizing, the leader will not be able to discern the big picture. In other words, the leader and the organization may be on the path to the wrong mission! Understanding systems and how they work is essential for effective leadership.

PERSONAL KNOWING

Empirical knowledge is an important foundation for leadership. Having knowledge of self helps one to use the empirical knowledge gained. Personal knowing may also be likened to what Bender (1997) called leadership from within. Leadership from within is grounded in reflective practice.

Reflective practice is based on three key assumptions:

1. Those who are committed to reflective practice are also committed to problem finding and solving. Problems faced by leaders today are complex and ill defined. Leaders must remain open to discovery and new ways of looking at old problems.
2. Reflective practice involves making ethical judgments about changes in people and systems.

3. Reflective practice goes beyond analysis and thought to some form of action (Cervero, 1988; Osterman & Kottkamp, 1993, Peters, 1991; Schon, 1987).

Reflective practice also involves assessing and taking risks and not being afraid to make mistakes and admit to those mistakes (Bender, 1997). Reflective practice involves asking such questions as suggested by Senge (1999):

1. Why am I doing this?
2. Do I understand what I'm doing and its consequences?
3. Am I willing to stay the course (if the course is right)?
4. Am I willing to accept the ambiguity?
5. Am I willing to change?
6. Am I prepared to rethink our organization's purpose?
7. What am I doing?
8. Do I have the energy to be fully engaged in this major transformation?
9. What do I personally stand for? (pp. 230–237)

Developing the skills of reflective practice and thus personal knowing provides one of the cornerstones of leadership education. In fact, Schmieding (1999) stated that preparation for reflective practice is an essential component of education for nurse leaders that is currently absent in the curricula. Further, she notes that this topic is absent in the major texts that support graduate programs for nurse administrators. Reflective practice in the traditional clinical courses also fosters personal knowing. Strategies for developing personal knowing include writing a personal mission statement, journaling, and engaging in leadership style assessments such as the Myers-Briggs Personality Type Inventory (Consulting Psychologist Press, 1998), True Colors (1988), and 360-degree evaluation processes (Frank, 1998). Strickland (2000) said that having emotional intelligence is a characteristic of outstanding performers. Therefore, using Goleman's (1998) multiple intelligence inventory may also be a part of leadership style assessment.

ETHICAL KNOWING

Ethical knowing transforms the empirical and personal knowing into doing what is right for self and organizations in which we work.

Ethical knowing leads us to cherish diversity within the organization and respect autonomy and privacy of individuals in the organization (Chinn & Kramer, 1999).

Ethical knowing is so important in a time of staffing shortages, fiscal constraints, and a rapidly changing regulatory environment (Marquis & Huston, 2000). Without some expertise in the area of ethical knowing, decisions might be made that are expedient and perhaps in the short run fiscally sound. In the short and long term, however, the persons within the organization and the clients the organization serves may be adversely impacted. Cost-benefit ratio is not only financial!

Ethical knowing helps the leader discern when rules and policies can be abandoned in favor of what is the right thing to do. Canner and Feigan (2000) noted that successful corporations such as Home Depot and Southwest Airlines know that people, not rules and procedures, drive companies. Legal considerations cannot be abandoned, of course. But a strong sense of ethical knowing can help the leader know the boundaries of proper decision making. Including frameworks for ethical decision making as well as knowledge of how organizations deal with ethical issues are important topics for leadership education across the curriculum.

AESTHETIC KNOWING

Aesthetic knowing is, according to Chinn and Kramer (1999), the blending of the empirical knowledge with the personal knowledge and intuitive knowing to weave a pattern of action that appears often effortless and without thought. In reality, the action has a strong foundation in the blending of the three other ways of knowing. Chinn, Maeve, and Bostick (1997) suggest that we can use the principles of reflective practice to examine the blend of all the ways of knowing. An application of such is having students use journals to reflecton their observations and experiences while working with preceptors and mentors. Aesthetic knowing is also using the knowledge from the humanities and the arts to understand and appreciate the world around us. Writing poetry, painting pictures, or molding a clay pot can help us to reflect on the situations we find ourselves in when exploring the notion of leadership. Reading poetry, viewing paintings and pottery, and journaling about the engagement with the creative works can do the same.

In sum, leaders are expert knowers who use knowledge to be continual expert learners and explorers. Vaill (1996) used the term "white water"—a metaphor that describes today's turbulent pace of change. The only certainty in this environment is the need for lifelong learning. According to Vaill, leadership is not learned but is learning. Leaders must also use the ways of knowing to go beyond mere learning into the realm of exploring. Vaill uses a fictional dialogue with the explorer, Sir Francis Chichester, to explain this critical competency for leaders today. "To be an explorer is not to know where, precisely, or concretely, one is going" (p. 207).

WHAT DO EXPERT LEADERS DO?

Being an expert knower and learner, of course is not enough. Leaders must also be expert doers. Leaders must be expert at building and designing effective and efficient organizations—organizations that are known as learning organizations. In order to build these effective and efficient organizations they must be experts at delegation and motivation.

LEADER AS BUILDER AND DESIGNER

In order to stay vibrant, and in many cases stay in business, organizations must transform themselves to match the continually changing environment. Much has been written on organizational structure and design. What is critical for this discussion is the leader's role in the transformation process.

Using all the ways of knowing, leaders guide their organizations in creating the vision for the organization and communicating that vision throughout the organization (Miles, 1999). In order to create the vision, leaders must have a strong propensity for systems thinking (Bradford & Cohen, 1998); or as Collins and Porras (1997) suggested, leaders are the "clock builders" who focus on all the processes of an organization and how they fit together rather than on a single great idea. Leaders weave together organizational transformations by being able to understand organizational competencies, strategies, structure and infrastructure, workforce skills, needs, diversity, and an organization's culture (Miles, 1999). Leaders can see what is and what needs to be if an organization is to become more effective and efficient. Within the nursing profession, making the organization efficient and effective is not only the responsibility of the formal leaders, but the informal leaders at the staff level.

LEADER AS MOTIVATOR AND DELEGATOR

As noted by Miles (1999), leaders cannot accomplish organizational goals without others. Leaders must create a climate wherein all the organization's members are motivated to participate in an organization's transformation. Then, the leaders must delegate authority for participation in the transformation. To create a climate wherein an entire organization is on the same pathway, leaders must recognize and respect the uniqueness that each person brings to an organization (Essex & Kusy, 1999). Within such a climate, leadership and followership at times merge into one.

Sharing power and information is an important first step in creating that climate and delegating authority and responsibility (Kouzes & Posner, 1999). Kouzes and Posner quote an old Chinese proverb:

> If you want one year of prosperity, grow grain.
> If you want ten years of prosperity, grow trees.
> If you want one hundred years of prosperity, grow people. (p. 235)

In sharing information, leaders focus on opportunities, rather than problems, and encourage people to take a local focus while keeping a broad and purposeful view (Cashman, 2000).

Creating this climate also means providing adequate resources, giving people important work and resources to do the tasks while allowing autonomy and discretion over the tasks. At the same time, leaders must let others know what are the expectations or outcomes desired (Kouzes & Posner, 1999). One strategy for helping others build strong relationships is to place those with less experience with mentors, preceptors, and others who can help accomplish the delegated tasks. The leader, as expert communicator, creates the climate wherein those strong relationships can be built (Haynor, Chapter 6). As an expert communicator, motivator, and delegator, the leader will create organizational teams that not only buy into the vision necessary for organizational transformation, but also have an active role in creating that vision.

The end result of knowing and doing is the creation of a learning organization that is not only responsive to the environment but operates in a proactive way—sees the coming changes and responds before it is forced to respond (Senge, 1990). And, all within the organization are constantly learning. Mistakes in decision making are seen as learning opportunities, rather than errors made. Learning organizations are best able to cope with the white water or uncertainty that exists in health care delivery today (Sparrow, 1998).

IMPLICATIONS FOR NURSING CURRICULA

Identifying what makes "the leader as expert" can give guidance to faculties in colleges, schools, or departments of nursing in developing curricula that will help prepare the leader as expert. This leader will be a creative thinker who always challenges the boundaries of what is. Fashioning undergraduate and graduate leadership curricula may seem fairly straightforward once faculty know what an expert, a visionary, a communicator, a critical thinker, and a mentor are. The challenge is, however, greater than at first glance. Nursing education creates a paradox. Our clinical education purports to educate critical thinkers, while often stressing the use of standardized languages of the North American Nursing Diagnosis Association (NANDA), the Nursing Intervention Classification (NIC), and the Nursing Outcome Classification (NOC) and critical pathways that seem necessary in an age of computer documentation and outcomes research. Students are focused on the standardized, while at the same time faculty want to educate the creative nursing leaders that will be needed to cope with the rapidly changing health care delivery system. By being aware of the importance of incorporating all the ways of knowing, faculty can help students deal with the paradox of having to function in a world that at the same time demands standardization and creative problem solving. Leadership education takes place at the undergraduate, graduate, and of course continuing education arenas, and all levels of education can make use of the ways of knowing and principles of creating student-centered learning environments to construct relevant curricula.

As previously alluded to, the ways of knowing suggest some learning strategies that promote the education of the leader as expert. More specifically, six central building blocks for implementation of the curricula for nursing leadership development—assessment, reflection, mentoring, case teaching, simulation, and practica—flow from the ways of knowing. Reflection has been discussed but to reinforce its importance, Vaill (1996) said that reflection helps learners to learn about learning, to gain an understanding of barriers to learning, and to learn new ways of learning. Reflection also helps learners to know why they do what they do, to accept ambiguity and to develop a sense of what they personally stand for (Senge, 1999). Leadership assessments have also been suggested. The assessments are not to identify the ideal leaders, but to increase self-awareness of a person's leadership abilities.

Mentoring is discussed in more detail by Vance (Chapter 7). Briefly, however, Harris and DeSimone (1994) suggest that mentoring relationships are important from two perspectives: life development and career development. Life development involves working with those older and wiser and career development is aimed at progression within the organization.

Case teaching, which may be likened to problem-based learning, has been the hallmark of teaching at the Harvard Business School. In the nursing education arena, Baker (2000) has used problem-based learning in a graduate nursing administration program. Problem-based learning does not rely on memorization and lectures but group work that enhances critical thinking. According to Barnes, Christensen, and Hansen (1994), this method of teaching shares the power of teaching between teacher and student, helps students take command of the material, and assists students to learn how to function in a group.

Ruben (1999) provided rationale for the inclusion of simulation and games in the curricula. Unlike case studies of situations that may have already occurred, simulation and games allow for interactivity with a created environment. Consequences of actions are learned, and in a collaborative group environment both the cognitive and affective domains of learning are addressed. Further, Silberman (1998) noted that simulations and games help participants see the whole before discussing the parts. A vast array of simulation and games are available through such organizations as the North American Simulation and Gaming Association (www.nasaga.org).

The final cornerstone of leadership education is the practicum experience. Two types of practica are used: the shadowing practicum and the integrative practicum. Silberman (1998) noted that observation or shadowing can be an effective way to learn if the learning involves reflection and an opportunity to dialogue with those whom one is shadowing. The integrated practicum allows a leader to have progressive responsibilities under the supervision and guidance of an experienced leader. Businesses often call this experience an internship.

All these building blocks can be incorporated into undergraduate and graduate curricula within a variety of courses, not just the traditional leadership and management courses at the undergraduate level and the role development courses at the graduate level. Other information that may be useful are the Essentials of Baccalaureate Education (1998) and the Essentials of Master's Education (1996), both available from the American Association of Colleges of Nursing, and the curricular guidelines from the Council on Graduate Education for Administration in Nursing (CGEAN) (Dienemann & Arioan, 1995), which are currently under revision.

At the undergraduate level the student should acquire the basic theoretical foundation for leadership in action. Personal exploration of values and learning one's learning preferences and basic psychological characteristics are appropriate topics to be included. The Myers-Briggs Personality Inventory might be used at the undergraduate level. The basic theoretical orientation comes from an introduction to the seminal ideas from organizational behavior, sociology, anthropology, psychology, education, and business. Case studies that are often included in textbooks at the undergraduate level help students apply the theoretical knowledge. Practica at the undergraduate level may involve primarily a shadowing experience along with completion of a small definitive project. If a student has little clinical experience, more circumscribed practica may be necessary at the clinical unit level.

At the graduate level, a more in-depth examination of the theories behind leadership and organizational structure and functioning is appropriate. This would include an acquisition of more in-depth knowledge related to the financial, legal, and clinical practice components of health care delivery systems. More advanced assessment techniques such as 360-degree evaluations could be undertaken (Frank, 1998). An integrative practicum experience is appropriate at this level.

All these strategies are predicated on the notion of adult learning and lifelong learning principles. Although he has been criticized, and in fact, many of us know those instances when his assumptions do not bear out in the real world of education, Malcolm Knowles does give guidance about the learners we encounter (Merriam & Cafferella, 1999). Knowles (Knowles & Associates, 1980; 1984) stated the following:

1. Adult learners are self-directed.
2. Life experiences are a rich resource for learning.
3. Readiness to learn is associated with the developmental tasks of the learner's social role.
4. Adult learners are future oriented and more problem centered rather than subject centered.
5. Adult learners are internally rather than externally motivated.

What this means in the classroom is that faculty are facilitators of learning and students become responsible for their own knowledge acquisition.

The notion of transformational learning is equally important to consider when designing curricula. According to Vaill (1996), leadership development is an "on-going process of action" that is "occurring all the time in executive life" (p. 319). Formal coursework is important, but bringing to bear the learning that occurs in organizations, including health care and on campus co-curricular and extra curricular organizations, is also crucial. Mezirow (1990) reinforced this notion by saying that active participation in the real world and critical reflection facilitate leadership education.

Creating curricula that will prepare leaders for the present and future health care delivery is a challenging task for nursing faculty. By incorporating all the ways of knowing in the curricular design and implementing those curricula in a learner-centered environment, we can provide our students with a strong foundation for their lifelong quests to become leaders as experts.

REFERENCES

American Association of Colleges of Nursing. (1996). *The essentials of master's education for advanced practice nursing.* Washington, DC: Author.

American Association of Colleges of Nursing. (1998). *The essentials of baccalaureate education for professional nursing practice.* Washington, DC: Author.

Baker, C. M. (2000). Using problem-based learning to redesign nursing administration master's programs. *Journal of Nursing Administration, 30*(3), 41–47.

Barnes, L. B., Christensen, C. R., & Hansen, A. J. (1994). Teaching and the case method (3rd ed.). Boston: Harvard Business School Press.

Bender, P. U. (1997). *Leadership from within.* Toronto, Canada: Stoddard.

Bradford, D. L., & Cohen, A. R. (1998). *Power up: Transforming organizations through shared leadership.* New York: Wiley.

Canner, N., & Feigan, M. (2000, August 28). Verizon strike: A wake-up call for better service. *Wall Street Journal,* p. A18.

Carper, B. (1978). Fundamental ways of knowing in nursing. *Advances in Nursing Science, 1*(1), 13–23.

Cashman, K. (2000). *Leadership from the inside out.* Provo, UT: Executive Excellence.

Cervero, R. M. (1988). *Effective continuing education for professionals.* San Francisco: Jossey-Bass.

Chinn, P. L., & Kramer, M. K. (1999). *Theory and knowledge: Integrated knowledge development.* St. Louis, MO: Mosby.

Chinn, P., Maeve, M. K., & Bostick, C. (1997). Aesthetic inquiry and the art of nursing. *Scholarly Inquiry for Nursing Practice, 11,* 83–96.

Collins, J. C., & Porras, J. I. (1997). *Built to last.* New York: HarperCollins.

Dienemann, J., & Arioan, J. (1995). *Essentials of baccalaureate nursing education for nursing leadership and management and master's nursing education for nursing administration advanced practice.* Retrieved April 2, 2002, from http://www.unc.edu/~sengleba/CGEAN/index.html

Essex, L., & Kusy, M. (1999). *Fast forward leadership.* London: Prentice-Hall.

Fralic, M. A. (1999). Nursing leadership for the new millennium: Essential knowledge and skills. *Nursing and Health Care Perspectives, 20,* 260–265.

Frank, B. (1998). Performance management. In J. Dienemann (Ed.). *Nursing administration: Managing patient care* (2nd ed. pp. 461–484), Stamford, CT: Appleton and Lange.

Garone, S. J. (1999). *Concepts for the new leadership.* New York: The Conference Board.

Goleman, D. (1998). *Working with emotional intelligence.* New York: Bantam Books.

Harris, D. M., & DeSimone, R. L. (1998). *Human resource development.* Ft. Worth, TX: The Dryden Press.

Hodgkinson, C. (1982). *The philosophy of leadership.* Oxford, UK: Blackwell.

Knowles, M., & Associates (1980). *The modern practice of adult education: From pedagogy to andragogy.* Chicago: Follett.

Knowles, M., & Associates (1984). *Andragogy in action.* San Francisco: Jossey-Bass.

Kouzes, J. M., & Posner, B. Z. (1999). Strengthen others: Sharing power and information. In J. A. Shotgren (Ed.), *Skyhooks for leadership* (pp. 235–257). New York: American Management Association.

Lemire, J. (2001). Preparing nurse leaders: A leadership education model. *Nursing Leadership Forum, 6*(2), 39–44.

Marquis, B. L., & Huston, C. J. (2000). *Leadership roles and management functions in nursing: Theory and application* (3rd ed.). Philadelphia: Lippincott Williams & Wilkins.

Merriam, S. B., & Cafferella, R. S. (1999). *Learning in adulthood: A comprehensive guide.* San Francisco: Jossey-Bass.

Mezirow, J. (1990). *Fostering critical reflection in adulthood: A guide to transformative learning.* San Francisco: Jossey-Bass.

Miles, R. H. (1999). Leading corporate transformation: Are you up to the task? In J. A. Conger, G. M. Spreitzer, & Edward E. Lawler III (Eds.), *The leader's change handbook: An essential guide to setting direction and taking action* (pp. 221–267). San Francisco: Jossey-Bass.

Miller, T. W. (2000). Keeping informed. In F. L. Bower (Ed.), *Nurses taking the lead: Personal qualities for effective leadership* (pp. 297–329). Philadelphia: W. B. Saunders.

Myers, I. B., & Brigs, K. C. (1998). *Myers-Briggs Type Indicator.* Palo Alto, CA: Consulting Psychologist Press.

Osterman, K. F., & Kottkamp, R. B. (1993). *Reflective practice for educators: Improving schooling through professional development.* Newbury Park, CA: Corwin Press.

Peters, J. M. (1991). Strategies for reflective practice. In R. G. Brockett (Ed.), *Professional development for educators of adults: New directions for adult and continuing education* (No. 51). San Francisco: Jossey-Bass.

Ruben, B. D. (1999). Simulations, games and experienced-based learning: The quest for a new paradigm for teaching and learning. *Simulation and Gaming, 30,* 498–505.

Schmieding, N. J. (1999). Reflective inquiry framework for nurse administrators. *Journal of Advanced Nursing, 30,* 631–639.

Schon, D. A. (1987). *Educating the reflective practitioner.* San Francisco: Jossey-Bass.

Senge, P. M. (1990). *The art and practice of the learning organization.* New York: Doubleday.

Senge, P. M., Kleiner, A., Roberts, C., Roth, G., Ross, R., & Smith, B. (1999). *The dance of change: The challenges of sustaining momentum in learning organizations.* New York: Doubleday.

Shotgren, J. A. (Ed.). (1999). *Skyhooks for leadership.* New York: American Management Association.

Silberman, M. (1998). *Active training.* San Francisco: Jossey-Bass.

Sparrow, J. (1998). *Knowledge in organizations: Access to thinking at work.* Thousand Oaks, CA: Sage.

Strickland, D. (2000). Emotional intelligence: The most potent factor in the success equation. *Journal of Nursing Administration, 30*(3), 112–117.

True colors: Keys to successful business leadership profile booklet. (1988). Corona, CA: Communications Companies International.

Vaill, P. B. (1996). *Learning as a way of being: Strategies for survival in a world of permanent white water.* San Francisco: Jossey-Bass.

ACKNOWLEDGMENTS

The author gratefully acknowledges the contributions of Dr. Joyce Johnson, DNSc, FAAN, Senior Vice President, Operations Georgetown University Hospital, whose initial work on this article was invaluable, and to Denise Blair, RN, BS, graduate student, who helped to clarify a very important idea.

CHAPTER FOUR

Leader As Achiever

Jaqueline A. Dienemann

A leader's singular job is to get results (Goleman, 2000). First, they need to identify a vision or desired future for their scope of responsibility. Results demonstrate the leader's ability to invigorate others to work in collaboration to achieve a mutually desired future. Without a supportive environment that challenges everyone to contribute to progress, obstacles arise that are insurmountable. Thus, leadership is not charisma, or following a certain style or set of processes. It is the degree that a leader facilitates the achievement of desired outcomes with and through others (Warden, 1999). The evidence of leadership is achievements; organizational achievements are the evidence of effective and efficient processes.

In communicating their vision and working with others to define and plan how to achieve it, leaders must balance individual power and humility. Leaders who do not solicit new ideas and feedback are not viewed as effective by subordinates since they do not truly collaborate or integrate new information that only subordinates know (Greenleaf, 1996). In fact, a leader risks alienation and sabotage when acting in isolation or not publicly acknowledging the contributions of others. Looking across and up the organization, peers and those higher in the organization also provide invaluable support and assistance to a leader's achievements. The leader who fails to seek and acknowledge their counsel not only lacks all the information needed to develop a vision that may have the most impact, but also risks the backlash of others when they step forward and present themselves as solely responsible for their achievements. Conversely, work relationships can induce freedom for the leader and their collaborators to achieve personal potential, perceive meaning in work, and feel fulfilled through mutual achievements (DePree, 1989).

Change may be evolutionary or revolutionary. Evolutionary change is achieved through incremental improvement in achievement of a desired future. Performance Improvement (PI) is a powerful framework for creation of evolutionary change. Performance Improvement is based upon the selection of criteria for monitoring quality and a team approach to improving work processes through reducing variation or preventing sentinel (dangerous) events. Incremental change can be effective when introducing a shift in work processes or mix in types of team members. Leaders recognize this is always the preferred mode when time allows, because there is less resistance when change is paced to fit an employee's ability to process and integrate new expectations into their daily work life.

Revolutionary change, or a rapid and dramatic change in work processes or strategic direction, is chosen when it is determined that a needed change is so complex that the timeframe for incremental change would be ineffective or a crisis requires rapid, large scale change for organizational survival. Revolutionary change requires a period of adjustment in order to demonstrate systemic, positive results. At first disjointed and uneven levels of functioning are shown across the organization as people integrate new, daily work processes and changed expectations. Time is also required to identify and resolve unanticipated issues that arise with revolutionary change.

When examining results of change one should examine the revenue streams generated and the bottom line balance of cost and quality. The shift from measuring results from the perspective of professional actions carried out to *financial efficiency* and *patient outcomes* has been revolutionary in health care. This shift has created a new definition of quality patient care and determines what data should be collected and analyzed to measure achievements of leaders. Financial efficiency data should include price, volume, services provided, and comprehensiveness of services provided. Patient outcomes data should include measures of functional disability, pathology, co-morbidity, mortality, quality of life, satisfaction, risk reduction behaviors, and adherence. These data can then be aggregated for analysis of value and sustainable service. This is a revolutionary change, and the involvement of all health care providers and administrators in this new paradigm remains uneven (Wilson & Porter-O'Grady, 1999). Most collect and use data on some of the parameters listed above, but few collect all and systematically use them for making decisions. Leaders are increasingly being held accountable for achieving financial gains and desired rates of clinical outcomes.

LITERATURE REVIEW: THEORY AND RESEARCH

Sociotechnical system design is the leading organizational theory on how to configure organizations to be successful under today's conditions of high uncertainty and rapid change. This theory describes the ideal organization as a *self-designing system*, having a specific strategic direction (also called vision or long-term goal) and a chosen set of strategies to achieve that direction. Strategies are continuously adapted or changed in response to consumer (population served) demands and environmental changes in technology, professional functions, and society. The work processes and production technologies are aligned and responsive to trends in measures of results achieved and opportunities for performance improvement (Nadler & Tushman, 1997). Its defining characteristic is the autonomy of workers to lead the response to external demands though collaborating with managers to redesign work and initiate new ventures, resulting in improved financial and clinical performance. This theoretical approach builds upon a half century of research by organizational psychologists. The organization is viewed as continuously being redesigned. The system is *self-regulating*, responsive to its context, has fast, focused, and *flexible work processes*, and uses autonomous work teams. For a further description see Dienemann's (1998) summary of organizational theory.

Leadership in this context requires knowledge and understanding of the critical competencies outlined in the Leadership Education Model (LEM). The effective leader is an expert in the work of this organization, a critical thinker, a visionary, a communicator, an achiever, and a developer of self, others, and the organization. Leaders for specific changes may be direct care providers or managers working together for effective change.

ACHIEVING QUALITY OF PATIENT CARE

For nurses, as well as other professionals, the move from evaluating the quality of work based on work processes, such as asepsis, to improvement in patient outcomes is a difficult change. It is a major *paradigm shift* from a professional to a *patient focused orientation*. Previously, quality care was performed when the nurse or other professional acted professionally, that is, followed established procedures and policies. Now quality care is that which documents achievement of desired patient outcomes. Leaders have made this shift and seek information to validate their achievements.

For a health care organization to justly hold its leaders accountable for patient outcomes, however, executives must know the relationship of organizational structures and processes to *patient outcomes*. A person should only be held accountable for that which they can control, in this case the context for professional practice—organizational structures and work processes. Identifying this relationship has been a complex endeavor for nursing since nursing work is integrated with that of other professionals and the infrastructure supporting its delivery. Studies have been done to identify the patient outcomes that are directly the result of nursing work in various work settings. Those found are called *nurse-sensitive indicators* of quality nursing care. Measuring these indicators allows the assessment of quality of nursing care delivered. For example, recent studies by Aiken and others of the relationship of nurse staffing to specific, negative patient outcomes (Smith, 2002) have demonstrated that lower levels of staffing are directly associated with more negative patient outcomes.

The American Nurses Association (ANA) report card has been developed for acute care settings to guide agencies in choosing nurse sensitive indicators to collect to assess the quality of nursing interventions delivered (ANA, 1997). Less is known about patient outcomes directly associated with quality of nursing care for community health, ambulatory care, home health care or long-term care nurse practice settings. The new data collection required for all Medicare and Medicaid patients using the Outcome Assessment and Information Set (OASIS) in home care and the minimum data set (MDS) in long-term care may provide future standards for measurement of nurse-sensitive indicators in these settings, although recent studies have not been promising (Adams, DeFrates, & Wilson, 1998). Thus, more is known in acute care about which patient outcomes to collect to assess if a leader for a unit or service line is effective in bringing about quality nursing care.

Another approach to identifying *nurse-sensitive indicators* has been the Nursing Intervention Classification/Nursing Outcome Classification (NIC/NOC) project at University of Iowa that builds upon nursing diagnoses promoted by the North American Nursing Diagnosis Association (NANDA). Some progress is being made to test these relationships and incorporate these measures into clinical pathways to standardize care and present a standard for measurement of quality care. Adoption remains controversial since the language used is unique to nursing and not inclusive of all health care providers. Work is being done at the National Library of Medicine, however, to integrate nursing, medical, and other profession-specific languages for information retrieval in the Metathesaurus for a Unified Medical Language (UMLS). The UMLS has included NANDA, the Omaha System, the Home Health Care Classification, and NIC. These are all computer-based systems for describing nursing assessments, interventions, and patient outcomes in various settings (Hannah, Ball, & Edwards, 2000).

A parallel endeavor to measure quality and support improvement over time has been the development of *national guidelines*, lists of *best practices* and *standards of care*, and *standards of professional practice*. Standards are based on evidence of effectiveness for diagnosis and treatment of certain conditions and diseases which has been financed by the Agency for Healthcare Research Quality (AHRQ) and other health care related agencies of the federal government, as well as professional specialty organizations and consulting businesses such as Millman and Robertson. Slow adoption of these guidelines in practice is evidence of the slow pace of change from individual, professionally oriented decision making to aggregate population, patient-focused decision making in health care (McLaughlin & Kaluzny, 1999).

Simultaneously, organization-specific *case management* programs to incorporate best practices and national guidelines using *clinical pathways* have been developed to both profess a desired timing and choice of treatment for common conditions, surgeries, and diseases and identify accountable compliance by health care providers. Often pathways include designation of the health provider responsible for a specific parameter or action within a specific time frame. This is a revolutionary change for professionals who are still in the process of being accepted and incorporated in many settings.

Leaders need to address documentation policies, risk management, status of the health information system, choice of quality indicators that have evidence of their relationship to nursing practice, provision for updates, and level of professional team development of the health providers. Evolutionary change with the inclusion of physician leadership appears to be the most efficient mode of incorporation of quality measures of patient outcomes (Wilson & Porter-O'Grady, 1999; Zander, 1999).

Historically, nursing documentation has focused primarily on assessment with a secondary emphasis on intervention and minimal recording of outcomes. One step needed to establish both accountability and plan performance improvement is *documentation* of assessment, intervention processes, and outcomes. Outcome data that are not linked to processes will reveal status, but not cause and effect. For example, to evaluate results of a health education program on managing hypertension by recording a patient's blood pressure over time will indicate control or lack of control of hypertension. Without notation of baseline data on risk reduction behaviors, dose and frequency of health teaching regarding risk reduction behaviors and adherence to a medical regime and measurement of intensity and frequency of change in risk reduction behaviors and adherence to medical regime, the connection of the intervention to the outcome is unknown.

In fact, many medical patient records do not include data on patient outcomes other than pathology parameters or adverse incidents. No data are collected on health, function, or disability. Documentation is episode- and site-oriented with no connection being tracked between interventions (desired changes in behavior and patient outcomes or of patient change over time across multiple providers in different settings). Therefore the outcomes for many interventions are unknown. Without intervention, patient behavior, and appropriate outcome data, leaders cannot evaluate the worth or value of nursing interventions. This is an area of inquiry that leaders are pursuing.

FISCAL ACCOUNTABILITY

The fact that nursing remains embedded in the room cost for inpatient care makes documentation of the *financial costs and revenues* generated by nursing services difficult. This will be made even more difficult for all professions with new changes in billing and payment across settings toward global payment or prospective payment or capitation. Financial accountability is likely to move from individuals or single professions to programs with teams providing health and disease care for populations of people such as the current case management programs for high cost users.

These changes, however, will not change the need for organizations to identify their costs and develop means to monitor *fiscal efficiency*. Possible financial revenue or expense measures directly related to nursing actions and nurse administrator actions fall into three categories: patient data, nurse data, and system data. Patient data may include supply costs per patient day, timeliness of patient admission documentation, actual time of patient leaving after discharge has been ordered, tracking denials of payment due to lack of nursing documentation, rates of adverse events and malpractice suits, and patient satisfaction survey results. Nurse data aggregated by unit or office may include nurse staffing ratios, nurse turnover rates, recruitment and orientation costs, rate of certified competencies, career development costs, vacancy time before hire by position, overtime and temporary nursing personnel costs, rate of job-related nurse injuries and illnesses, and results of surveys of physician or multidisciplinary team satisfaction with nursing care. System data might include nurse suggestions for new ventures that result in additional revenues, nurse participation in PI or re-engineering teams that result in cost reductions, and nurse capital expenditure proposals. Nurse leaders need to develop systems to collect and analyze these data within a shared governance context. For example, all staff at Holy Cross Hospital share in a bonus if the hospital meets its fiscal goals (Taylor, 1998).

Often, agency accounting systems have several systems in place with differing aggregations such as cost centers, nursing units, admitting physician, and service line. New software is increasingly being created to increase crossover of information to support evaluation of cost and revenues that can be sorted by multiple parameters. As these *health information systems* allow alignment of financial revenue and cost accounting and patient clinical data, the likelihood of financial and clinical outcome accountability for nurse leaders will increase.

The issues of cost of data collection and timeliness of reporting also are relevant when looking at how a leader can be held accountable for patient and fiscal outcomes. This has been facilitated by the upgrading of health information systems in many organizations, but remains problematic in others. Where appropriate measures of quality are in place with efficient data collection, aggregating for information and reporting, they become the vehicle for not only accountability by leaders and work teams, but also for signs of the need for quality improvement and validation when it occurs.

SHARED GOVERNANCE

This shift to patient-focused outcomes and *accountability* has implications for nurses in clinical positions providing direct patient care. There is an increasing trend for agencies to develop or expand their shared governance structures and processes. Staff nurses are expected to assume *emergent leadership roles* as they serve on task forces and committees. These groups make decisions regarding both patient care and fiscal control. Examples of decisions include organizational policies regarding evidence-based nursing practice, PI recommendations for increasing quality at a reduced cost, job redesign, capital improvements, and the development of new services. This heightened expectation of leadership by nurses not working in management roles moves their influence beyond the bedside to the organization as a whole. This change has personal and professional implications for nurses, those that educate them, and their workplace (Wilson & Porter-O'Grady, 1999).

Another group impacted by increasing shared governance is the nurses holding *administrative leadership positions* within nursing care delivery systems and within other areas of health care delivery systems. The role of the manager in today's health care environment is to create a context for professional work and to hold staff accountable for fiscal and patient outcomes, not to monitor how staff chooses to carry out their work. They are expected to coach, assist, and be a resource for the work team providing care within a collaborative rather than a hierarchical relationship. This requires a higher level of communication skills than in the past (Laschinger & Havens, 1998).

LEADERSHIP DEVELOPMENT

Pfeffer and Veiga (1999) summarize recent research and identify the following seven *leadership development* practices of successful organizations (those that achieve their vision). These are:

1. employment security (supports the risk of creative innovation);
2. selective hiring requirements (includes critical skills and attributes desired which are difficult to change through training);
3. peer control of work through self managed teams (increases motivation and commitment);
4. comparative high compensation linked to team performance (increases commitment and motivation);
5. extensive training (difficult to measure return on investment, but is integral to success);
6. reduction of status differences (more equality in space, dress, titles); and
7. sharing of information (employees that know organizational financial, strategy, and operational measures of success are more likely to try to increase profits).

For nurses, training often needs to focus on fiscal language and measures and standards for accountability since basic nursing education often does not include any content in economics or financial management. Agencies that provide a work environment and investment in employees described above have more employees that are successful in achieving expectations for fiscal and clinical performance of the scope of work they are accountable for.

REWARDS AND PUNISHMENTS FOR ACHIEVEMENTS

Accountability of leaders for fiscal and clinical outcomes should be over time and not merely quarterly or annual increments. In some ways this runs counter to the American passion for quick results and the current trend for fast-track promotion through early career professionals frequently changing organizations. In order to be identified as "fast track" one needs to show short-term change, for example, new initiatives or re-engineering with early profits before long-term benefits or the lack of them are known (Applebaum & Batt, 1994).

Vision is a *long-term view*, with organizational growth over time as the key measure of success. To achieve this vision, many health care systems need to redesign to become responsive to *market forces* and leader rewards. They also need to reward risk taking and creation of new market-driven ventures. New ventures are needed to align mix of services to market niches for specific target populations, for example, people who desire e-services using new information technologies, those who will access convenient professional services located where they gather (the fitness center nurse or the parish nurse), or ethnic groups who desire alternative therapies or diets mixed with traditional services (Peters, 1999). Herzlinger (1997) urged leaders in health care to create ventures that include greater patient involvement in their own health care resulting in patient mastery of health promotion and disease and disability management to achieve long term health status improvement or maintenance despite chronic illness. Accountability for these ventures should realistically project the start-up costs and timing needed for profitability to prevent "punishment" of leaders who do not generate quick profits.

An issue that arises when examining health care leadership and the success of nurses in assuming leader roles is *gender*. What difference does gender make? Increasingly research is finding many stereotypes do not apply, but some differences do exist. One way to describe these differences is that men are socialized to view life as combat and the successful leader possesses the qualities of a warrior. Most women are socialized to view the world as a village where the leader considers that lives and interests of coworkers are intimately connected. This leads to differing ways that may achieve similar results. Men and women may also use different language when describing similar results. Also men and women often hold differing perspectives on how a leader or team member should behave to be successful leading to conflict within a team. When assessing the performance of a person of the other gender, the nurse needs to be aware of these gender differences and assess if they are influencing the evaluation (Cummins, 1998; Kearney & White, 1994).

Another relevant issue regarding achievement as a leader is the ability to work effectively with others who have *cultural differences*. These differences may be due to ethnic heritage, life circumstances, or socioeconomic differences. From these differences arise differing perceptions of personal success, appropriate behavior, balance of family and work commitment, and what is an award. Leadership-training programs should include sessions on cultural self-awareness, tolerance of difference, and standards for respect and cooperation for effective achievement of work goals (Dienemann, 1997). Leaders need to be aware of what others see as a reward in order to design systems that link rewards to achievement.

RELATED CONCEPTS AND SKILLS FOR BACCALAUREATE COMPLETION AND MASTER'S STUDENTS

Related concepts are in italics throughout the previous literature review. These concepts and skills need to be introduced throughout the curriculum to all baccalaureate completion (RN/BS) and master's degree students and not isolated in a "leadership and management" or "organizations" course.

At the master's level, those choosing health care administration as a major or emphasis will take specific courses with in-depth subject matter related to financial management, organizational and environmental assessment, and planning and implementing change. RN/BS students need to gain familiarity with the language of patient-focused outcomes and the theoretical basis for the cost and quality achievement processes they are likely to have seen and participated in as part of their practice. Master's students preparing for advanced practice roles or advanced level positions in nursing such as researcher, educator, or administrator need to be familiar with identifying desired patient-focused outcomes and related costs, linking them to specific interventions and designing program evaluation systems or research projects to measure achievement.

TEACHING STRATEGIES

The RN/BS student comes with a clinical background that the curriculum not only needs to recognize, but also capitalize upon during learning experiences through faculty asking for case examples and active dialogue. Often, students are less willing to accept theory that is not linked to practice and are also more interested in the technical and theoretical rationale for practices they have seen at work than generic students. They need experiences in teaching others, aggressive analytic interchange, group facilitation, and career planning.

One approach to teaching the linking of interventions to outcomes is independent learning experiences integrated into the curriculum wherein students are asked to write measurable learning objectives, describe measures of different levels of achievement, and then report on processes used, opportunities seized, and barriers overcome to achieve their goals. Including both patient and fiscal goals helps them to realize the importance of both. Often this occurs in practicums or when a major project is required for graduation.

Another opportunity occurs in teaching the research process. Assignments to hone critical thinking and assist in focusing on achievement include (a) identifying the research support for best practices; (b) designing a clinical research project; (c) critiquing research reports for use in their practice; (d) identifying measures for clinical and cost outcomes; and (e) verifying that an intervention is appropriate for a certain patient population. These learning experiences increase a student's grasp of the assessment, intervention, and evaluation process.

At the master's level, more in-depth content on the health care delivery system, measurement of fiscal accountability, and program evaluation of an unit, service, or ambulatory practice and managed care is vital for successful future role performance. Also experiences in planning the student's own program of study, reviewing his or her own practice, and assessing personal learning needs prepare the student for applying performance improvement at a personal level.

Graduate students often benefit from working on performance evaluation projects as part of a practicum experience. In didactic classes they should develop skills to use the Internet to gather comparative financial information on a health care delivery system and to research evidence to verify practice or recommendations for best practices. Simulation experiences such as a performance evaluation project using mock data on costs and quality to create a story board report is often meaningful when discussing financial, marketing, or PI issues. Another useful assignment may be to identify what their market value will be on graduation.

CONCLUSION

Leadership is now an expectation for nurses in all types of positions. Educators need to incorporate leadership skill development within all aspects of the curriculum to prepare new graduates for the expectations of the workplace. Nurses are being asked to achieve quality patient care with scarce resources. To meet these expectations, they need to know the evidence of what factors influence quality outcomes and what the agency must provide to realistically support achievement.

REFERENCES

Adams, C. E., DeFrates, D. S., & Wilson, M. (1998). Data-driven quality improvement for HMO patients. *Journal of Nursing Administration 28*(10), 20–25.

American Nurses Association. (1997). *Implementing nursing's report card: A study of RN staffing, length of stay, and patient outcomes.* Washington, DC: Author.

American Nurses Association. (1999). *Principles for nurse staffing.* Washington, DC: Author.

Applebaum, E., & Batt, R. (1994). *The new American workplace.* Ithaca, NY: ILR Press.

Cummings, S. (1998). Atilla the hun versus Atilla the hen: Gender socialization of the American nurse. In E. Hein (Ed.), *Contemporary leadership behavior* (5th ed.). Philadelphia: Lippincott.

DePree, M. (1989). *Leadership is an art.* New York: Dell.

Dienemann, J. (1997). *Cultural diversity in nursing: Issues, strategies and outcomes.* Washington, DC: American Academy of Nursing.

Dienemann, J. (1998). Assessing organizations. In J. Dienemann, (Ed.), *Nursing administration managing patient care* (pp. 267–283). Stamford, CT: Appleton & Lange.

Goleman, D. (2000). Leadership that gets results. *Harvard Business Review, 78*(2), 78–90.

Greenleaf, R. K. (1996). Power, management, and organizations. In D. M. Frick & L. C. Spears (Eds.); *On becoming a servant leader* (pp. 31–40). San Francisco: Jossey-Bass.

Hannah, K. I., Ball, M. J., & Edwards, M. J. A. (2000). *Introduction to nursing infomatics* (2nd ed). New York: Springer.

Herzlinger, R. (1997). *Market driven health care.* Reading, MA: Addison-Wesley.

Kearney, K. G., & White, T. I. (1994). *Men and women at work.* Hawthorne, NJ: Career.

Laschinger, H. K., & Havens, D. S. (1998). Staff nurse work empowerment and perceived control over nursing practice. In E. Hein (Ed.), *Contemporary Leadership Behavior* (5th ed., pp. 177–186). Philadelphia: Lippincott.

McLaughlin, C. P., & Kaluzny, A. D. (1999). *Continuous quality improvement in health care: Theory, implementation and applications* (2nd ed.). Germantown, MD: Aspen.

Nadler, D. A., & Tushman, M. L. (1997). *Competing by design: The power of organizational architecture.* New York: Oxford University Press.

Peters, T. (1999). *The circle of innovation: You cannot shrink your way to greatness*. New York: Vintage Press.

Pfeffer, J., & Veiga, J. F. (1999). Putting people first for organizational success. *The Academy of Management Executive 13*(2), 37–48.

Smith, A. P. (2002). Evidence of our instincts: An interview with Linda H. Aiken. *Nursing Economic$, 20*(2), 58–61.

Taylor, C. (1998). Changing rewards to match expectations. In J. Dienemann (Ed.), *Nursing administration: Managing patient care* (2nd ed., pp. 485–491). Stamford, CT: Apppleton Lange.

Warden, G. L., (1999). Leadership some things to think about. *Journal of Healthcare Management 44*(2), 85–86.

Wilson, C. K., & Porter-O'Grady, P. (1999). *Leading the revolution in health care* (2nd ed., pp. 1–38). Gaithersburg, MD: Aspen.

Zander, K., & Bower, K. (1999). *Case management: Solving the crisis du jour*. Natick, MA: The Center for Case Management.

CHAPTER FIVE

Leader As Critical Thinker

Judith A. Lemire

Over the last 10 years there has been a focus within the nursing world on leadership centers, leadership courses, leadership seminars/workshops, leadership retreats, and measuring the leadership skills and characteristics of nurses. Thousands of books and articles published in the literature over the last 25 years support these activities. Much of this literature, however, is a rehashing of the same issues and theories with little progress toward the development of a validated model for leadership education and development. Consequently, nursing continues to struggle with the development of the leadership knowledge, skills, and attributes that will contribute to the stability, growth, and effectiveness of the profession (Lemire, 2001).

Defining a nursing leadership profile to guide the education and ongoing leadership development of nurses has been an excellent starting point. Because leadership development is continuous and progressive it is in the best interests of the profession that this education begin in the academic setting. This article presents the leader as critical thinker module that includes the four most significant survey items of: (a) critical thinking, (b) systematic problem solving, (c) advanced critical thinking skills, and (d) complex problem solving.

DESCRIPTION OF CRITICAL THINKING MODULE AND CONCEPT DEFINITIONS

Leader as critical thinker evolves from the constructs of critical thinking (CT) and problem solving (PS). A leader possesses the knowledge and skills to think critically and to process complex problem solving in a systematic and timely manner. Considering the profession's opportunity and desire to impact the future of health care, a commitment to CT skills is essential. The emergence of nursing's advanced practice role and the continuous advancement in scientific and technological patient care make it imperative that nurses possess the knowledge to utilize complex CT and PS processes that are the foundation to reflect on one's thinking. Critical thinking involves a complex thinking order, metacognition, and problem solving that evolve from a General Systems Theory (GST) foundation. The literature abounds with definitions of CT that are so varied that a common definition is difficult to find.

Three of the more widely accepted definitions of CT are utilized for this article. First, Watson and Glasser (1980) defined CT as a composite of attitudes, knowledge, and skills in the following manner:

> This composite includes: (1) attitudes of inquiry that involve an ability to recognize the existence of problems and an acceptance of the general need for evidence in support of what is asserted to be true; (2) knowledge of the nature of valid inferences, abstractions, and generalizations in which the weight or accuracy of different kinds of evidence are logically determined; and (3) skills in employing and applying the above attitudes and knowledge. (p. 1)

Second, in the Delphi research project conducted by Facione (1990) a consensus statement noted that "We understand critical thinking to be purposeful, self-regulatory judgement which results in interpretation, analysis, evaluation, conceptual, methodological, criteriological, or contextual considerations upon which that judgement is based . . ." (p. 3). Third, Bandman and Bandman (1995) defined CT as "the rational examination of ideas, inferences, assumptions, principles, arguments, conclusions, issues, statements, beliefs, and actions. This examination covers scientific reasoning, decision making, and reasoning in controversial issues" (p. 7). Integrating the three definitions above, thinking critically involves the acquisition of knowledge, reasoning and rational appraisal skills, analytic problem-solving behaviors, and reflective thinking.

The ability to solve complex problems evolves from a framework of advanced CT knowledge and skills and GST thinking. Problem solving is a purposeful and goal-directed effort using a systematic process to choose from alternative actions. There is a fairly strong consensus on the definition of PS in the literature, with some variation in the definition and arrangements of the specific steps in the process. Problem solving and decision making continue to be used synonymously in the literature, however, and that simply is not the case. Problem solving is an intellectual and complex process that begins with the identification of a problem and culminates in the implementation and evaluation of a resolution, whereas decision making is a specific step in the PS process involving the selection of an available alternative for the purpose of goal attainment. The kind of decision making practiced by nurses requires skillful PS supported by CT. Also, PS is not just the responsibility of managers and advanced practice nurses, but also an important aspect of every nurse's role (Kontryn, 1999).

REVIEW OF THE LITERATURE

There is consensus that nurses need effective PS skills in order to make the autonomous and group decisions frequently required in the professional role (Adams, 1999; Boney & Baker, 1997) and that CT is essential to leadership (Duchesne, 1999; Facione, Sanchez, Facione, & Gainen, 1995). Critical thinking provides the framework for responsible thinking that facilitates good judgment and thus competent quality care (Beeken, Dale, Enos, & Yarbrough, 1997; Brigham, 1993; Glen, 1995; Miller & Malcolm, 1990). The acquisition of refined CT skills facilitates the development of effective PS skills (Boney & Baker, 1997; Dary, 2000; Martin, 1996; Miller, 1992; Watson & Glaser, 1964). Brooks and Shepherd (1990) showed a significant correlation between CT and decision making in 50 seniors in ADN, diploma, BSN, and RN to BSN programs. Adams reviewed 20 studies from 1977 to 1995 that employed changes in the CT abilities of nursing students; 19 of the studies suggested that CT is synonymous with PS and decision making. The PS associated with nursing involves complex problems demanding the use of higher order reflective CT skills. For this discussion of the CT and PS aspects of leadership, CT is presented as the theoretical construct from which effective PS evolves.

A world of continuous and rapid change in both personal and professional arenas has contributed to an emphasis on the need for CT knowledge and skills (Facione, 1990; Kerka, 1992; Shell, 2001; Tucker, 1996). These skills are especially important to the graduate student preparing for the advanced practice role who is involved in high-level PS in the organization of 2000 and beyond (Rieley & Crossley, 2000). Schrag (1992) and Kerka suggested that the changing nature of the workplace requires individuals with greater cognitive abilities and CT skills. The literature abounds with writings on the attributes of CT, beginning with Dewey (1933), who suggested a major goal of education should be the acquisition of reflective thinking skills that he defined as the collection and evaluation of evidence for the purpose of drawing a conclusion. Dary (2000), Shell (2001), and Watson and Glaser (1964) noted the importance of CT to learning and that thinking critically should be considered a priority of higher education.

A number of studies demonstrated a positive correlation between CT and education (Duchesne, 1999; Miller, 1992; Pascarella, 1989; Pearson, 1991; Sullivan, 1987). Howe and Warren (1989) stated that "the ability to think critically is essential if individuals are to live, work, and function effectively in our current and changing society" (p. 3). Experts in CT suggest that developing CT skills prepares one for the complex change associated with every aspect of one's life (Davis & Botkin, 1995; Kerka, 1992; Penner, 1995).

Several similar concepts have been identified with CT, such as thinking about one's thinking (Facione & Facione, 1996), multidimensional metacognitive activity (Beeken, et al., 1997), composite of inquiry attitudes and knowledge (Miller, 1992), higher order thinking skills (Glen, 1995), and an affective dimension or way of behaving (Paul, 1992; Perkins, 1985). The Delphi Project identified the dispositions exhibited by critical thinkers: inquisitiveness, self-confidence, open-mindedness, honesty, and fair-mindedness. Also noted was that without such dispositions one is unlikely to apply learned CT skills (Facione, 1990; Facione, et al., 1995). Several theorists support Facione's finding that CT has both disposition and cognitive dimensions (Brookfield, 1991; Halpern, 1993; Paul). Yet a correlational study of senior BSN students by Colucciello (1999) showed that the students had very inadequate critical thinking dispositions.

By the late 1980s the need for CT skills as a foundation for effective PS was well accepted and the integration of CT concepts into college curricula emerged. Even though the profession advocates developing CT skills in nurses, studies of the results are disappointing. No consistent evidence shows that nursing curricula increase the CT abilities of students (Adams, 1999; Glaser & Resnick, 1991; Hickman, 1993). Longitudinal studies with measurements on entry and exit from a nursing program show no significant gains in CT skills (Bauwens & Gerhard, 1987; Berger, 1984; Sullivan, 1987). Brigham (1989) and Dungan (1986) found no significant difference between any groups of nursing students. Other studies showed that the RN to BSN and MSN students scored significantly higher on the CT measurement than ADN and diploma students (Brooks & Shepherd, 1992; Lynch, 1988; Pardue, 1987). Hickman (1993) suggested that higher RN to BSN and MSN student scores might indicate a relationship between CT abilities and life experiences. A study to elicit the perceptions of nurse educators concerning their perceptions of barriers to the implementation of CT teaching strategies suggested "that nurse educators continue to use teaching methods that hinder higher thinking development and that recent nursing graduates are lacking in their ability to think critically" (Shell, 2001, p. 290).

In summary, although there is consensus on the importance of CT to effective PS, studies of nursing students and new graduates showed inadequate CT skills and dispositions. The nursing profession still struggles with the development of an educational paradigm that integrates CT into nursing education with measurable results on a consistent basis.

THEORETICAL FRAMEWORK

General Systems Theory provides a conceptual framework from which leadership attributes and characteristics evolve and prosper. Utilizing CT and PS skills within a GST framework provides the opportunity to see the whole picture and achieve a greater understanding of a situation. Wilson and Porter-O'Grady (1999) stated that "the greater the systems we comprehend, the greater will be our knowledge and the more potent the solutions" (p. 337). GST proposes that systems are wholes composed of interconnected subsystems with significant interaction. Therefore, change in one area affects all areas, including the supraenvironment within which the system exists. These subsystems are connected in one of four ways, operating (a) simultaneously, (b) in tandem, (c) parallel, or (d) in a series with each other. Mastering systems thinking and the interactions between subsystems enables an individual to develop strategies and methodologies with the total picture in mind. The GST concepts of input-transformation-output model, holism, feedback, multiple goal seeking, and equifinality complement the elements of CT and PS processes and form the basis from which high level thoughts, integration, and synthesis occur (Kast, Fremont, & Rosenzweig, 1981).

Vaske (1998) posited a conceptual framework of critical thinking for the adult learner based on an extensive review of the literature. He summarized the framework in the following statement:

> Critical thinking is composed of two dimensions: (1) cognitive skills, and (2) dispositions. Cognitive skills consist of higher order thinking skill, problem solving, metacognition, and reflective thinking. Dispositions include both cognitive and affective dispositions consisting of reflective thinking, explore and imagine, and skepticism. . . . It is possible to measure each of these indicators of critical thinking. (p. 119)

Higher order thinking and PS include five cognitive skills: interpretation, analysis, evaluation, inference, and explanation. The principles of metacognition emphasize the following learning activities and processes with higher cognitive learning goals: (a) the interaction of cognitive, metacognitive, and affective aspects of learning; (b) deep cognitive processing and awareness of one's learning strategies; and (c) self-regulation skills. Reflective thinking is an important aspect of individual cognitive and disposition dimensions (Vaske, 1998). The disposition dimension of the model addresses the effect of a person's experiences, values, beliefs, and attitudes upon their ability to think critically. The belief that the cognitive skills and dispositions of an individual interrelate to create CT ability has been widely accepted.

STAGES OF CRITICAL THINKING AND PROBLEM SOLVING EDUCATION

The acquisition and application of CT and PS skills is progressive and is refined through life long learning and experience. Developing CT skills though achievement in higher education is important to this learning. Critical thinking and PS expertise are acquired through sequential learning, beginning with a sound knowledge base of the CT composite and PS strategies. Critical Thinking and PS learning occur at an individual pace when the elements of CT are integrated into all courses. In addition to classroom learning, students need a practicum experience that facilitates successful application of learned concepts to ensure the ultimate goal of synthesis.

Figure 5.1 suggests a progressive plan for integrating CT concepts into the curriculum. The undergraduate baccalaureate nursing student needs to acquire a thorough understanding of basic CT skills and GST. The CT concepts described as continuous and progressive are integrated into undergraduate and graduate curricula because the learning process relating to these concepts is on-going and enhanced by an individual's maturity and expertise. Advanced CT concepts would be integrated into the graduate program curriculum. Progressive learning allows students to develop a solid understanding

Offer a rationale for learning the skills.
Actively involve students in the learning.
Allow sufficient time for students to reflect on the questions asked or problems posed.
Ask open-ended questions.
Promote interaction among students as they learn.
Model problem-solving techniques.
Provide practice of thinking skills in multiple settings.
Use multiple learning strategies.
Use examples that are similar to the situations in which the skills will be used.
Teach for transfer.
Use intrinsic motivational techniques.
Promote metacognitive attention to thinking.

FIGURE 5.1. Guidelines for teaching higher order thinking skills.

of the basic CT skills and knowledge that will provide the foundation for learning and for applying the more advanced concepts.

CRITICAL THINKING TEACHING STRATEGIES

Adult educators facilitate learning through strategies that utilize the adult learner characteristics of experiential learning, re-evaluation of childhood values and beliefs, intellectual curiosity, and willingness to take responsibility for their learning. The classroom environment that promotes critical thinking has the following characteristics: (a) encourages questions and the challenging of ideas; (b) facilitates student discussions focused on reasoning and valid premises; (c) supports nonjudgmental consideration of the ideas and arguments of peers; and (d) fosters active learning that inspires students to take responsibility for their learning (Brookfield, 1991).

This description of classroom environment indicates the need for adjusting the faculty role and teaching methods to actively involve both faculty and students in the learning process. Open-ended questions and core studies similar to solutions in which the skills will be used also facilitate learning (Kerka, 1992). In recent years there has been faculty resistance to teaching CT, faculty being unprepared to teach CT, and faculty lacking adequate knowledge to teach CT (Hass & Keeley, 1998; Keeley, Shemberg, Cowell, & Zinnbauer, 1995; O'Sullivan, Blevins-Stephens, Smith, & Vaughan-Wrobel, 1997; Shell, 2001). Nurse educators are pressured to teach enormous amounts of content, requiring strategies that may be inconsistent with the development of CT skills and knowledge. A challenge to the profession is not only embracing CT as an essential component of education, but also ensuring that faculty members have sufficient class time and that the CT knowledge and teaching strategies will facilitate student's acquisition of CT skills.

Articles and books authored by experts can guide the pursuit and commitment to embrace CT. For example, Vaske (1998, p. 35) identified 12 guidelines for teaching higher order thinking skills (Figure 5.2). Faculty for adult learners must use a variety of teaching methodologies that support the objectives, purpose, and content of subject matter to successfully implement these guidelines. Discussion, case method, inquiry exercises, nominal group technique, oral and written presentations, and experiential learning are described below and serve as examples for teaching CT and PS.

DISCUSSION

Group discussion and assessment are conducive to the development of CT and PS skills. Through discussion, cognitive and affective ends can be achieved, particularly those of PS, concept exploration, inquiry, and reasoning. A discussion group's degree of success will be related to the faculty role and student activity. Using this strategy, faculty provide unobtrusive structure and guidance to facilitate learning and meet educational objectives. Group members must participate fully in the discussion process to develop higher level thinking skills. Robertson and Rane-Szostak (1996) stated in their article concerning group dialogues that "students must learn to critically evaluate dialogues as they occur, which requires well-integrated critical thinking ability" (p. 553). Faculty can facilitate this experience by identifying and assessing reasoning skills, using diverse approaches, welcoming the unanticipated, attending to the emotional dimension, and analyzing errors in thinking (Brookfield, 1991; Robertson & Rane-Szostak, 1996).

CASE METHOD

Case method is an approach to instruction based on real-life or lifelike examples and includes three components: case study, case analysis, and case discussion. The case study describes a complex lifelike problem designed to provoke an analysis of alternative solutions and consideration of possible consequences of implementation. The case analysis of a complex situation should be constructed to assist students to consider all aspects of the case. The key to a quality analysis is based on factual data depicted in the case study. The third phase, case discussion, consists of simulating reality with perceptions and proposed actions based on factual data (Marsick, 1990). The real challenge of the case method is designing intricate case studies that focus on real-life, complex problems, and whose analysis will meet the objectives of the planned learning. To ensure a productive analysis, faculty should anticipate and facilitate dialogue that will meet the objectives to be achieved, utilize the critical points of the case study analysis to discreetly guide the discussion, and ensure the application of high level CT and PS skills.

INQUIRY EXERCISES

The inquiry approach evolves from the premise that humans are inquisitive by nature. Kurfiss (1988) reviewed numerous college level studies in which the inquiry method proved effective in developing CT skills. Joyce, Weil, and Showers (1992) described a teaching process for an inquiry exercise that focuses on both content and process objectives. The process includes the following five phases:

1.   presentation and analysis of the problem;
2.   collection and analysis of data;
3.   development of causal hypotheses;
4.   explanation of the phenomena;
5.   and analysis of the inquiry process to identify areas for improvement.

Faculty have a variety of opportunities to facilitate the achievement of higher order thinking as they guide the discussion and student's critiques of the inquiry process.

ORAL AND WRITTEN PRESENTATIONS

Individual oral presentations and written assignments provide an opportunity to assess CT and PS abilities of a student's independent work. It also allows students to explore an idea or situation of special interest. Although much of an individual's CT and PS occur in groups, it is essential that students demonstrate those abilities when working independently and without cues from others. This is an important aspect of a person's effectiveness and includes responding to inquiries.

NOMINAL GROUP TECHNIQUE

Nominal group technique has been widely utilized in academia. Anticipated outcomes from a nominal group process evolve from a foundation of defined individual and group objectives, productive group dynamics, a defined and agreed upon group processing model,

Basic critical-thinking skills for RN to BSN students	
Comprehension of CT concepts	Development of cognitive skills
Comprehension of one's thinking	Exploration of the relationship between premises
Recognition of patterns	Explanation
Deductive reasoning	General Systems Theory
Continuous and progressive critical thinking concepts for RN to BSN and graduate students	
Inquiry skills	Analysis
Evaluation and exploration of assumptions	Reasoning to make valid inferences
Validation of reasoning and inferences through logic	Exploration of one's dispositions, values, and beliefs
Metacognition	Assessment of the relevance of information
Interpretation of arguments	Evaluation
Advanced critical thinking skills for graduate students	
Inductive thinking	Identifying inconsistencies in reasoning
Formulating valid and relevant hypotheses	Conjecture
Synthesis of CT constructs	Evaluation of arguments
Assessing disposition	Self-regulation
Nurturing CT in others	Critical Thinker 1

FIGURE 5.2. Progression for integrating critical thinking concepts into the curricula.

and cognitive CT skills. The effectiveness of this technique results from sharing ideas in a context of high-level CT and PS. Ludden and Wood (1986) identified the following four-step nominal group technique model:

1. Participants are asked to respond to a question or statement by generating a written list of responses.
2. The group facilitator asks each member to contribute an idea from her or his list in a round-robin approach.
3. Group members are given the opportunity to discuss and clarify any of the ideas that have been selected.
4. Group members are asked to rank or rate each item.

EXPERIENTIAL LEARNING

Experiential learning consists of a practicum for the purposes of integrating, synthesizing, and applying the learned concepts of CT and PS in practice. Process and outcome objectives specific to the clinical experience should be mutually developed to serve as criteria for measuring the student's ability to transfer classroom learning to the real world. An important component of this process is student logs/journals, to be utilized as the springboard for the student's conferences with faculty. The log/journal format should be structured to stimulate CT by addressing areas such as the validity of the premises upon which reasoning is based.

THE EVALUATION OF CRITICAL THINKING

Evaluation criteria evolve from the structural, process, and outcome standards of both the program curriculum and student learning objectives. Process standards can be measured from course to course as the student progresses through the program, whereas the outcome standards measured at program completion can be compared with program entry measurements. The evaluation of curriculum and student achievement is specific to each program, with case study analysis, student presentations, and student writings utilized for evaluation. Case studies evaluated according to predetermined criteria measure a student's ability to utilize high-level CT and PS skills to plan strategically and resolve real life situations. Oral presentations demonstrate the ability to progress from using CT skills and PS processes in writing to articulating ideas and influencing others.

There are several valid and reliable tests that measure the CT outcome of a student's learning experience. Dary (2000) compiled comparative data on tests to assess CT, PS, and writing by measuring cognitive variables. Sponsored by the National Center for Education Statistics, this is a valuable sourcebook for developing an evaluation plan. Dary compared 12 assessment tests and 22 writing assessments. Since all methods for evaluating CT and PS skills have limitations, an efficient assessment plan would include a combination of methods for both formative and summative purposes.

SUMMARY

Members of the nursing profession acknowledge the importance of thinking critically to leadership and complex problem solving; however, the endeavors to teach CT have been less than successful. General Systems Theory framework forms the basis for CT learning, with CT teaching strategies integrated into the entire curriculum in a progressive fashion. Teaching CT is difficult and requires changes in teaching methodologies and the creation of new roles for nurse educators. Faculty who understand what CT really is and demonstrate proficiency in CT can be successful in developing this proficiency in students.

REFERENCES

Adams, B. L. (1999). Nursing education for critical thinking: An integrative review. *Journal of Nursing Education, 38,* 111–119.

Bandman, E. L., & Bandman, B. (1995). *Critical thinking in nursing* (2nd ed.). Norwalk, CT: Appleton & Lange.

Bauwens, E., & Gerhard, G. (1987). The use of the Watson-Glaser critical thinking appraisal to predict success in a baccalaureate nursing program. *Journal of Nursing Education, 26,* 278–281.

Beeken, J. E., Dale, M. L., Enos, M. F., & Yarbrough, S. (1997). Teaching critical thinking skills to undergraduate nursing students. *Nurse Educator, 22,* 37–39.

Berger, M. C. (1984). Critical thinking ability and nursing students. *Journal of Nursing Education, 23,* 306–308.

Boney, J., & Baker, J. D. (1997). Strategies for teaching clinical decision-making. *Nurse Education Today, 17,* 16–21.

Brigham C. F. (1989). *Critical thinking skills in nursing students progressing through a nursing curriculum.* Unpublished doctoral dissertation, Ball State University, Muncie, IN.

Brigham, C. (1993). Nursing education and critical thinking: Interplay of content and thinking. *Holistic Nurse Practitioner, 7,* 48–54.

Brookfield, S. D. (1991). *Developing critical thinkers, challenging adults to explore alternative ways of thinking and acting.* San Francisco: Jossey-Bass.

Brooks, K. L., & Shepherd, J. M. (1990). The relationship between clinical decision-making skills in nursing and general critical thinking abilities of senior nursing students in four types of nursing programs. *Journal of Nursing Education, 29,* 391–399.

Brooks, K., & Shepherd, J. (1992). Professionalism versus general critical thinking abilities of senior nursing students in four types of nursing curricula. *Journal of Professional Nursing, 8,* 87–95.

Colucciello, M. L. (1999). Relationships between critical thinking dispositions and learning styles. *Journal of Professional Nursing, 15,* 294–301.

Dary, E. (2000). *The NPEC sourcebook on assessment, Volume 1: Definitions and assessment methods for critical thinking, problem solving, and writing* (Report No. NCES-2000-195). Jessup, MD: Educational Publications (ERIC Document Reproduction Service No. ED 443 891)

Davis, S., & Botkin, J. (1995). *The monster under the bed.* New York: Simon & Schuster.

Dewey, J. (1933). *How we think: A restatement of the relation of reflexive thinking to the educational process.* Lexington, MA: Heath.

Duchesne, R. (1999). Critical thinking, developmental learning, and adaptive flexibility in organizational leaders. In *Academy of Human Resource Development (AHRD) Conference Proceedings: Managers and Learning.* (ERIC Document Reproduction Service No. ED 431 938).

Dungan J. M. (1986). *Relationship of critical thinking and nursing process utilization.* Presented at the University of Minnesota School of Nursing Research Conference, Minneapolis, MN.

Facione, N. C., & Facione, P. A. (1996). Assessment design issues for evaluating critical thinking in nursing. *Holistic Nurse Practitioner, 10,* 41–53.

Facione, P. (1990). *Critical thinking: A statement of expert consensus for purposes of educational assessment and instruction.* (ERIC Document Reproduction Services No. ED 315 423)

Facione, P., Sanchez, C., Facione, N., & Gainen, J. (1995). The disposition toward critical thinking. *The Journal of General Education, 44*(1), 1–25.

Glaser, R., & Resnick, L. (1991). *National research center on student learning.* (Report No. EDO-TM-91-7). Washington, DC: Office of Educational Research and Improvement. (ERIC Document Reproduction Service No. ED 338 704)

Glen, S. (1995). Developing critical thinking in higher education. *Nurse Education Today, 15,* 170–176.

Halpern, D. F. (1993). Assessing the effectiveness of critical-thinking instruction. *The Journal of General Education, 42,* 239–254.

Hass, P., & Keeley, S. (1998). Coping with faculty resistance to teaching critical thinking. *College Teaching, 46*(2), 63–67.

Hickman, J. S. (1993). A critical assessment of critical thinking in nursing education. *Holistic Nurse Practitioner, 7,* 36–47.

Howe, R. W., & Warren, C. R. (1989). *Teaching critical thinking through environmental education.* (Report No. EDO-SE-22). Washington, DC: Office of Educational

Research and Improvement. (ERIC Document Reproduction Services No. ED 324 193)

Joyce, B., Weil, M., & Showers, B. (1992). *Models of teaching.* Boston: Allyn & Bacon.

Kast, Fremont, & Rosenzweig. (1981). General systems theory: Applications for organization and management. *The Journal of Nursing Administration, 11*(7), 32–41.

Keeley, S., Shemberg, K., Cowell, B., & Zinnbauer, B. (1995). Coping with student resistance to critical thinking: What the psychotherapy literature tells us. *College Learning, 43,* 140–145.

Kerka, S. (1992). *Higher order thinking skills in vocational education.* (Report No. EDO-CE-92–127). Washington, DC: Office of Educational Research and Improvement. (ERIC Document Reproduction Service No. ED 350 487)

Kontryn, V. (1999). Strategic problem solving in the new millennium. *Association of Perioperative Registered Nurses Journal, 70,* 1035–1044.

Kurfiss, J. F. (1988). *Critical thinking: Theory, research, practice, and possibilities.* Washington, DC: Association for the Study of Higher Education.

Lemire, J. (2001). Preparing nurse leaders: A leadership education model. *Nursing Leadership Forum, 6*(2), 39–44.

Ludden, L., & Wood, G. S., Jr. (1986). *Identifying the adult literacy, research needs of Indiana: Utilization of the nominal group technique.* Proceedings of the Midwest Research-to-Practice Conference in Adult, Community and Continuing Education, Muncie, IN.

Lynch, M. H. (1988). *Critical thinking: A comparative study of baccalaureate and associate degree nursing students.* Unpublished doctoral dissertation, Vanderbilt University, Nashville, TN.

Marsick, V. J. (1990). Case study. In M. W. Galbraith (Ed.), *Adult Learning Methods* (pp. 225–246). Malabar, FL: Krieger.

Martin, G. W. (1996). An approach to the facilitation and assessment of critical thinking in nurse education. *Nurse Education Today, 16,* 3–9.

Miller, M. A. (1992). Outcomes evaluation: Measuring critical thinking. *Journal of Advanced Nursing, 17,* 1401–1407.

Miller, M. A., & Malcolm, N. S. (1990). Critical thinking in the nursing curriculum. *Nursing & Health Care, 11,* 67–73.

O'Sullivan P., Blevins-Stephens, W., Smith F., & Vaughan-Wrobel, B. (1997). Addressing the National League for Nursing critical-thinking outcome. *Nurse Educator, 22*(1), 23–29.

Pascarella, E. (1989). The development of critical thinking: Does college make a difference. *Journal of College Student Development, 30,* 19–26.

Pardue, F. (1987). Decision making skills and critical thinking among associate degree, diploma, baccalaureate and master's prepared nurses. *Journal of Nursing Education, 26,* 354–361.

Paul, R. (1992). Critical thinking: What, why, and how. In Cynthia Barns (Ed.), *Critical thinking: Educational Imperative.* San Francisco: Jossey-Bass.

Pearson, C. V. (1991). *Barrier to success: Community college students' critical thinking skills.* Washington, DC: U.S. Office of Education. (ERIC Document No. ED 340 415)

Penner, K. (1995). *Teaching critical thinking*. Paper presented to Linda Cannell, Professor of Learning and the Art of Teaching, Regent College.

Perkins, D. N. (1985). General cognitive skills: Why not? In S. F. Chipman, J. W. Segal, & R. Glaser, (Eds.), *Thinking and learning skills* (pp. 339–364). Hillsdale, NJ: Lawrence Erlbaum.

Rieley, J. B., & Crossley, A. (2000). Beyond 2000: Decision making and the future of organizations. *National Productivity Review, 19,* 21–27.

Roberson, J. F., & Rane-Szostak, D. (1996). Using dialogues to develop critical thinking skills: A practical approach. *Journal of Adolescent & Adult Literacy, 39,* 552–556.

Schrag, F. (1992). Critical thinking. In *Encyclopedia of education research* (Vol. 1, pp. 254–256). Toronto, Canada: Macmillan.

Shell, R. (2001). Perceived barriers to teaching critical thinking by BSN nursing faculty. *Nursing Health Care Perspectives, 22*(6), 286–291.

Sullivan, E. J. (1987). Critical thinking, creativity, clinical performance, and achievement in RN students. *Nurse Education, 12,* 12–16.

Tucker, R. W. (1996). Less than critical thinking. *Adult Assessment Forum, 6,* 2–8.

Vaske, J. M. (1998). *Defining, teaching, and evaluating critical thinking skills.* Unpublished doctoral dissertation, Drake University, Des Moines, IA.

Watson, G., & Glaser, E. M. (1964). *Watson-Glaser critical thinking appraisal (WGCTA).* New York: Harcourt Brace Janovich.

Watson, G., & Glaser, E. M. (1980). *Watson-Glaser critical thinking appraisal (WGCTA).* San Antonio, TX: Harcourt Brace.

Wilson, C. K., & Porter-O'Grady, T. (1999). *Leading the revolution in health care: Advancing systems, igniting performance* (2nd ed.). Gaithersburg, MD: Aspen.

CHAPTER SIX

Leader As Communicator

Patricia M. Haynor

The nurse leader performs a myriad of communication activities, routinely interacting with patients, families, peers, professional and nonprofessional team members, inter- and intra-organizational colleagues, sales and marketing representatives, members of the press, spiritual representatives, and others involved intimately as well as tangentially in the delivery of health care. The role requires the skills of an interpreter, marketer, collaborator, questioner, advocate, coordinator, promoter, reflector, negotiator/peacemaker, soother/healer, truth teller, reality checker, teacher, documenter, conduit, correspondent, problem solver, brainstormer, influencer, organizer, envisioner, delegator, consensus builder, and follower. This requires panache, grace, and a clear head. The communication must be seamless and must be delivered effortlessly, clearly, precisely, and sensitively across personal, professional, cultural, organizational, departmental, and developmental boundaries. It must be delivered effectively, appropriately, and use diverse thinking done with benign intent so as to "do no harm." The timing is critical and the mode changes with the time and situation. Three modes of communication are required: verbal, nonverbal, and written. It is the duty of a professional nursing education program to understand the nature of the skills required, and their importance, and to cultivate them in each student.

LEADERS, COMMUNICATION, AND DEFINITIONS

Although it is commonly agreed that communication is a vital skill for leaders, it is often the reason for leader ineffectiveness. Leaders who are effective communicators are good listeners who validate what is heard and seek clarification (Bower, 2000). The elements basic to the communication model include a sender, message, mode of transmission, and receiver. Both the sender and the receiver are influenced by internal and external climates. The values, beliefs, temperament, and stress levels of the individuals will impact on the message sent and received. Many external factors such as power, position, weather condition, and physical space may also affect the climate of the sender and receiver. Messages are transmitted in three modes (verbal, nonverbal, and written), with each mode having its own barriers to success.

Tappen (1995) defined communication as the sharing of thoughts, feelings, and ideas that occurs whenever two or more people are working together. Huber (1996) on the other hand stated that communication is the art of being able to structure and transmit a message that can be easily understood or accepted. Vestal (1995) saw communication as "the exchange of meanings between and among individuals through a shared system of symbols (verbal and nonverbal) that have the same meaning for both the sender and receiver of the message" (p. 34). Manion (1999) discussed communication as the

> act of interchanging or importing thoughts, opinions, ideas or information by speech, writing or other signs . . . the sender may either perceive a change in the receiver's behavior or actually be told that the message has been received . . . this feedback closes the communication loop. (p. 54)

Taking a wider view, Poole and Hirokawa (1985) saw communication as a social catalyst and the medium for coordination and control of group activities.

Each of these definitions has similarities, but perhaps Berlo's (1960) coining communication as a process integrates the definitions. He offered four elements inherent in the process; (a) action or acts, (b) a continuous change in time, (c) advancement or progress over time, and (d) a goal or result. Each of these elements affects all of the others and thus brings us to the interdependence of the sender and receiver(s) in a fluid environment. These definitions support the basic model of communication and prepare us to explore the characteristics of effective communication, the effects of communication on the culture of an organization, and the importance of feedback.

At least two people are involved in every communication regardless of the mode: a sender and a receiver (Hackman & Johnson, 1991; Matusak, 1997; Swanburg, 1996). And since communication is a human process involving interpersonal relationships, the ability to use effective language patterns, actively listen, and establish and retain rapport are critical to communication effectiveness (Dickenson-Hazard & Root, 2000). Because individuals are unique (they make decisions and perceive communications differently), it is necessary to discuss language patterns that may present barriers to ensure that listeners (receivers) comprehend the meaning attached to the message.

LEADERS, COMMUNICATION, AND LANGUAGE BARRIERS

Four major language patterns create problems for us in communicating effectively: deletion, distortion, use of vague pronouns, and nominalization (McKay, Davis, & Fanning, 1995). Deletion means that information is left out of the message and leaves the receiver with a need to have "the blanks filled in." This relates to the definition of communication by Huber (1996) that suggests that the transmitted message should be easily understood or accepted. Distortion appears in several forms and is the result of our personal values, our prejudices, and how we see the world, which might occur as a result of cause and effect. That is, I respond to your behavior as a sender and have no choice. Mind reading is another form of distortion in which the receiver claims to know what the sender is thinking about without any communication. Vestal (1995) stated that communication is "an exchange of meanings between and among individuals . . . through a shared system of symbols" (p. 34). Although this definition requires an exchange or communication it is easy to make the link to mind reading if the two parties do have a shared system of symbols that are both verbal and nonverbal. Another distortion pattern that is frequently experienced involves presuppositions or the belief that if the first part of the statement is true, so is the second part.

Vague language and nominalizations complete the most common distortions. Vague language refers to the use of pronouns and verbs that create confusion for the receiver. For instance, "it worked yesterday." What does "it" refer to? The receiver experiences nominalization when the sender uses language that appears precise, but is not. The receiver needs additional information to visualize the message. The message may include such terms as "problems," "solutions," " successful," but provide no explanation as to what "solutions" are at hand, what "help" is needed. Words should be carefully chosen to assure the sending of a clear and concise message. Attention, however, also needs to be paid to the mode that delivers the message.

LEADERS, COMMUNICATION, AND MODE OF DELIVERY

The delivery mode of communication can easily affect the outcome of the message sent. Usually the more direct the communication, the greater the possibility it will be received clearly. Leaders are involved in four modes of communication: (a) written, (b) face-to-face, (c) nonverbal, and (d) telephone. Written communication is one of the most common modes of communication in all organizations (Swanburg, 1996). Written communication requires attention and deliberation on the part of the sender because the communication is open to interpretation and distortion. Unless intentionally planned, that is, having another person read the message prior to sending, receiver feedback mechanisms are usually not built into this mode of communication. Today's written communications are more and more often e-mail messages that do not contain clearly constructed thoughts. Quick messages, with little direction, many pronouns, several ideas, and disjointed thoughts, are often found in e-mail messages. Clarity, readability, direction, and sensitivity to the audience are still critical items in written communications, whether it is a memo, letter, policy statement, or e-mail message.

Leaders communicate verbally in face-to-face communication to several audiences. This mode is used with individuals and groups both formally and informally. Face-to-face communications offer the most opportunity to be assertive and solicit feedback. Remember, however, that the number of people participating in the communication can distort reception. Assertive behavior in communication means allowing individuals to express themselves directly and honestly with concern for the other person's rights and sensitivities. Although many believe that communication is either assertive or passive, it may also be passive-aggressive or aggressive. Passive communication occurs when an individual remains nonresponsive even when they feel strongly about an issue. Aggressive behaviors are usually characterized by hostile behaviors that infringe on another's rights. Passive-aggressive communication may be exhibited by withdrawal behaviors or limited verbal exchange with contrary action. The assertive communicator can maintain influence through reflection, repeated assertion, restating, or questioning (Marquis & Huston, 1998).

Nonverbal communication occurs anytime that the leader is visible. Nonverbal communication includes facial expression, body movements, cues, and gestures, and also includes the emotional component of a message that is transmitted along with the verbal message. The congruency of verbal and nonverbal communication is significant to leader effectiveness. Incongruence usually leads the receiver to disregard the verbal message and believe the nonverbal message instead. The nonverbal message cues are affected by environment, outward appearance, eye contact, body posture, gestures, facial expressions, and the tone and volume of voice.

Telephone communication is another form of verbal communication that can be a quick way to communicate, but it lacks nonverbal cues. With voice mail and other types of delayed retrieval systems, the receiver has the opportunity to listen to messages and interpret meaning before responding. Telephonically recorded and received messages do have their problems: they are often too long, too rambling (not directed or focused), and incomplete. This mode of communication in today's instant message network must be used more carefully and deliberately than the face-to-face conversation or interactive telephone message. Modes of communication are the same whether they involve an individual or a group. Feedback can assist the communicator to improve ineffective communication patterns.

LEADERS, COMMUNICATION, AND FEEDBACK

Perhaps the most challenging aspect of communication for the leader is giving and receiving feedback. Although we tend to think of feedback in a negative sense (Hathaway, 1990), in reality it is one of the best ways to achieve positive results. When discussing concrete or tangible issues it is possible to receive feedback by observing the receivers' reaction or behavior. It is naïve on the part of the sender, however, to assume that the message sent is the one received. Giving and receiving feedback can be a resource for accomplishing the leader's goals and improving relationships. Giving and receiving feedback in an environment of gentle honesty can strengthen a relationship, increase trust, and add creativity to problem solving. Foster (1997) stated: "To tell the truth, you build a bridge. It's a bridge of words . . . one end is anchored by your reason for telling the truth . . . other end is anchored by needs of person you're telling the truth to" (p. 271).

In giving unsolicited feedback, Hathaway (1990) offers four steps to ensure success: preparation, timing, permission, and specificity. Preparation should include rehearsing what one wants to say, anticipating responses from the receiver, and reflecting on how to offer support for change. Timing includes a time and place wherein the receiver is not stressed or distracted and seeks permission to give feedback. Specificity requires that the sender give concrete examples of behavior or thoughts that need clarification or change. Feedback is a critical skill for the leader who must be competent in interpersonal communication. McCall, Lombardo, and Marison (1998) in their research about successful leaders, found that leaders spent a great deal of energy protecting their self-image. Their study demonstrated the need for leaders to reflect on unsolicited feedback and to increase their own self-awareness or self-feedback. Increasing self-awareness through introspection and feedback from constituencies will lead to more effective communication regardless of the communication mode. The best way to gain this is through the technique of active listening.

LEADERS, COMMUNICATION, AND ACTIVE LISTENING

Communication must be clear, simple, and precise, and the sender is responsible for ensuring that the message is received and understood. The sender should seek feedback, which is the next critical factor in effective communication: the ability to actively listen. This factor is important to both the sender and receiver. Listening is not a physiological process like hearing, but rather an active interpretation process. The work done by Devito (1995) demonstrated that listening requires the following five processes:

1.   Receiving a message from a speaker;

2. Striving to learn the meaning of the speaker's verbal and non-verbal messages;
3. Using understanding to help in recall;
4. Evaluating the speaker's message; and
5. Responding.

Active listening is a commitment required by both sender and receiver to maintain effective communications. McKay and colleagues (1995) recommended several behaviors to increase listening ability, among them maintaining good eye contact, leaning forward when listening, reinforcing what is heard by nodding or paraphrasing, clarifying meaning, and committing to listen to the speaker. Effective listening results in two people hearing each other, beneficial information transmitted for decision making, and a better relationship between sender and receiver. Matusak (1997) said that the "effectiveness of leaders rises and falls . . . [with] their willingness to be active, positive listeners" (p. 80).

As listeners, active and positive leaders open the pathways to relationship building experiences for their followers. Relationship-building occurs when senders are able to adjust their body language, verbal language, and tone to the individual or members of the group. It is necessary to synchronize the different experiences, values, and meanings held by each so that similarities can be drawn on and differences understood. Over time, establishing rapport will increase the trust between sender and receiver(s) and lead to more open and meaningful communication. Remembering that communication is a process involving two or more people with different value sets and perceptions will assist leaders to establish and maintain relationships within their setting. The leader, however, may be limited by the organization's culture in establishing effective communication patterns.

LEADER, COMMUNICATION, AND ORGANIZATIONAL CULTURE

Organizational culture is the "rules of the game" (Nelson, 1997, p. 64) or the total of an organization's beliefs, norms, values, philosophies, traditions, and sacred cows. Cultures of organizations include artifacts, values, language, assumptions, and behaviors from the past. The artifacts in organizations take many forms. They may be physical, behavioral (rituals), or verbal. Verbal artifacts come from shared values and beliefs that include traditions, heroes, the party line, ceremonies, and metaphors. Metaphors are used to characterize work style and personalities that create a language of their own. Such words as captain, tight ship, quarterback, novice, sitcom, well-oiled machine, and top dog come from several arenas. The military, sports teams, animal kingdom, television, and anthropology have contributed language to our organizational culture. The guidelines or "rules of the game" emanating from organizational culture tell members how to communicate with one another and the content of the communication (Nelson).

Recent literature (Nelson, 1997; Ryou, Oestreich, & Orr, 1996) reports a growing trend toward open discussions in organizations. Slowly the walls of denial in organizations are breaking down, allowing individuals to speak up without fear of punishment. This new culture encourages employee participation in decision making that emphasizes customers, stockholders, and employees and creates a more positive and dynamic environment and certainly one that creates new challenges for the leader.

Leaders influence both the organizational culture and the climate as they direct work output. Organizational climate is the personality of an organization, the subjective perceptions and feelings shared by its members. An important aspect of climate is the sense of trust displayed by leaders as they communicate. Trust is developed through clear communication of goals, effective sharing in the decision-making process, cooperation, leader effectiveness, openness, and effectiveness of teamwork and problem solving. Studies have demonstrated that a positive work climate resulting from a corporate culture promotes more satisfied employees and customers (Campbell, 1986). The organization's culture and climate are created by the intertwined and multiple series of conversations experienced within it as well as the language used to describe it. The sharing of a common language and culture is necessary for common action in an organization (Harkins, 1999) and sets the stage for giving and receiving feedback to meet organizational needs.

LEADERS, COMMUNICATION, AND ORGANIZATIONAL NEEDS

Communication is the process that enables the leader to give voice to the role of visionary, critical thinker, achiever, mentor, and expert. Matusak (1997) reported, "the total effectiveness, of leaders rises and falls in direct proportion to their ability to communicate with meaning, their willingness to enthusiastically share their goals and vision and their willingness to be active, positive listeners" (p. 80). Like leadership, communication is relational and requires constant exchange. Over the years, authors have continued to conduct research and write about communication and yet we are still searching for new ways to teach how to communicate effectively. While we are continuing to strive for the perfect communication interaction, skill, or technique, many new avenues of information exchange have opened up and have added new complexity to the communication arena.

Today's organizational structures are highly interdependent and require effective communication to enable employees and managers to do the work of organizations. Swanburg (1990) reported that depending on one's position (manager or staff) up to 80% of available time may be spent in communication. The multidisciplinary nature of health care demands excellent interpersonal communication skills between individuals and within groups. Group cohesiveness and the ability to meet organizational goals is dependent both on the group and the leader's ability to communicate direction and vision. Successful leaders use communication as a tool to reach their ends and match their behaviors with their goals (Hackman & Johnson, 1991). They must communicate and define reality as both they and their followers envision it. A sense of shared meaning through communication encourages the development of trust and prompts the question "now what?" According to DePree (1992) communication comes to fruition when it is clear enough to enable action in a forward moving manner.

Leaders use communication with three specific ideas in mind: advancing their agendas, sharing learning, and strengthening relationships (Harkins, 1999). Effective communicators are able to develop higher levels of trust and gain better results while creating meaningful relationships with individuals and groups. Because a group communicates differently from individuals, however, the leader must have an understanding of group dynamics.

LEADERS, COMMUNICATION, AND GROUP DYNAMICS

Communicating with groups can complicate issues in an already complex environment. Leaders must be sensitive to group needs and always ask the question: "Is this a group need or an individual need?" Groups have increased feelings of ownership and responsibility and the relationship with the leader is key to accomplishing goals embraced by the group (Manion, 1999).

The leadership communication function in groups varies throughout the stages of a group interaction. Tuckman and Jensen (1977) labeled the stages of group development as forming, storming, norming, and performing. Each of these stages requires different skills from the leader. In the forming phase the leader must be able to establish relationships with other members and communicate what is acceptable behavior. Storming requires the leader to clearly set out goals for the group and manage resistance to the task at hand. Cooperation in the norming phase occurs as the leader influences group cohesion and performing. The last phase witnesses problem resolution and task performance. A group's organizing process functions to create an evolutionary process to reduce the complexity of information (Weicks, 1979). The leader is the "medium" in the process, and is the " mediator" between the group and informational environment.

Delegation is a subsystem of the interaction process involved ingroup or individual communications that requires effective interpersonal communication skills. Delegation can relate the message that "you are important and valued by this organization" or can impart the message of "just more work." Delegation includes assigning routine tasks, problems for resolution, and developmental tasks. Each of these areas assumes clear, consistent messages and behaviors that avoid confusion. The individual or group must understand the expectations of the job, work relationships, and expected outcomes. Feedback from both sender and receiver is important in maintaining dynamic interpersonal relationships as they develop.

LEADERS, COMMUNICATION, AND EFFECTIVENESS

Effective leaders are skilled communicators who are versatile in all modes of communication whether with individuals or groups. They use judgment in each situation to ascertain the most appropriate mode to send a message and continually evaluate effectiveness through feedback. These communicators cultivate language patterns that deliver clear and concise messages, develop meaningful interpersonal relationships, and support the development and maintenance of a culture conducive to open communication. In establishing rapport with individuals and groups, leaders encourage communication that focuses on the topic at hand and the goals of the organization. Leaders use communication to influence others to see the common vision and to reach for it.

APPLICATION BY NURSING EDUCATORS

Nursing educators should also be models of excellent communication themselves and they need to become familiar with communication theory and models including gender communication research. Some useful communication models include those of Shortell (1991) and Daft and Steers (1986). Also useful is Hurst's self-examination activity for communication skills, a tool found in Yoder-Wise (1999). Skill-building experiences for students include role play, case studies, memo rewrites, e-mail communication, reflective journals, Myers-Briggs Inventory (short version), and the reactive to proactive grid by Rakich, Longest, and Darr (1992). The experiences that the educator selects should be commensurate with the level and degree of communication skills of the students.

FUTURE DIRECTIONS

Following are five future goals for the Leadership Education Model (LEM) Task Force:

1. Developing teaching methodologies and systems for evaluating learning;
2. Providing additional seminars to introduce the LEM and its curriculum integration;
3. Providing curriculum development consultation to faculty;
4. Evaluating the LEM developmental process; and
5. Measuring the outcomes.

In addition, current communication research should be broadened to include its application to nursing leadership. Nursing research applying communication theory should be made a priority. As teachers of tomorrow's nurse leaders, we must remember that we all use communication to advance agendas, share learning, and strengthen relationships.

REFERENCES

Berlo, D. (1960). *The process of communication.* New York: Holt, Rinehart and Winston.

Bower, F. L. (2000). *Nurses taking the lead: Personal qualities of effective leadership.* Philadelphia: W. B. Saunders.

Campbell, L. R. (1986). What satisfies . . . and doesn't. *Nursing Management, 8,* 78.

Daft, R. L., & Steers, R. M. (1986). *Organizations: A micro/macro approach.* Reading, MA: Addison-Wesley.

DePree, M. (1992). *Leadership jazz.* New York: Doubleday.

DeVito, J. A. (1995). *The interpersonal communication book.* New York: HarperCollins.

Dickenson-Hazard, N., & Root, J. A. (2000). Communicating effectively. In F. L. Bower (Ed.), *Nurses taking the lead.* Philadelphia: W. B. Saunders.

Foster, C. (1997). *There's something I have to tell you: How to communicate difficult news in tough situations.* New York: Harmony Books.

Hackman, M. Z., & Johnson, C. E. (1991). *Leadership: A communication perspective.* Prospect Heights, IL: Waveland Press.

Harkins, P. (1999). *Powerful conversations: How high-impact leaders communicate.* New York: McGraw-Hill.

Hathaway, P. (1990). *Giving and receiving feedback.* Menlo Park, CA: Crisp.

Huber, D. (1996). *Leadership and nursing care management.* Philadelphia: W. B. Saunders.

Manion, J. (1999). *From management to leadership.* Chicago: American Hospital Publishers.

Marquis, B. L., & Huston, C. J. (1998). *Management decision making for nurses* (3rd ed.). Philadelphia: Lippincott.

Matusak, L. K. (1997). *Finding your voice: Learning to lead . . . anywhere you want to make a difference.* San Francisco: Jossey-Bass.

McCall, M. W., Lombardo, M. M., & Marison, A. M. (1998). The lessons of experience: *How successful executives develop on the job.* Lexington, MA: Lexington Books.

McKay, M., Davis, M., & Fanning, P. (1995). *Messages: The communication skills book* (2nd ed.). Oakland, CA: New Harbinger.

Nelson, R. W. (1997). *Organizational troubleshooting: Asking the right questions, finding the right answers.* Westport, CT: Quarum Books.

Poole, M. S., & Hirokawa, R. Y. (1986). *Communication and group decision-making.* Beverly Hills, CA: Sage.

Rakich, J. S., Longest, J. R., & Darr, K. (1992). *Managing health services organizations.* Baltimore: Health Professions Press.

Ryan, K. D., Oestreich, D. K., & Orr, G. A. (1996). *The courageous messager: How to successfully speak up at work.* San Francisco: Jossey-Bass.

Shortell, S. M. (1991). *Effective hospital-physician relationships.* Chicago: Health Administration Press.

Swanburg, R. C. (1996). *Management and leadership for nurse managers.* Boston: Jones & Bartlett.

Tappen, R. M. (1995). *Nursing leadership and management* (3rd ed.). Philadelphia: F. A. Davis.

Tuckman, B. W., & Jensen, M. A. C. (1977). Stages of small group development revisited. *Group Organization Studies, 2*(4), 419.

Vestal, K. W. (1995). *Management concepts for the new nurse* (2nd ed.). Philadelphia: Lippincott.

Weicks, K. E. (1978). The spines of leaders. In M. McCall and M. Lombardo (Eds.), *Leadership: Where else can we go?* Durham, NC: Duke University Press.

Yoder-Wise, P. S. (1999). *Leading and managing in nursing.* Philadelphia: Mosby.

Dr. Haynor is an associate professor at Villanova University, College of Nursing. She has been an educator for 12 years involved primarily in graduate education for administration of health services. Prior to her academic career, Dr. Haynor held chief nursing officer positions in both university and community hospital settings. Her areas of research interest are: nurse manager development, leadership in nursing, and long-term care/the Eden Alternative.

CHAPTER SEVEN

Leader As Mentor

Connie Vance

In the not too distant past, the "Old Order" leadership paradigm was the predominant model in most organizations. It was enacted within strict structures and bureaucracies in which rules and regulations were rigidly followed. It was a "Great Leader" approach, in which one strong leader with particular inherited or acquired traits and abilities made decisions and gave orders in isolation from the followers. The leader operated from a command-and-control, power-over-others stance—from a position of unquestioned authority, power and control. This all-knowing, individualistic, and non-systemic leadership worldview was appropriate in an environment that was predictable, orderly, and simple. In a world now characterized by flux, change, ambiguity, and chaos—described by Vaill (1996) as permanent "white water"—a new form of leadership is required. Our quantum world teaches us that there are no prefixed, predetermined patterns; instead, there are "potentials" (Wheatley, 1999) and the constant flux of dynamic processes (pp. 10–11). Leaders must reflect the inherent transformational nature of contemporary organizational life.

The New Order leadership in an evolving world is increasingly characterized by the values and behaviors of mentorship, collaboration, and empowerment. This means that leadership is a complex human interaction between leaders and members of the social-organizational environment (Fiedler, 1996). Organizational members, therefore, are viewed as colleagues, partners, learners, and team members, not as a collection of passive followers. In today's organizational culture, leaders must evolve from macho to *maestro* (Bennis & Townsend, 1995), from ordering to *empowering*, from control to *connection*, from telling to *teaching*. Clearly, the leadership paradigm is shifting from independence to interdependence, from individualistic to group, and from exclusion to inclusive partnerships, mentor connections, and networks (Capezio & Morehouse, 1997; Lipman-Bluman, 1996; O'Neil, 1997). Leadership is transformational, in that leaders mentor, motivate, energize, inspire, and create change in individuals, teams, and organizations (Hunt, 1999; Maccoby, 2000). Clearly, contemporary health care and educational organizations demand a new type of leader—a transformational leader whose responsibilities are developmental in nature (Moeller & Johnson, 1992).

The successful leader of today and the future must first and foremost be a mentor—a developer and teacher of others. The crucial work of the leader entails developing the talents of others, that is, polishing gifts (De Pree, 1989; 1992). The leader must believe in and hold high expectations of associates and create environments where growth, development, and learning assume primacy. The leader can create the Pygmalion effect—instilling hope, belief, and optimism in the potential and performance of individuals, teams, and organizations. This is a self-fulfilling prophecy in which leaders and their colleagues possess reciprocal high expectations of each other and the organization (Eden, 1992; Livingston, 1988). Research consistently has shown that "leaders not only shape the expectations and productivity of their subordinates but also influence their attitudes toward their jobs and themselves . . . if leaders are skillful and have high expectations, their co-workers' self-confidence will grow, their capabilities will develop, and their productivity will be high" (Livingston, 1988, p. 130). Further, it has been found that leaders produce change by influencing the worker's self-concept and that workers in turn influence the leader's self-schema, both individually and collectively (Lord, Brown, & Freiberg, 1999).

Leadership is learning. Ongoing learning must be the preeminent characteristic of all leadership. The developmental leader's responsibility is to build learning organizations in which "people continually expand their capacity to create the results they truly desire, where new and expansive patterns of thinking are nurtured, where collective aspiration is set free, and where people are continually learning how to learn together" (Senge, 1990a, p. 3). In an authentic learning organization, the leader is responsible for teaching and learning and for "building organizations where people are continually expanding their capabilities to shape their future" (Senge, 1990b, p. 3; Senge, 1999). In other words, the leader's roles should include those of Teacher-Learner and Mentor-Developer.

LEADER AS TEACHER-LEARNER

The true leader recognizes that continuous development, lifelong education, and collective learning are essential. This is a dynamic mutually inclusive process, because leaders and colleagues must help each other learn as well as gain more accurate approaches to reality and their work. The leader is a teacher-learner rather than a patron-patriarch. The leader as teacher-learner helps people "restructure their views of reality to see beyond the superficial conditions and events into the underlying causes of problems—and therefore to see new possibilities for shaping the future" (Senge, 1990b, p. 6). This futuristic systems thinking is critical for today's ever-changing environment, in which there are no clearly defined guidelines and rules that always work. The leader maintains as a core value the ongoing growth and developmental needs of others—the belief that learning is liberating and empowering, essential for sparking the human spirit and for promoting creativity and excellence in goal achievement.

It has been said that the art of leadership should necessarily reside in the future—in recognizing and growing new leaders (De Pree, 1989). This means that the effective leader believes in the potential growth of people and sets the foundation for helping them to realize their potential in a learning environment. The leader must, therefore, establish structures wherein individual and collective learning opportunities are continuously offered. Developmental leaders will provide the necessary structures and resources to assist people expand their repertoire of thinking and behaving, risk taking, and changing. Learning partnerships and networks will be encouraged, including the establishment of informal and formal structures for individual and team development. "Organizations of the future will not survive without becoming communities of learning" (Noer, 1997, p. 176). A key leadership competency, therefore, is the ability to engage others in a collective dialogue of inquiry and innovative behavior. According to Drath and Palus (1993), the process of creating meaning and learning in a collective environment is the essence of the leadership process. Clearly, collective problem solving and creative learning will be essential in the constantly changing climate of contemporary organizational life.

Learning groups should be established in organizations in which the responsibility for learning is spread among peers as well as the learning leader. The learning leader's task is to create an environment for professional growth and development where all can benefit from the diverse experience, knowledge, and support of both group members and leaders (Kaye & Jacobson, 1995). Learning groups can be characterized by learning partners, mentor connections, small group learning networks, knowledge work teams, professional and specialty associations, and entire departments or organizations (Sorrells-Jones & Weaver, 1999).

The social learning theory of Bandura (1977, 1986) provides a theoretical foundation for understanding the role of leader as teacher-learner. This theory is based on the imitation of modeling behavior of another person. The active learner acquires a larger and better integrated behavior pattern more effectively and efficiently by watching, listening, and being guided by a leader-teacher. Various studies in nursing and other disciplines attest to the importance in the neophytes' socialization and development of learning relationships with more experienced persons. Formal leaders at all levels serve crucial functions in such developmental relationships as teacher, mentor, role model, and professional guide.

LEADER AS MENTOR-DEVELOPER

Mentoring may be one of the highest forms of leadership (Henry & Gilkey, 1999). The leader-mentor plays an essential developmental role in the professional socialization and the personal and career development of colleagues. In the older, more established professions and in business, it has been widely recognized that the careful nurturing and coaching of aspiring professionals through mentor relationships is essential in ensuring the highest levels of achievement, success, and satisfaction. Harris and DeSimone (1998) suggested that mentor relationships have two perspectives: life development and career development. The life development aspect means that the young need meaningful relationships with older, wiser adults; while the career development aspect suggests that mentors assist protégés in organizational and career socialization and growth. An important role, then, of contemporary leaders entails mentoring others— enabling and empowering them to grow and develop. Serving as a mentor is both an obligation and a privilege. The mentor serves as professional guide, role model, sponsor, teacher, partner, advocate, and counselor (Bell, 1998; Levinson, 1996; Levinson, Darrow, Klein, Levinson, & McKee, 1978; Sinetar, 1998; Vance, 1982).

The concept of mentoring is supported by Erikson's theory of human development (1963, 1968), in which the stage of "generativity" is manifest by the human need to reach out to others to provide guidance and nurturance. There is the acceptance of responsibility for passing on wisdom to the next generation. Both the giver and the receiver in this relationship experience mutually beneficial outcomes. Various life and career developmental models acknowledge the central importance of helping and developmental relationships, including mentorship, throughout the career and life cycle (Bateson, 1990; Kegan, 1982; Levinson, 1996; Levinson et al., 1978; Super, 1957, 1963).

The mentor connection is a developmental, empowering, and nurturing relationship extending over time in which mutual sharing, learning, and growth occur in an atmosphere of respect, collegiality, and affirmation (Vance & Olson, 1998). Traditionally, the mentor was always older, more experienced, and further advanced in a career; the protégé was always a younger neophyte; however, another mentor connection model has evolved in which there is an inherent reciprocity in the relationship for both mentor and protégé. This model is characterized by greater inclusiveness and diversity-of age, experience, gender, culture, ethnicity, and race (Vance, 2000a, 2000b). "The mentor's gifts come from their life experiences, knowledge, and wisdom. The mentor guides, models, encourages, and inspires the protégé. The protégé receives the mentor's gifts and returns these gifts by her or his contributions to the profession and by eventually mentoring others" (Vance, 1999, pp. 201–202). Indeed, according to Bolman and Deal (1997), leadership is a subtle process of mutual influence and mentorship that fuses thought, feeling, and action to produce cooperation in the service of the values, purposes, and goals of both the leader and the led. Research and anecdotal reports have consistently demonstrated the benefits of mentoring relationships: preparation for leadership roles, career success and advancement, professional and personal satisfaction, and strengthening of the profession and organization. In the nursing profession, mentoring should be viewed as a professional obligation and privilege, a work environment necessity, and a way to attract and retain talent.

Clearly the best leaders and the best organizations are those that are "people growers" and "leader growers" (Bennis & Townsend, 1995). The leader-mentor creates an environment that encourages the development of both individual and collective mentor relationships. These relationships are particularly important during entry into a discipline and entry into advanced specialty work. A study of nurse managers reported that their most influential mentoring experiences occurred during the early years of their career, particularly with their leaders and colleagues (Boyle & James, 1990). Mentor connections are also important at transitional points in a career, at which time the mentor's guidance, support, and coaching are particularly valuable (Vance, 1982). Leaders, therefore, have a clearly defined responsibility in shaping learning environments in which mentor relationships can occur easily at all levels in the organization and the profession. Mentoring creates an impact on the entire organization and profession, influencing job satisfaction and performance (Appelbaum, Ritchie, & Shapiro, 1994).

In the mentoring-learning organization, two types of mentor relationships are present: informal and formal. Informal mentoring consists of the traditional expert-to-novice relationship and the peer-peer relationship. These mentor relationships occur through mutual attraction, shared interests and goals, a mutual desire to learn and work collaboratively, and personal "chemistry." Research and anecdotal studies illustrate that these unique support relationships in the nursing profession can endure for many years (Olson & Vance, 1993; Vance & Olson, 1991, 1998). Formal or planned mentor relationships are the organizational application of informal mentoring relationships. These relationships promote ongoing learning, excellence, and creativity in work, as well as commitment to the organization. Formal mentor programs match mentors and proteges with respect to mutual goals and needs. These formal programs require careful planning, orientation, training, support, and follow-up of the participants (Vance, 1999; Vance & Bamford, 1998). Formal mentor programs provide heightened focus and visibility to mentoring, and create enhanced communication, motivation, and productivity (Duff & Cohen, 1993; Kaye & Jacobson, 1995; Murray & Owen, 1991; Wickman & Sjodin, 1997).

The nursing profession and its leaders are increasingly embracing mentorship as an essential professional and leadership development ingredient. Assuming responsibility for assisting future generations of nurses and nursing leadership should be the norm, not the exception (Olson & Vance, 1999). The recruitment and retention of talent, as well as the ongoing development and support of talent, requires the adoption of formal mentor programs and expansion of mentor connections throughout the profession. Leaders grow leaders. Mentoring relationships will develop future leaders who will in turn leave their legacy to the profession.

TEACHING THE MENTOR COMPONENT OF LEADERSHIP

> Each of us as teacher-mentor must seek opportunities to mentor our students. This means that we involve ourselves with students as partners in learning; we actively nurture and encourage them; we share our networks with them; we draw them in with us through professional meetings and events; we help them dream and imagine their potential. Mentoring means that we keep "caring" as a core value in our teaching. It means that in relationship with students, we help them tap into their unique strengths and become more powerful in both their personal and professional lives. (Vance, 1995, p. 3)

Teaching-learning approaches that develop the mentor component of leadership for RN-BSN and graduate students occur through three avenues: (a) the student-teacher relationship; (b) the classroom; and (c) the practicum experience.

THE STUDENT-TEACHER RELATIONSHIP

Teaching and learning always occur in relationship to one another. Mentoring also is a relational phenomenon and is, therefore, a natural component of the teaching-learning process. For example, the teacher provides essential experiential learning in leadership development by serving as an active leader-mentor to students in various encounters—advisement, clinical teaching, and in the classroom. The teacher in essence models the New Order leadership paradigm of mentorship, collaboration, and empowerment, in contrast to the authoritarian, compliance, power based model. Humanistic learning theory guides the mentoring approach to teaching the concept of leadership. The focus of the humanistic perspective in teaching and learning is the promotion of human potential, self-esteem, and self-actualization— the same goal of a good mentor relationship (Combs, 1994; Glasser, 1969; Maslow, 1954, 1962; Rogers, 1961, 1969). In a caring curriculum the teacher's role is to interact with students as persons of potential, intelligence, and dignity. Through these interactions, students will be liberated to learn and grown as strong leaders (Bevis & Watson, 2000). "Only a mentor/preceptor/teacher modeling a humanistic, caring ethic and having dialogue with students that underscores constructed knowing and encourages them to be personally related to the ethical issues involved can facilitate and enhance students in their moral development for life and for nursing" (Bevis & Watson, p. 184). This certainly applies to the development of leaders in the profession.

The teacher as mentor serves in various roles: as intellectual-guide, role model, promoter-coach, visionary-idealist, and advocate-believer (Vance & Olson, 1998). The teacher-mentor inspires, guides, models, encourages, facilitates, and nurtures students in their learning journey. Anecdotal and research studies report that students' communication, critical thinking, organizational and technical skills, self-esteem and self-confidence, and professional satisfaction—all leadership skills— are enhanced by mentoring relationships with their teachers (Olson & Vance, 1999).

Teachers can develop meaningful mentor relationships with students in both informal and formal ways. Informal mentoring occurs when teachers possess a mentoring attitude in their relationships with students—when they view themselves as collaborative learning partners with their students, actively guide and encourage students to find their voice, advocate for students and believe in their dreams, and serve as role models of committed leadership in the profession. Nursing schools are also establishing formal mentor programs in which faculty expand the usual repertoire of teaching beyond course and clinical work into larger professional and career development areas. Faculty and students are formally linked as mentors and protégés through a school-supported program; discussion and action occur across a broad range of academic, professional, and personal life issues. These relationships are developed through a mutually agreed-upon time period and may continue beyond the student-protégé's academic program. Both mentors and protégés also should have a consensus on the professional and personal development goals in their relationship.

Leadership skill development is unquestionably facilitated by the presence of active, knowledgeable mentors in the teaching-learning enterprise. The following examples of teaching-learning objectives and content are recommended:

- *Objective*: Serve as an active advocate and mentor with students.
- *Content*:

1. Discuss with students the contribution of mentor relationships in leadership development, including the initiation and nurturing of the relationship, qualities, and responsibilities of mentors and protégés, goals, and benefits of successful mentor relationships.
2. Use the term "mentor" in contacts with students to raise consciousness about the mentor connection and to promote intentionality in developing mentor relationships among peers, faculty, and clinical colleagues.

- *Objective*: Arrange mentor connections, vis-à-vis a formal matching process with students through various avenues: a school-wide mentor program, the classroom, practicum, clinical connections, and informal experiences.
- *Content*:

1. Discuss the formation of formal mentor programs with students and faculty, including various approaches, necessary resources, and support.
2. Encourage students and faculty colleagues to establish mentoring opportunities where students study and work.

The Classroom

A major role of the classroom teacher in introducing mentoring as a leadership component is to establish a classroom culture that emphasizes mentor connections among faculty and students and between student-peers. The mentoring classroom emphasizes high expectations and high performance along with supportive collaborative and collegial interactions. The mentor concept is studied formally as well as experienced through classroom interactions among all participants. The classroom should be viewed as a "place of realized potential" (DePree, 1997). This suggests that high value must be placed on the development of each learner's leadership potential, which entails intentional, careful mentoring in the learning process. According to DePree (1997, 1989), much of the language of potential has to do with the language of teaching and learning. Students can develop leadership competencies through receiving and applying mentorship in both the technical and the relational areas of leadership. These are best learned through a variety of classroom experiences and may include the following:

- observation and assessment of leaders in written and audiovisual formats
- interactive learning and simulations (Ruben, 1999; Silberman, 1998)
- leadership dialogues
- writing and journal writing (Billings & Halstead, 1998)
- analysis of research and case studies of leaders (Barnes, Christensen, & Hansen, 1994)
- storytelling about mentoring experiences among leaders (Boykin & Schoenhofer, 1991; Daloz, 1986; Kirkpatrick, Spickerman, Edwards, & Kirkpatrick, 2001; Schank, 1990)
- interviewing leaders about their mentor connections

The following objectives and content are suggested to guide these learning experiences:

- *Objective*: Use the mentor concept as an overall framework for designing and implementing leadership learning experiences in the classroom. These can include establishing a mentoring classroom environment, as well as structuring dialogue groups and learning circles that promote peer mentoring for peer feedback and evaluation, coaching, and support.
- *Content*: Explicate the mentor concept, including the roles and characteristics of mentor and protégé, the mentor relationship and professional career stages, and the establishment of formal and informal mentor programs in nursing schools and clinical organizations, including expert to novice and peer-to-peer relationships.

- *Objective*: Develop presentations and discussion for exploring the mentor component of leadership, using research and anecdotal literature.
- *Content*: Provide various learning experiences that illustrate the mentor concept to students, including research analysis, leadership case studies, storytelling, journal writing, and interviews of leaders.

THE PRACTICUM EXPERIENCE

Experiential learning opportunities provides students with observational and hands-on experiences that enliven theoretical material, promote personal skill development, and provide networking for a leadership career path. The number, length, and settings of these practicum experiences vary, depending on the curriculum plan and learning objectives. Developing the mentor component of leadership can be woven into other leadership learning components, such as communication, critical thinking, interpersonal skills, group and system dynamics, and organizational-managerial activities. The practicum experience provides an opportunity for leader-mentors to develop future leaders and mentors. This is accomplished for the learner by observation of behavior modeling by the leader-mentor and hands-on experiences with the facilitation and guidance of seasoned leader-mentors. The mentor must be a willing and generous professional career guide, who serves as an expert role model and who coaches and opens doors for the developing leader. Sharing networks by the leader-mentor is another important contribution to the future career enhancement of the student leader.

A major strength of the practicum experience for students, whether observing or doing, is the opportunity to engage in reflective learning. Learning as a way of being (Vaill, 1996) and mentoring as a way of being (Vance & Olson, 1998) entail reflection and insight into one's goals, strengths, and developmental needs. Merriam and Caffarella (1991) suggest that there are two basic processes involved in reflective learning and practice: reflection-on-action, or the analysis of an experience and exploring new perspectives, assumptions, and behaviors and reflection-in-action, or the conscious attention and learning in the moment-the here and now. The practicum experience is rich in possibilities for critically examining one's leadership skills as well as consciously exploring the development of mentor relationships, connections, and networks.

Developing a relationship with a leader-mentor in an organizational setting can influence a developing leader's career path in powerful ways and lead to leadership succession. Adams and Beard (1998) described their long-term mentoring relationship that began when Beard served as an administrative intern with Adams, the vice president of patient services. Through this mentor connection, they modeled professionalism and mutual respect, and engaged in ongoing discussion and debate of critical leadership issues. Beard eventually assumed the role of vice president of patient services on Adam's retirement.

Sample objectives and content for the mentor-leadership practicum are:

- *Objective*: Explore the mentor connection in the practicum experience.
- *Content*: Keep a learning journal to reflect on one's development of mentor relationships with clinical leaders and teachers.
- *Objective*: Collect data from selected formal leaders in the clinical setting to determine the presence of their mentor connections, both as mentors and protégés.
- *Content*. Interview leaders at various career stages to gain information about their mentor relationships and mentoring activities.

EXAMPLES OF STUDENT EVALUATION

Although evaluation of the mentor component in the curriculum is complex and difficult to quantify, there are several evaluation strategies that may be employed to assess student development. These may include the following:

- Reports (oral and written) about students' formal and informal mentoring experiences (peer:peer and expert:novice) in teacher and student relationships, in the classroom, and the practicum experience
- Journal writing, including literature and research summaries.
- Oral presentations summarizing research and anecdotal and case studies about the mentor connection.

CONCLUSION

Leadership, learning, and mentoring are phenomena that in some form have occurred universally among all people, regardless of culture, from antiquity through contemporary society. The process by which a wiser and more experienced person guides, teaches, and nurtures a less experienced, often younger, person is as old as the bonds between parent and child, master and disciple, teacher and student. One of the first descriptions of mentoring came from Greek mythology in Homer's Odyssey (1961). Athena, the goddess of wisdom disguised as Mentor, taught, guided, advised, and protected Odysseus's son during his 10-year absence from his homeland. Likewise, it is now believed that the concepts of leadership and mentorship involve certain qualities and skills—interpersonal, technical, and intellectual— that can be learned (Bass, 1981, 1990). Levinson and colleagues (1978), who extensively studied mentor relationships in the developmental life of adult men, observed that a mentor serves as a teacher, sponsor, guide, exemplar, and counselor.

The first documented evidence of the presence of mentoring in the nursing profession, and specifically its value to the development of nursing leaders, appeared in the doctoral investigation of Vance (1977) entitled, "A Group Profile of Contemporary Influentials in American Nursing." The 71 nursing leaders in this study reported a high level of mentoring activity, both in the receiving and giving of mentoring guidance and support to students and colleagues who were aspiring leaders. The benefits of mentor connections in the nursing profession are (a) the promotion of career success and advancement; (b) increased personal and professional satisfaction; (c) enhanced self-confidence; (d) preparation for leadership roles; and (e) commitment to and strengthening of the profession (Vance & Olson, 1998). Growing evidence suggests that those who have been mentored will mentor others, and that mentor-leaders will grow other leaders. Good mentoring seems to beget good mentoring (Hardcastle, 1988). It is, therefore, essential that baccalaureate and graduate students in leadership education be provided relational, theoretical, and experiential opportunities in mentoring. Although this is a relatively new area of the nursing curriculum, continuing research and anecdotal studies document its relevance to the education of future nursing leaders. Thirty-three research studies on mentorship in nursing education were summarized in a review by Olson and Vance (1999), in which they report a paucity of literature on mentoring for graduate students, particularly in the educational development of leadership qualities and skills. It was recommended that mentoring phenomena should be studied through the use of case studies, longitudinal studies, and other qualitative methods that capture the developmental character and complexity of the process. Documentation of formal and informal mentoring activities for students in the nursing education literature is still sparse.

FUTURE DIRECTIONS

Research and anecdotal literature in all professional fields points to the value and necessity of promoting mentoring relationships in leadership development. Clearly the teacher as leader-mentor can promote students' leadership development through intentional mentoring, behavior modeling, and facilitation of leadership experiences in the classroom, practicum experience, and interactions with students. Curriculum planning should entail discussion and inclusion of the mentorship component in leadership courses and the promotion of mentoring as a way of being with students. Because the research literature is still relatively scarce in the description and measurement of leadership skill development through mentoring in nursing programs, it is recommended that:

1. Curriculum and course material in leadership include the mentoring component through theoretical and experiential activities;
2. faculty development be provided in the area of mentorship and leadership development;
3. Students be offered a variety of opportunities to explore and experience the mentor connection as an essential professional leadership activity;
4. Curriculum incorporating the mentor concept be reported in the literature for guidance and replication; and
5. Research be conducted on curricular and course development and outcomes in mentoring, as well as planned mentoring programs in schools of nursing.

REFERENCES

Applebaum, S. H., Ritchie, S., & Shapiro, B. T. (1994). Mentoring revisited: An organizational behavior construct. *The International Journal of Career Management, 6*(3), 3–10.

Adams, M., & Beard, E. (1998). Mentoring for succession. In C. Vance & R. Olson (Eds.), *The mentor connection in nursing* (pp. 25–28). New York: Springer.

Bandura, A. (1977), *Social learning theory.* Englewood, NJ: Prentice-Hall.

Bandura, A. (1986). *Foundations of thought and action: A social-cognitive theory.* Englewood, NJ: Prentice-Hall.

Barnes, L. P., Christensen, C. R., & Hansen, A. J. (1994). *Teaching and the case method* (3rd ed.). Boston: Harvard Business School Press.

Bass, B. M. (1981). *Stogdill's handbook of leadership: A survey of theory and research.* New York: Free Press.

Bass, B. M. (1990). *Bass & Stogdill's handbook of leadership: Theory, research, and managerial applications.* New York: Free Press.

Bateson, M. C. (1990). *Composing a life.* New York: Penguin.

Bell, C. R. (1998). *Managers as mentors: Building partnerships for learning.* San Francisco: Berrett-Koehler.

Bennis, W., & Townsend, R. A. (1995). *Reinventing leadership: Strategies to empower the organization.* New York: William Morrow.

Bevis, E. O., & Watson, J. (2000). *Toward a caring curriculum: A new pedagogy for nursing.* Sudbury, MA: Jones and Barlett.

Billings, D. M., & Halstead, J. A. (1998). *Teaching in nursing: A guide for faculty.* Philadelphia: W. B. Saunders.

Bolman, L. G., & Deal, T. E. (1997). *Reframing organizations: Artistry, choice, and leadership.* San Francisco: Jossey-Bass.

Boykin, A., & Schoenhofer, S. (1991). Story as link between nursing practice, ontology, epistemology. *Image: Journal of Nursing Scholarship, 23*(4), 245–248.

Boyle, C., & James, S. K. (1990). Nursing leaders as mentors: How are we doing? *Nursing Administration Quarterly, 15*(1), 44–48.

Capezio, P., & Morehouse, D. (1997). *Secrets of breakthrough leadership.* Franklin Lakes, NJ: Career Press.

Combs, A. W. (1994). *Helping relationships: Basic concepts for helping professions* (4th ed.). Boston: Allyn & Bacon.

Daloz, L. A. (1986). *Effective teaching and mentoring: Realizing the transformational power of adult learning experiences.* San Francisco: Jossey-Bass.

DePree, M. (1997). *Leading without power.* San Francisco: Jossey-Bass.

DePree, M. (1989). *Leadership is an art.* New York: Doubleday.

DePree, M. (1992). *Leadership jazz.* New York: Dell.

Drath, W. H., & Palus, C. J. (1993). *Making common sense: Leadership as meaning making in a community of practice.* Greensboro, NC: Center for Creative Leadership.

Duff, C. S., & Cohen, B. (1993). *When women work together: Using our strengths to overcome our challenges.* Berkeley, CA: Conari Press.

Eden, D. (1992). Leadership and expectations: Pygmalion effects and other self-fulfilling prophesies in organizations. *Leadership Quarterly, 3*(4), 271–305.

Erikson, E. (1963). *Childhood and society* (3rd ed.). New York: Norton.

Erikson, E. (1968). *Identity: Youth and crisis*. New York: Norton.

Fiedler, F. E. (1996). Research on leadership selection and training: One view of the future. *Administrative Science Quarterly, 41*(2), 241–250.

Glasser, W. L. (1969). Schools without failure. New York: Harper & Row.

Hardcastle, B. (1988). Spiritual connections: Protégés' reflections on significant mentorships. *Theory into Practice, 27*(3), 201–208.

Harris, D. M., & DeSimone, R. L. (1998). *Human resource development*. Fort Worth, TX: Dryden Press.

Henry, J., & Gilkey, R. (1999). Growing effective leadership in new organizations. In R. Bilkey (Ed.), *The 21st century health care leader* (pp. 101–110). San Francisco: Jossey-Bass.

Homer (1961). *The odyssey*. (R. Fitzgerald, Trans.). New York: Doubleday.

Hunt, J. G. (1999). Transformational/charismatic leadership's transformation of the field: An historical essay. *Leadership Quarterly, 10*(2), 129–144.

Kaye, B., & Jacobson, B. (1995, April). Mentoring: A group guide. *Training & Development*, 23.

Kegan, R. (1982). *The evolving self: Problem and process in human development*. Cambridge, MA: Harvard University Press.

Kirkpatrick, M., Spickerman, S., Edwards, M. K., & Kirkpatrick, J. (2001). Storytelling: An approach to teaching leadership values. In H. R. Feldman (Ed.), *Strategies for Nursing Leadership* (pp. 15–25). New York: Springer.

Levinson, D. (1996). *The seasons of a woman's life*. New York: Knopf.

Levinson, D., Darrow, C., Klein, E., Levinson, M., & McKee, B. (1978). *The seasons of a man's life*. New York: Knopf.

Lipman-Bluman, J. (1996). *The connective edge: Leading in an interdependent world*. San Francisco: Jossey-Bass.

Livingston, J. S. (1988). Pygmalion in management. *Harvard Business Review, 66*(5), 121–130.

Lord, R. G., Brown, D. J., & Freiberg, S. J. (1999). Understanding the dynamics of leadership: The role of follower self-concepts in the leader/follower relationship. *Organizational Behavior and Human Decision Processes, 78*(3), 167–203.

Maccoby, M. (2000). Understanding the difference between management and leadership. *Research Technology Management, 43*(1), 57–59.

Maslow, A. (1954). *Motivation and personality*. New York: Harper & Row.

Maslow, A. (1962). *Toward a psychology of being*. Princeton, NJ: D. Van Nostrand.

Merriam, S. B., & Caffarella, R. S. (1991). *Learning in adulthood: A comprehensive guide*. San Francisco: Jossey-Bass.

Moeller, A. D., & Johnson, K. (1992), Shifting the paradigm for health care leadership. *Frontiers of Health Services Management, 8*(3), 28–30.

Murray, M., & Owen, M. (1991). *Beyond the myths and magic of mentoring*. San Francisco: Jossey-Bass.

Noer, D. M. (1997). *Breaking free: A prescription for personal and organizational change.* San Francisco: Jossey-Bass.

Olson, R., & Vance, C. (1993). *Mentorship in nursing: A collection of research abstracts with selected bibliographies; 1977–1992.* Houston, TX: University of Texas Printing.

Olson, R., & Vance, C. (1999). Mentorship in nursing education. In K. Stevens, & V. Cassidy (Eds.), *Evidence-based teaching: Current research in nursing education* (pp. 23–69). Sudbury, MA: Jones and Barlett Publishers and National League for Nursing.

O'Neil, J. (1997). *Leadership Aikido.* New York: Harmony Books.

Rogers, C. R. (1961). *On becoming a person.* Boston: Houghton Mifflin.

Rogers, C. R. (1969). *Freedom to learn.* Columbus, OH: Charles E. Merrill.

Ruben, B. D. (1999, December). Simulations, games and experience-based learning: The quest for a new paradigm for teaching and learning. *Simulation & Gaming, 30,* 298–505.

Schank, R. C. (1990). Tell me a story: *Narrative and intelligence.* Evanston, IL: Northwestern University Press.

Senge, P. M. (1990a). *The fifth discipline: The art and practice of the learning organization.* New York: Currency Doubleday.

Senge, P. M. (1990b). The leader's new work: Building learning organizations. *Sloan Management Review,* 1–16.

Senge, P. M., Roberts, C., Ross, R., Smith, B., Roth, G., & Kleiner, A. (1999). *The dance of change: The challenges of sustaining momentum in learning organizations.* New York: Doubleday.

Silberman, M. (1998). *Active training.* San Francisco: Jossey-Bass.

Sinetar, M. (1998). *The mentor's spirit.* New York: St. Martin's Press.

Sorrells-Jones, J., & Weaver, D. (1999). Knowledge workers and knowledge-intense organizations, part 1: A promising framework for nursing and healthcare. *The Journal of Nursing Administration, 29*(10), 12–18.

Super, D. E. (1957). *The psychology of careers.* New York: Harper.

Super, D. E. (1963). *Career development: Self-concept theory.* New York: Entrance Board.

Vaill, P. B. (1996). *Learning as a way of being: Strategies for survival in a world of permanent white water.* San Francisco: Jossey-Bass.

Vance, C. (1977). A group profile of contemporary influentials in American nursing (Doctoral dissertation, Teachers College, Columbia University, 1977). *Dissertation Abstracts International, 38,* 4734B.

Vance, C. (1982). The mentor connection. *The Journal of Nursing Administration, 12*(4), 7–13.

Vance, C. (1995). The teacher as mentor. *The International Nurse, 8*(2), 3.

Vance, C. (1998). Mentorship. In J. J. Fitzpatrick (Ed.), *Encyclopedia of nursing research.* New York: Springer.

Vance, C. (1999). Mentoring—The nursing leader and mentor's perspective. In C. Andersen (Ed). *Nursing student to nursing leader: The critical path to leadership development.* (pp. 200–211). New York: Delmar.

Vance, C. (2000a). Discovering the riches in mentor connections. *Reflections on Nursing Leadership, 26*(3), 24–25.

Vance, C. (2000b). Mentoring at the edge of chaos. *Nursing Spectrum, 12*(17), 6.

Vance, C., & Bamford, P. (1998). Developing caring connections: Mentorship in the academic setting, *Dean's Notes, 19*(4), 1–3.

Vance, C., & Olson, R. (1991). Mentorship. In J. J. Fitzpatrick, R. Taunton, & A. Jacox (Eds.), *Annual Review of Nursing Research*, (Vol. 9, pp. 175–200). New York: Springer.

Vance, C., & Olson, R. (1998). *The mentor connection in nursing.* New York: Springer.

Wheatley, M. J. (1999). *Leadership and the new science: Discovering order in a chaotic world.* San Francisco: Berrett-Koehler.

Wickman, F., & Sjodin, T. (1997). *Mentoring: A success guide for mentors and protégés.* New York: McGraw-Hill.

Connie Vance, RN, EdD, FAAN, is professor at The College of New Rochelle, School of Nursing, in New Rochelle, New York.

PART TWO

Educating With an Academic Focus

CHAPTER EIGHT

Using Nursing History to Educate for Leadership

Sandra B. Lewenson

In 1934, the Committee on the Grading of Nursing Schools recommended in its final report to nursing educators, "It is important that all students admitted to schools of nursing in the future be of a professional type, capable of leadership" (Committee on the Grading of Nursing Schools, 1934, p. 131). The expectation that nurses would assume leadership roles meant that professional preparation included the skills necessary for students to become nurses and for all nurses to become leaders.

History provides insight into leadership principles and skills only when we seek history to learn these lessons. The strategy presented in this chapter describes the use of nursing history to teach students about leadership. Today, nursing history is integrated throughout nursing curricula. For the most part, students and faculty have a smattering of knowledge of the historical antecedents to nursing practice, education, and research. Lack of substantive knowledge about nursing history often leads educators and practitioners to ignore the study of how leaders in the past dealt with issues they faced or the strategies they used while building the profession. By studying the leadership strategies of the pioneers of the profession, students and practicing nurses can begin to understand the skills required to make change and to reflect on nursing's history.

WHY USE NURSING HISTORY TO STUDY LEADERSHIP IN NURSING?

In 1917, the Committee on Education of the National League for Nursing Education (NLNE) published the *Standard Curriculum for Schools of Nursing* in order to raise standards among nursing schools, and it served as a model for all schools of nursing to strive toward. The architects of this ideal curriculum wrote that it was not expected that all schools would be able to implement all parts of the curriculum because of the difficulty training schools faced in implementing the suggested innovations. Yet one of the concerns that all schools should have addressed was the need to train sufficient number of nursing leaders in education and administration. The Committee on Education of the NLNE (1917) wrote

> In positions of leadership especially, we are suffering from the lack of well-trained women. Hospitals and training schools are looking every-where for competent women to undertake the important duties of superintendents, supervisors, teachers, and technical experts in many different departments. Unless the hospital itself selects good women and gives them a broad substantial foundation to begin with, there is lit-tle hope that we will develop many of the kind of leaders who are need-ed for our very responsible educational and administrative work." (p. 6)

In the 1917 version of the Standard Curriculum, the study of nursing history was included under the heading of Social and Professional Subjects. Nurses needed to have the knowledge that their past could provide. The recommended course was titled, "Historical, Ethical and Social Basis of Nursing" and two objectives of the 15-hour course included the following:

1. To arouse interest and enthusiasm in nursing as an occupation, by introducing the pupil nurse early to the long and splendid history of nursing, and the great leaders who have established its traditions and ideals.
2. To make them appreciate some of the obstacles that have been overcome in making the profession what it is, and some of the opportunities which are open to them in the future. (p. 121)

Educating nurses who were leaders and who appreciated and were enthusiastic about nursing was crucial to perpetuating the profession.

Case studies, discussion, and readings were among the suggested teaching strategies that would engender enthusiasm and help students "catch the spirit of the great leaders" (Committee on Education of the NLNE, 1917, p. 126.)

In more recent times, Lynaugh (1996) notes that "history is our source of identity, our cultural DNA; it affords us collective immortality" (p. 1). This understanding of who past leaders were and how they accomplished their goals enables current and future nursing leaders to be armed better in their roles. In a doctoral level course on the role of nursing educators, students were encouraged to look at the writings of former nursing administrators and educators to assist them in finding solutions that they sought in their own practice. They reviewed the published standard curriculum and its revisions, and they explored the readings that nursing educators read and wrote. This exercise gave them a better understanding of how women in the earlier part of the twentieth century employed leadership skills and strategies to make change.

STRATEGIES THAT PROMOTE LEADERSHIP DEVELOPMENT

An educational strategy I have used with students and practicing nurses is to have them read speeches, articles, or books prepared by nursing leaders and educators reflecting an earlier period in nursing. These real case studies highlight the dilemmas, strengths, and issues behind the development of the nursing profession. For example, at a workshop I conducted at the National League for Nursing, participants read selected speeches from leaders of the American Society of Superintendents of Training Schools and the National League of Nursing Education, forerunners of the National League for Nursing, between 1893 and 1952 (Birnbach & Lewenson, 1991). The selections included a speech by Agnes Brennan who presented the debate between too much theory versus too much practice in 1897. Time was allotted for participants to work in groups to identify leadership strategies used and why they were used. In addition, they were encouraged to discuss whether these strategies would be useful in contemporary times and why they would or would not work. The workshop concluded with each group presenting to the larger group some of the ideas that were generated.

In nursing courses that address leadership roles in nursing, I have used a similar exercise where students select an address found in *Legacy of Leadership: Presidential Addresses from the Superintendents' Society and the National League for Nursing Education, 1894–1952* (Birnbach & Lewenson, 1993). Students examine the context in which the speech was presented, the message that was conveyed, and the person who presented the speech. They also focused on the leadership style, strategies used, and outcomes achieved, in addition to how it relates to current issues in nursing leadership, whether in education, practice, or research. By using historical documents such as these speeches that were presented to nurses some 100 years ago, leadership strategies and principles can be taught and incorporated into real-life situations.

Another assignment that I have successfully used in nursing history courses and in beginning professional nursing courses is to ask students to identify a nursing leader from a collected list of names of people that have been identified as leaders. Students examine this person's life, including family, social, and educational background and the contributions this person made to the nursing profession. Part of the assignment includes reflecting on the leadership style and strategies the person used to make change in the profession. In doing this assignment, students must critique the social, political, and economic period in which the person lived and led and how these factors may have influenced the leadership strategies used. Students can complete this assignment by reviewing the literature about the individual and the period they are studying. In some instances where the nursing leader is still alive, students are encouraged to interview that person, collecting an oral history.

When students place the nursing leader and accomplishments in the context of the period in which the person lived, they learn about the history of their profession. Students write their findings as scholarly papers and are expected to present this person to the class as well. Time is spent at the end of the presentations to discuss leadership strategies and how they might differ from one individual to another, and how the period influenced their style.

Students "meet" the leaders by studying their writing, speeches, and other relevant literature, but what is most compelling is when they can meet the leader in person. This can be accomplished by inviting living nursing leaders to class. At the Lienhard School of Nursing at Pace University, I had the pleasure of introducing Mary Elizabeth Carnegie, an outstanding nurse historian, educator, and researcher, to the entire student body. As part of a Web-assisted course, Historical Issues in Nursing, students in the class read about Dr. Carnegie and prepared questions for her presentation. We opened the course to the entire university community, advertising Dr. Carnegie's prominence in nursing and recommending readings to prepare for the talk. This provided a wonderful venue for informing students (nurses and non-nurses) and faculty about this important historical leader in nursing. Dr. Carnegie gave an informal presentation about her life, her role in nursing, and her leadership style. The question and answer period that followed enabled students and guests to ask about her leadership style, how she felt as a leader, and what made her do what she did in the profession. Students responded warmly to Dr. Carnegie's comments and noted how they could not believe what a "real person" she was and how meeting someone of her stature influenced them to work harder and "never give up." Excerpts from notes that students wrote to Dr. Carnegie following her talk include:

> Thank you for your talk. I will always remember that "rejection can be a challenge."
> It was a great honor to meet you and hear you speak of your great accomplishments. You are an inspiration for nurses, and women all over. It was amazing to have met someone who I have read and learned about.
> From sharing your experience in the nursing profession, I am more determined to become a nurse and make a difference like you did.

TARGET POPULATION FOR THIS STRATEGY

Using nursing history to teach leadership skills and strategies lends itself to several groups of people. Students in their pre-licensure education benefit from learning about the profession and the strength and expertise of pioneers who led nursing from an apprenticeship model of training to a university-based model of nursing education. As students learn the role of the professional nurse it is essential they connect with past role models. In 1969, noted nurse historian Theresa Christy wrote about the dilemma that young nursing students experienced in identifying with nurses, in part because they never learned about leaders in the past as people they could identify with. Christy noted:

> This lack of awareness of the great leaders in nursing may stem in part from the inattention to the role of these women in the historical development of the profession. It would seem that greater familiarity with the lives of Miss Nutting, Miss Dock, Miss Stewart, Miss Goodrich, and Mrs. Robb could aid young nurses in this identity problem by offering them true heroines of whom they can be justly proud, women of courage and conviction. (1969a, p. 20)

To remedy this loss of identity, Christy (1969a, 1969b, 1969c, 1969d, 1970a, 1970b, 1975) wrote a series of articles, titled "Portrait of a Leader," that focused on leaders such as Nutting, Robb, Dock, Stewart, Wald, and others who could provide students with a historical source of their professional identity. I still assign Christy's articles in several of my courses, especially when teaching nursing history. Students who seek out past leaders learn that these extraordinary pioneers were people who shared similar experiences in their professional lives and were able to overcome significant odds to accomplish their goals.

The second group of students that would benefit from studying historical records, speeches, and other important literature on nursing history are students in post-licensure programs, such as the RN to BS and graduate programs leading to the master's or doctorate in nursing. As students progress in their studies in higher education, it is essential that they understand how nursing leaders have changed the profession, what strategies they used, and if these same strategies would be useful today. Critical analysis needs to take place at these higher levels, but before that can be accomplished, students at all levels need to understand the development of the profession.

Role models for students in master's and doctoral level programs are not always readily identifiable or available. By encouraging nurses to look at the lives of other nurses, they are better able to find role models among the many who came before. For example, two emergency room nurses who were completing their master's project at our school were interested in how triage developed in their institution. To accomplish this goal they conducted oral histories on three nurses who had worked in their hospital for over 25 years. By interviewing these nurses, the students were able to learn how triage changed over time and how these nurses implanted innovative triage strategies in the emergency room. From a distance these students could see how the leadership strategies employed by these nurses enabled the changes to be successful. It also allowed them the opportunity to look at how other strategies may have created a more successful outcome.

Nurse educators comprise a third group that is integrating history into the curriculum. Although educators have expertise in particular content and in teaching strategies, they may not have a sufficient knowledge of historical antecedents that would facilitate discussions about nursing history and how it informs our practice today. Educators may not be comfortable applying leadership strategies to the nursing leaders that they may have studied as heroines of the past. Therefore, it is important that similar exercises be presented at professional meetings, faculty development workshops, or teaching colloquia that would raise the level of awareness among educators.

PROS AND CONS OF USING NURSING HISTORY AS A STRATEGY

Using nursing history to teach the next generation about leadership provides the cultural DNA that Lynaugh (1996) described. For example, by understanding the political strategies that nurses used to pass state licensure laws beginning in 1903, we gain a better understanding of the leadership methods used by many of these women. Focused on protecting both their profession and the public from those who would call themselves a nurse without nurses' training, nursing leaders successfully used a variety of methods, including persuasion, letter-writing campaigns, and collective action, in order to make legislative changes (Lewenson, 2002). Until 1920, women did not have the vote, and since nurses were mostly women, they relied on these kinds of strategies to make change. Nursing administrators and educators practiced their skills of persuasion on physicians, hospital boards, and legislative leaders and were successful to some degree in making necessary inroads in the profession. Thus, learning about how leaders, such as Lavinia Dock and Lillian Wald help students better understand how change is made, the context in which it is made, and the strategies that can be used.

Meeting the "living legends" of nursing also allows for students to relate to nurses and see how perseverance, hard work, and the ability to take criticism contribute to the success of many leaders. In addition, reading critiques of nursing history, case studies, speeches, and biographical sketches allows nursing leaders of today, including students, practicing nurses, and nurse educators, to view the success and sometimes failure of the strategies used. Thus, history gives us perspective that other strategies may not be able to provide. It is difficult for me to suggest any drawbacks to using history as a way to study nursing leadership styles and strategies. An interpretation using "present-mindedness," however, must be cautioned against when using history to understand leadership styles. Present-mindedness—"using a contemporary perspective when analyzing data collected from an earlier period" (Lewenson, 2003, p. 209)—may cloud the students' interpretation. For example, when nursing leaders argued for state registration laws, some opposed professional nursing organizations' support for women's suffrage because they felt it might jeopardize their relationship with politicians and, therefore, would work against them as they sought this protective nursing legislation. Although Dock and many others supported organizational advocacy for the suffrage campaign, the activities of nurses at that time could be and often were judged using a present-mindedness lens of contemporary feminists and thus the strategies invoked by early twentieth-century nursing leaders may have been misinterpreted.

EXPECTED AND SERENDIPITOUS OUTCOMES

Learning about leaders in nursing through the reading of speeches and texts on nursing history, studying primary and secondary sources, and meeting nursing leaders provides a sense of connection with the past. It allows for understanding and interpreting past events, leading to insight into what can be done in the future. Serendipitous findings are the surprise expressed by students when they recognize the number of enduring issues from a century of nursing. Issues such as nursing shortages, nurse practice acts, nursism, entry into practice debates, and recruitment remain continuing concerns of the nursing profession. On course evaluations, students write of the importance nursing history plays in their professional leadership development. They comment that "nursing history should be a requirement" for all nurses.

Learning directly from the source, whether in person or through historical speeches, commentaries, or published works provides an excellent way to learn about leadership. Faculty must find creative ways for students to understand nursing's rich heritage and to study the ways in which we have succeeded and failed in order for us to continue to grow.

REFERENCES

Birnbach, N., & Lewenson, S. B. (1991). *First words: Selected addresses from the National League for Nursing, 1894–1933.* New York: NLN.

Birnbach, N., & Lewenson, S. B. (1993). *Legacy of leadership: Presidential addresses from the Superintendents' Society and the National League of Nursing Education.* New York: NLN.

Christy, T. E. (1969a). Portrait of a leader: M. Adelaide Nutting. *Nursing Outlook, 17*(1), pp. 20–24.

Christy, T. E. (1969b). Portrait of a leader: Isabel Hampton Robb. *Nursing Outlook, 17*(3), pp. 26–29.

Christy, T. E. (1969c). Portrait of a leader: Lavinia Lloyd Dock. *Nursing Outlook, 17*(6), pp. 72–75.

Christy, T. E. (1969d). Portrait of a leader: Isabel Maitland Stewart. *Nursing Outlook, 17*(10), pp. 44–48.

Christy, T. E. (1970a). Portrait of a leader: Lillian D. Wald. *Nursing Outlook, 18*(3), pp. 50–54.

Christy, T. E. (1970b). Portrait of a leader: Annie Warburton Goodrich. *Nursing Outlook, 18*(8), pp. 46–50.

Christy, T. E. (1975). Portrait of a leader: Sophie F. Palmer. *Nursing Outlook, 23*(12), pp. 746–751.

Committee on Education of the National League of Nursing Education. (1917). *Standard Curriculum for Schools of Nursing,* Baltimore: Waverly Press.

Committee on the Grading of Nursing Schools. (1934). *Nursing schools today and tomorrow: Final report.* New York: Author.

Lewenson, S. B. (2002). 2: Pride in our past: Nursing's political roots. . In D. J. Mason & J. Leavitt (Eds.), *Policy and Politics for Nurses* (4th ed., pp. 19–30). Philadelphia: Saunders.

Lewenson, S. B. (2003). Historical research method. In H. J. Streubert Speziale & D. R. Carpenter (Eds.), *Qualitative research in nursing: Advancing the humanistic imperative* (3rd ed., pp. 207–223). Philadelphia: Lippincott Williams & Wilkins.

Lynaugh, J. E. (1996). Editorial. *Nursing History Review, 4,* p. 1.

CHAPTER NINE

Reflective Journaling: Bridging the Theory-Practice Gap

Debra A. Morgan
Jewett G. Johnson
Deborah R. Garrison

The real world is dynamic. There are no preset solutions to real life problems. Each situation and patient encounter is unique and each practitioner views the encounter through the lens of his or her own experience. Likewise, each individual will arrive at a unique interpretation of an encounter. If, indeed, these statements are true, how are we as nurse educators going to prepare students to make sound clinical decisions in the practice arena? The answer is to help them learn to think critically. We must help them bridge the gap between theory and practice. One strategy for accomplishing this is through the use of reflection and reflective journaling, which is the focus of this chapter.

THEORETICAL FRAMEWORK, DEFINITION, PURPOSE

Acquiring greater knowledge and insight into practice through reflection is not a new concept. In his classic work *The Reflective Practitioner*, Schon (1982) asserts that the educational preparation of professionals should be centered on enhancing the practitioner's abilities to reflect, that is, to recapture an experience, think about it, mull it over, evaluate it, and then learn from it. Reflective thinking is essential to identifying, analyzing, and solving complex problems. Reflection is active, persistent, and careful consideration of a situation, encounter, or idea. The process is not only cognitive in nature; it also involves exploration of feelings and emotion. Reflection generates greater understanding of a situation and promotes clarification and prioritization of personal values and ideals (Fonteyn & Cahill, 1998; Webster, 2002). It can stem either from an interest in examining an experience and then drawing on theoretical concepts, or from testing out theoretical concepts through experience. Both approaches cause the individual to critically examine experiences—to think critically.

WHY USE REFLECTION TO TEACH LEADERSHIP

Although leadership theorists have yet to come to consensus on a definition of leadership, there is little debate concerning the roles of a leader. A leader is a decision maker, communicator, evaluator, facilitator, visionary, risk taker, change agent, advocate, role model, coach, priority maker, creative problem solver, and critical thinker, and the list goes on. Acquiring insight into the practice of leadership requires developing a knowledge base of leadership principles, having opportunities to practice leadership skills, and creating a mechanism for internalizing these principles and skills. Reflection and reflective journaling can provide such a mechanism. Because the skills associated with leadership are conceptual in nature, journaling provides a framework for exploring and internalizing these skills.

BENEFITS OF REFLECTIVE JOURNALING

Without question, reflection is beneficial for learning (see Table 9.1), but reflection with the addition of appropriate feedback produces even greater learning. Journaling offers opportunities for students and practitioners to reflect on their practice, explore reactions, discover relationships, and connect new meaning to past experiences. Appropriate feedback can bring about positive changes in an individual's ability to think critically. Journaling provides a structure for reflection and a mechanism for feedback. Reflective journaling is a

TABLE 9.1. Benefits of Reflective Journaling

Students	Faculty	Faculty and student
Promotes autonomy	Assesses student learning	Fosters faculty/student relationship
Encourages self-appraisal	Evaluates student growth	Shares responsibility for evaluation
Cultivates communication	Provides insight into student thinking mechanism	Enhances faculty/student communication
Fosters critical thinking	Establishes/maintains a relationship with students	Humanizes faculty/student relationships
Aids in conflict resolution	Provides a dialogical teaching tool	Facilitates recognition of student growth
Encourages values clarification		Allows the sharing of perceptions about critical incidents

valuable tool for acquiring leadership skills; it has the potential for turning every experience into a learning experience. Writing about experiences enables practitioners to make explicit the knowledge that is implicit in their action and provides an avenue for critical thinking that is fundamental to growth as a leader and that more fully engages students in the learning process.

Journaling fosters self-appraisal. A fundamental assumption of adult education is that adult students are independent beings who have developed self-concept based on an accumulation of life experiences. Journaling provides a formal mechanism for examining these life experiences and it improves observational skills and increases cognitive awareness. Journaling prompts individuals to assess their strengths and weaknesses and strive for personal growth. Journaling develops the skill and, equally important, the habit, of self-monitoring and self-appraisal (Fonteyn & Cahill, 1998; Jasper, 1999; Webster, 2002). As one student wrote in her clinical journal:

> Keeping a clinical journal forced me to look back on my clinical experiences. It made me evaluate what I did and to ask myself what I should have done. I was also forced to examine the events and relate them to management/leadership principles. As a result of writing and thinking about each clinical day, I believe I have learned more about leadership and more about myself than I would have had journaling not been required.

Through journaling, students identify what went really well and what activities had a less than satisfactory outcome. Learning becomes more personal and is more readily internalized.

Journaling also cultivates communication skills by helping to develop and hone written communication. As a dialogical tool, journaling promotes self-talk and exploration of feelings. In journaling, questions can be raised, questions that might otherwise never have been asked, and issues can be scrutinized from every angle. Journaling provides a means for students to define experiences in their own words and to have their thinking processes reflected back to them through faculty feedback. Through journaling, students are better able to synthesize and evaluate information, increase conceptual clarity, and engage in problem solving and critical thinking—all factors essential to leadership development (Kennison & Misselwitz, 2002; Kok, 2002).

Finally, journaling provides students with a safe outlet for personal concerns and frustrations. Students should be encouraged to explore areas of concern, situations that produce frustration, and areas of cognitive dissonance. Journaling is useful in managing conflict and clarifying values. On the other hand, journaling is an acceptable way to "toot your own horn," to share a moment in time in which the student performed in an exemplary fashion. As one student wrote:

> Today was a great day. I didn't really expect it to be. To meet one of my clinical objectives, I volunteered to go to a junior high school career day. It was a hands-on learning event for girls only. These young girls were so enthusiastic and so excited, as my friends and I talked with them about nursing and let them touch and play with nursing tools. I left thinking we had done something good, something worthwhile. It felt great.

Reflective journaling is not without benefit for the faculty as well. It provides a tool for assessing students' accomplishments, personal growth, and skill development. It presents a window into a student's thinking and a picture of the learning that is taking place and allows the teacher to see, from the students' own perspective, how the students are doing. In this way, the journal becomes a form of self-assessment allowing the evaluation process to be shared between teacher and student. Perhaps of equal importance is that journaling serves to humanize the faculty/student relationship. Students come to see faculty as "real people" with wisdom to share. A mentoring relationship often develops as a result of sharing thoughts and ideas through journal entries (Landeen, Byrne, & Brown, 1995; Spalding & Wilson, 2002; Webster, 2002). One bonus is that journaling provides a permanent record of thoughts and experiences for students and faculty to examine again at a later time.

BARRIERS TO REFLECTIVE JOURNALING

The benefits to reflective journaling are many, yet there are barriers to overcome, or at least to consider, when using this strategy. Trust is perhaps the biggest hurdle, and the lack of trust runs both ways. Students may not feel safe in revealing their thoughts for fear of repercussion. Faculty may doubt the students' veracity in relating events. Clearly, for journaling to be most effective, a trusting and safe environment is a prerequisite (Riley-Doucet & Wilson, 1997; Spalding & Wilson 2002). A second barrier is that journaling takes time—time to think and write on the part of the student, and time to read, think, and provide feedback on the part of the teacher. In a culture that is definitively busy, allowing adequate time for reflection is no small obstacle. A third and final barrier is student readiness for this type of self-directed learning. Reflection is not a naturally occurring phenomenon. As early as 1933, Dewey stated that although thinking was natural, reflective habits of the mind needed to be taught. If journaling is to be the strategy for reflection, students must believe they are in a safe learning environment. They must feel free to express themselves fully, to articulate their own points of view, and to know that their journals will remain confidential.

TEACHING REFLECTION

We must help students to understand that "telling" and "reflecting" are not the same. Simply describing an event does not constitute reflection. Reflection is more. First, an individual has a particular encounter or experience; the reflective process is initiated when the individual returns to the experience, recalls what has taken place, replays the experience, then reevaluates the experience and her or his response to it (Wong, Kember, Chung, & Yan, 1995). Reflection is active and deliberate. It is a process that leads to a greater understanding of the situation. Concepts central to the art of leadership can be explored, evaluated, and internalized through the process of reflective journaling. Insight is gained with journaling as it enables the student to structure thoughts and recollections more objectively. Since the 1980s, leaders in higher education have encouraged a transition from teacher-centered models to learner-centered models of education (Huba & Freed, 2002). Reflective journaling is highly student-centered. Students construct knowledge as they reflect upon the real world experiences of the practice arena.

One strategy for teaching reflection is to provide feedback on thinking strategies the student used in journal entries. To clarify this point, an illustration might be helpful. Fonteyn and Cahill (1998) had students do journaling each week about their clinical experiences. Specific feedback was given identifying what type of thinking was demonstrated in the journal. Five distinct thinking types were identified: recognizing a pattern, forming relationships, generating hypotheses, providing explanations, and drawing conclusions. Through journaling and faculty feedback that identifies the specific thinking strategies used, students became more aware of how they were thinking and improved thinking skills became apparent. An example of how this strategy can be applied to leadership is provided in Table 9.2.

TEACHING LEADERSHIP PRINCIPLES THROUGH REFLECTIVE JOURNALING

Schon (1999) describes "reflection on action" as an approach to contemplating practice retrospectively, usually away from the setting in which the practice took place. This involves identification, description, and determination of the significance of each incident. Journaling provides the perfect vehicle for such reflection. An important way to enhance learning is to strengthen the link between the learning experience and the reflective activity that follows it. This can be accomplished by using guiding questions to promote reflection. For example, when learning about the roles of a leader, a student first may be assigned to spend a day with a nurse manager. Following the clinical day, the student would be expected to reflect on the experience and answer specific questions or address particular issues posed by the teacher.

TABLE 9.2. Thinking Strategies Evident in Reflective Journaling

Thinking strategy	Definition	Sample journal entry
Recognizing a pattern	Identifying characteristic pieces of data that fit together	The nurse manager used several strategies to resolve conflict on the unit including compromising, smoothing, and collaborating.
Forming relationships	Connecting information to further understanding	I'm starting to see a connection. All the nurse managers in the in the hospital have at least a BSN and several years of experience.
Generating hypotheses	Asserting tentative explanations that account for a set of facts	Conflict seems to happen most when staffing is short. I wonder if conflict always occurs when there is a staffing shortage?
Providing explanations	Offering reasons for actions, beliefs, or remarks	When the nurse manager tells the staff why a new policy was put into effect, they seem more willing to follow the policy.
Drawing conclusions	Reaching a decision or forming an opinion	The personnel budget was not increased this year, it is not likely that a new RN position will be approved.

SAMPLE QUESTIONS

Questions may be tailored to a specific clinical experience or a standard set of questions may be used for reflection following any clinical experience dealing with leadership. For example:

* What have I learned from this experience?
* How would I behave given a similar situation?
* In what ways do nursing or leadership theories predict or explain this situation?

Another set of questions considers the many roles and characteristics of a leader. Students are asked to evaluate the day spent with the nurse manager and then reflect upon the following questions:

* Which roles/characteristics of a leader were evident in the nurse manager you followed? How did she/he demonstrate these roles?
* Given the benefit of hindsight, might the nurse manager have handled the situation differently and how so?
* What went exceptionally well? Why do you think this is?
* What insight did you take away from this experience?

This approach allows students to engage in real-world leadership experiences and helps to bridge the gap between theory and practice. Even when what is seen in practice does not match theory, journaling about the experience provides a rich learning opportunity for the student. Journaling, with appropriate feedback, helps students see the connection between theory and practice. Further, these journaling exercises promote a sense of value and appreciation for theory. Theory becomes more real, more substantial, and more meaningful.

One caution when asking students to use journals to reflect upon their clinical experience is their tendency to focus writing upon what went wrong or what they perceive as poor practice. While this is very important and a valuable learning experience, students should also critically examine what went well. There is much to be learned about why something was successful. Behaviors leading to success can be learned. To this end, students should be asked to identify an incident that occurred in clinical in which they felt they made a positive difference in the care of a patient. The following directions are designed to facilitate this reflection:

* Reflect upon the incident to clarify, understand, and learn from it.
* Analyze the experience.
* What knowledge or skills were used?
* What insight was gained?
* What might you do to be able to achieve consistently such a positive outcome?

Regardless of the questions used or the topics explored through journaling, the goal of faculty feedback is to provide support, challenge assumptions, encourage deeper reflection, and assist students in making the theory-practice connection. Journaling is a powerful tool that can change the function of the teacher, the responsibilities of the learner, and the purpose and process of evaluation.

REFERENCES

Dewey, J. (1933). *How we think: A restatement of the relation of reflective thinking to the educative process*. New York: Heath.

Fonteyn, M., & Cahill, M. (1998). The use of clinical logs to improve nursing students' metacognition: A pilot study. *Journal of Advanced Nursing, 28*(1), 149–154.

Huba, M., & Freed, J. (2000). *Learner-centered assessment on college campuses: Shifting the focus from teaching to learning*. Boston: Allyn & Bacon.

Jasper, M. (1999). Nurses' perceptions of the value of written reflection. *Nurse Education Today, 19*, 452–463.

Kennison, M., & Misselwitz, S. (2002). Evaluating reflective writing for appropriateness, fairness, and consistency. *Nursing Education Perspectives, 23*, 238–242.

Kok, J. (2002). Reflective journal writing: How it promotes reflective thinking in clinical nursing education: A students' perspective. *Curationis, 25*(3), 35–42.

Landeen, J., Byrne, C., & Brown, B. (1995). Exploring the lived experiences of psychiatric nursing students through self-reflective journals. *Journal of Advanced Nursing, 21*, 878–885.

Riley-Doucet, C., & Wilson, S. (1997). A three-step method of self-reflection using reflective journal writing. *Journal of Advanced Nursing, 25*, 964–968.

Schon, D. A. (1982). *The reflective practitioner*. New York: Basic Books

Schon, D. A. (1999). *The reflective practitioner, How professionals think in action*. London: Ashgate.

Spalding, E., & Wilson, A. (2002). Demystifying reflection: A study of pedagogical strategies that encourage reflective writing. *Teachers College Record, 104*, 1393–1421.

Webster, J. (2002). Using reflective writing to gain insight into practice with older people. *Nursing Older People, 14*(9), 18–21.

Wong, K., Kember, D., Chung, L., & Yan, L. (1995). Assessing the level of student reflection from reflective journals. *Journal of Advanced Nursing, 22*(1), 48–57.

CHAPTER TEN

Integrating Leadership Content Into the Undergraduate Curriculum

Jewett G. Johnson
Deborah R. Garrison
Debra A. Morgan

One goal of faculty of baccalaureate nursing programs is that that their graduates become recognized as leaders in the profession and in their communities. It is therefore incumbent on faculty to integrate professional standards, leadership models and examples, and practical application of leadership skills throughout the curriculum from the students' introduction to nursing to their graduation. Often, the pressing realities of preparing students to assume their roles as staff nurses subjugates leadership principles and skills to those of technical nursing and management. This chapter describes an integrated curriculum approach to teaching leadership.

The nursing program at Midwestern State University makes the following assumptions regarding teaching leadership throughout the curriculum. Although not synonymous, the roles of professional and leader share many common characteristics (Drath & Palus, 1994). Although it may be assumed that preparation in one enhances and overlaps the other, that may not be the case. It is also incumbent upon faculty to be active members and leaders within the professional nursing community, as they are responsible for modeling and fostering implementation of such behavior throughout the baccalaureate experience. Modeling and role modeling are not sufficient, however, to instill predictably the habits, traits, and skills essential to producing graduates with the potential to become leaders. The faculty must provide multiple, safe opportunities to learn, implement, and practice leadership strategies, and provide examples drawn from the history of the profession and other professions and vocations.

INTEGRATION WITHIN THE
INTRODUCTORY CURRICULUM

As with most baccalaureate nursing programs, Midwestern State's program offers an introductory course designed to inspire those desiring to become nurses and provides the foundation to sustain them through the difficult course of study. The initial course utilizes the history of nursing as part of its framework, highlighting those individuals who are recognized leaders in nursing. The emphasis here is not on rote learning of historical fact, but rather on the elimination of common myths of leadership: that leaders are charismatic; leaders are born, not made; leaders exist only at the top of an organization; leaders control, direct, manipulate, and prod; and leadership is a rare skill. Students are encouraged to develop a reverence for these individuals and a pride in their accomplishments as a basis for developing their own sense of professional pride and community leadership. Historical nursing leaders are presented in light of their personal strengths and the circumstances in which they emerged so that students can discover what Wheatley and Kellner-Rogers (1996) state so eloquently:

> Life uses messes to get to well-ordered solutions. Life doesn't seem to share our desires for efficiency or neatness. It uses redundancy, fuzziness, dense webs of relationships, and unending trials and errors to find what works.
> Life is intent on finding what works, not what's "right." It is the ability to keep finding solutions that is important; any one solution is temporary. There are no permanently right answers. The capacity to keep changing, to find what works now, is what keeps any organism alive. (p. 13)

It is also important to provide the beginning student with a sense of immediacy regarding the profession and leadership by nurses.

Community leadership activities at all levels by the faculty and local nurse leaders are highlighted and presented as the expected norm, furthering a sense of professional pride as well as an expectation of participation. A guided interview with local nursing leaders and inquiry into their personal motivation for entry into nursing, philosophy of patient care, and interrelationships with other professionals benefits students by identifying the myriad of leadership roles in the many different working environments of professional nurses. As students share the results of the guided interviews, faculty emphasize that leadership is "a particular mode of engagement with life, requiring a lifelong commitment to growing toward human fulfillment" (Terry, 1993, p. 15). This same content and emphasis in the guided interview model is adapted using local nursing leaders as guest lecturers where there are time constraints within the curriculum.

These strategies are simple for faculty to implement and have had an excellent reception by the students. The introductory course is also a vehicle for stressing the uniqueness of the nursing student role and building a sense of pride and special being. By presenting and explaining the long hours of study and clinical practice as proof of their importance and worth to the community, a quality that sets them apart from any other baccalaureate level program, students begin to develop a sense of collegiality with one another. Membership in the Nursing Student Association (NSA) and in other campus groups is encouraged and supported by all faculty members and begins at this introductory level. Morgan (2001) found that membership in the NSA was significantly related to successful completion of the curriculum. Our course uses membership in the NSA as part of the course grade. Faculty participation in leadership roles in both professional and community organizations becomes paramount as students study the roles and expectations of the nurse, preventing the promulgation of a "do as I say, not as I do" culture.

The introductory course includes communication skills. These skills are learned through role-play rather than through traditional textbook exercises. Role-play allows students to develop and practice assertive communication skills in nonthreatening, low-risk environments. Additionally, students assume a leadership role in the course by taking responsibility for presenting integral, testable course content, such as the State Nurse Practice Act, historical leaders, and educational preparation in nursing. The outcomes of this exercise include the development of communication skills and demeanor appropriate to the advancement of the profession. Every leader develops a unique communication style, often through trial and error, and this course offers students an opportunity to discover and practice skills they will be able to incorporate into their own styles. In all, students emerge from their introductory nursing course with a set of communication skills as a foundation for accomplishing future goals in their professional development, developing a sense of pride in the importance of their profession, and becoming active members of the university community, existing within a microculture of shared norms and an ethic that supersedes cultural diversities.

INTEGRATION WITHIN CLINICAL COURSES

As students move into clinically based courses, the emphasis naturally shifts to ensuring clinical competence and the development of critical thinking skills so essential to practitioners. The principles of leadership and professionalism receive less emphasis in these courses as the body of knowledge to be mastered and the thought processes to be integrated are large, complex, and frequently overwhelming to the students. The fertile fields developed in the introductory course, however, are not left fallow. Often the inclusion of leadership topics based on observed clinical situations, along with further role-playing in assertive communication, are included in post-conferences. Again, the professional leadership of the faculty provides a modeling experience that is enhanced by inviting students to be active participants. This not only sets the importance of these activities firmly in the students' minds, but also begins the development of a sense of collegiality between faculty and students.

With appropriate guidance, students in advanced clinical practica identify their own needs, devise their own learning objectives, and make their own patient assignments, allowing them a sense of autonomy and control over their learning. This concept requires faculty to relinquish a modicum of control and has been found to be a useful strategy in clinical courses.

Including students in policy-making committees of the nursing department has become *de rigueur* in most baccalaureate programs. This is an excellent opportunity for students to form liaisons among their peers and the faculty and to further develop collegiality and assertive communication skills. At this point in their journey through the curriculum, most students have begun to identify with a particular faculty member or at least to see the activities of certain faculty members coinciding with their own interests. The provision of a mentoring program and the voluntary inclusion of students in the program is one of the most positive steps we have made as a faculty. The formation of mentoring relationships provides students with an anchor point, a sense of increased collegiality, and a feeling that the nursing program and being a nurse are special and different from other university programs.

The nursing management/leadership course is the place where we maximize and clarify the leadership role for students. Although they are frequently equated with one another and often overlap, management and leadership are, indeed, different and separate entities. There are certain management skills and concepts that must be mastered to ensure adequate preparation of new graduates. The inclusion of experiences and exercises promoting mastery of management techniques cannot be neglected or minimized, and should not be mistaken for teaching leadership. We include various group exercises that teach values clarification and prioritization, team building, team leading, and development of leadership traits, while providing students with a safe environment to spread their leadership wings, to make mistakes, and with guidance, to learn from them. At Midwestern State's program, providing a rich and supportive experience is the key to future movement into leadership roles by graduates. When students are encouraged and supported in risk-taking leadership behavior, they will be willing to take a risk again. We find that the management/leadership course is a great place to allow those risks to be taken. These exercises allow students to develop authenticity, ethical sensibilities, and integration of action with internal values. Students also learn that there is a set of features implicit or explicit in every action, and through those elements a leader can frame an issue for the group to solve (Mitstifer, 1995, 1998, n.d.).

The community nursing experience includes nursing leaders and allows students to begin the task of broadening the embraced vision to aggregates, communities, and society as a whole. Our curriculum divides the community experience into two courses: an introductory course providing a basis in public health issues in the junior year and a senior level course to integrate the concepts of community, nursing, and professionalism. Students in the final semester of study plan, lead, implement, and evaluate health fairs for selected populations. Completion of this course requirement demonstrates acquisition of leadership abilities necessary for becoming a contributing member of the nursing profession. Once again, the interrelationships among professionals and the impact of nursing on the quality of life of populations are emphasized, as they were in the introductory course.

The use of reflective journaling in both junior- and senior-level courses allows students to express themselves in a safe, confidential manner, provides a rich record of personal growth, and teaches them a method of actively and deliberately recalling an event, replaying the experience, and reevaluating the experience and their response (Wong, Kember, Chung & Yan, 1995). Using real-world examples, structured portions of journaling exercises are tailored to emphasize the true meaning of leadership action; if leadership action doesn't improve a situation, there is likely an error in issue framing (Mitstifer, 1995, 1998, n.d.). Toward the end of the baccalaureate program, students are growing in their realization of personal strengths, the integration of the skills and knowledge base they have acquired, and how the exercise of decision making in nursing activities reinforces their sense of self as a professional nurse. This growth is reflected in exit interviews with graduating seniors.

COMMITMENT TO LEADERSHIP ACTION

The inclusion of leadership action by graduates as an identified goal shared by all faculty throughout the nursing curriculum ensures its integration, beginning with simpler materials and ideas being presented and practiced, and progressing on to develop and incorporate more complex concepts. The attributes and outcomes relevant to the goal of leadership action (Table 10.1) guide the work of the curriculum and faculty. Demonstrated commitment to the goals by each faculty member provides students with a rich source of modeling and mentoring and the end result of preparing nurses who will lead the profession with spirit and élan. Terry (1993) puts it eloquently:

> Leadership is not a means to another end. It is not instrumental. Leadership is the act itself. . . . Leadership is a gift to be unwrapped and treasured; leadership is choice, to be claimed; leadership is part of a web of interdependent actions, to be made functionally whole; leadership is

TABLE 10.1. Curricular Goals for Leadership

Intrinsic leadership attributes	Extrinsic leadership outcomes
Sense of professional pride	Establishes a collegial relationship with students, faculty, and other health care professionals
Life-long learning habits	Participates within the wider nursing community
Cognizance of personal strengths and areas for growth	Evaluates positive and negative practices seen within the profession
View of nursing as a special, value-centered professional microculture	Participates in team building and leadership activities
Awareness of the impact of actions	Demonstrates assertive communication skills

participation, to be energized; leadership is adventure, to be embraced; leadership is creativity and innovation, to be playful. Leadership is total engagement offered for the well-being of the earth and all its inhabitants. (p. 273)

REFERENCES

Drath, W., & Palus, C. (1994). *Making common sense: Leadership as meaning-making in a community of practice.* Greensboro, NC: Center for Creative Leadership.

Mitstifer, D. (Ed.) (1995). Leadership. *Kappa Omicron Nu Dialogue, 5*(3), 1–4.

Mitstifer, D. (1998). Reflective human action. *A Leadership Journal: Women in Leadership—Sharing the Vision, 2*(2).

Mitsifer, D. (n.d.). *Reflective human action.* Retrieved November 20, 2003, from http://kon.org/rha_online_files/rha_manu.html.

Morgan, D. A. (2001). The impact of stress on integration and attrition in nursing education in Texas. Unpublished doctoral dissertation, Baylor University.

Terry, R. (1993). *Authentic leadership: Courage in action.* San Francisco: Jossey-Bass.

Wheatley, M., & Kellner-Rogers, M. (1996). *A simpler way.* San Francisco: Berrett-Koehler.

Wong, F., Kember, D., Chung, L., & Yan, L. (1995). Assessing the level of student reflection from reflective journals. *Journal of Advanced Nursing, 22,* 48–57.

CHAPTER ELEVEN

Using Group Process to Develop Caring Leaders

Linda D. Wagner

A s educators, we hope that one day our students will be leaders in the future of health care practice. Providing opportunities for them to develop the skills and values of humane leadership is essential to graduating nurses who advocate for change, support collaborative teams, and tolerate ambiguity. Concepts such as caring and leadership can only be understood through the personal context of the individual. Successful leadership entails working with other people, possessing strong communication skills and developing empathic understanding. Leadership based on caring relationships enriches the lives of all members in a relationship by enhancing their capabilities and self-confidence (Bondas, 2003; Boykin & Schoenhofer, 2001; Jung & Sosik, 2002; Watson, 2000). This chapter describes a strategy for teaching leadership skills through a group process experience. Discussion of the literature underlying caring and leadership extends the meaning of caring and the values of leadership when teaching undergraduate nursing students.

CARING LEADERSHIP

"At the core of becoming a leader is the need always to connect one's voice and one's touch" (De Pree, 1992, p. 3). A leader has to have self-knowledge, which will subsequently influence the leader's actions. "Thus implicit in the use of voice as an instrument of leadership is the notion that care and empowerment are leadership tasks" (Helgesen, 1990, p. 226). According to Felgen (2003), "the leadership practice of successful and caring executives includes. . ." (p. 213) personal knowing, active listening, empowerment, trust, and enhancing another's self-worth. Not only must leaders possess these characteristics, but they also should be able to confront conflict, be visible and competent, and promote team building through relationships (Hardt, 2001; Kouzes & Posner, 1993; Senge, 1990).

The metaphor of a web of connection is used frequently (Bishop & Scudder, 1991; Gilligan, 1982; Helgesen, 1990) to refer to relationships that are based on connection rather than hierarchy. Leaders who operate from a "web of inclusion" (Helgesen) as opposed to a hierarchy put themselves at the center of their organization, not at the top. An understanding of the position of leadership as a web as opposed to a hierarchy, with caring as a component, will allow nurses who are engaged in patient-care situations to practice as formal and informal leaders (Bishop & Scudder; Watson, 2000).

Literature on leadership within groups demonstrates that the main function of a leader is often to help the group achieve mutual goals (Nye, 2002) and a higher level of group performance, and to inspire a higher lever of commitment to a common mission or vision (Jung & Sosik, 2002). Members within the group have a significant influence over the leadership process, indicating a reciprocal process of leadership attributes, group cohesiveness, and common goals (Dirks & Ferrin, 2002; Jung & Sosik; Nye).

Several scholars speak about the importance of nurturing a caring relationship in leadership (Allen, 1998; Bolman & Deal, 1995; Kouzes & Posner, 1993; Senge, 1990; Watson, 2000; Wheatley, 1994). The elements of a caring relationship consist of listening, presence (Watson, 1988), trust and compassion (Roach, 1991), and the ability to create an environment that fosters another's growth (Mayeroff, 1971). A common theme that runs through the literature on caring and leadership is the importance of relationships. Leadership is about people forming relationships to change groups, organizations, and societies according to their mutual purposes (Felgen, 2003).

As health care dollars decrease, nurses who are positioned as primary advocates for patients and families will ultimately be the leaders in health care. Nursing care in the future will require individuals who have the ability to work in teams, coordinate care, and affect change (Allen, 1998; Boykin & Schoenhofer, 2001; Hardt, 2001; White & Rice, 2001). Leadership is more than good management, and nurses need not only to know the technical skills to provide care, but also to have the ability to intervene and promote healing through an understanding of how leadership influences practice.

Other studies on leadership in formal positions have helped to further define how constituents view leaders in organizational settings. Helgesen (1990) explored women's ways of leadership through interviews with four female executives. She conducted diary studies through observation and interview. She found that these women often viewed leadership from a web structure, "which affirms relationships, seeks ways to strengthen human bonds, simplifies communications, and gives means an equal value with ends" (p.52). From her interviews, Helgesen concluded that while a vision is imperative to leadership, it couldn't exist without a voice. A voice finds its form in the process of interaction. By this, Helgesen means that the value of connectedness is nurtured through the process of interaction of which "voice" or communication is present.

TEACHING CARING LEADERSHIP

It is important that nurse educators understand that knowledge and practice are inseparable in the study and performance of nursing. Nursing is a profession in which caring, knowledge, critical thinking, and compassion help to shape informed practice (Boykin & Schoenhofer, 2001). Nurse educators have the responsibility to create learning environments where leadership and caring can be experienced as process. When faculty serve as role models to facilitate learning activities where students experience reciprocal caring or are empowered as leaders, a learning community is established that fosters the development of caring leadership qualities that may persist into practice (Allen, 1998; Grams, Kosowski, & Wilson, 1997; Jung & Sosik, 2002).

Establishing small groups within a nursing program allows students the opportunity to share, listen, and provide peer support in a nonthreatening environment. Everyone enters the group as an equal participant, and grades do not represent a threat or reward. Although there needs to be a balance of task needs and socioemotional needs, it is up to group members to determine direction. It is also important that a cohesive environment be established and that it be developed on supportive, not defensive, communication (Jung & Sosik, 2002). Supportive communication occurs when group members are more accepting of the opinions and diversity of others and are willing to listen and learn from each other.

Caring groups have been used in nursing programs as a way for students and faculty to develop self-awareness, and to recognize that caring for oneself precedes caring for others (Beck, 1992; Grams et al., 1997). Grams and others described the lived experience of being in a caring group in an associate degree in nursing program. The three themes that emerged from their qualitative study were: creating the caring community, experiencing the reciprocity of caring, and being transformed. Their study assists educators to define how caring is experienced between students and supports the belief that "participants reported a strong desire to recreate the caring group experience in their future nursing practices" (p.15).

Recommendations from studies on caring groups have stressed the need to identify methods by which faculty can nurture and sustain the ability of students to care (Beck, 1992; Grams et al., 1997). These studies highlight peer group interactions as an environmental context within which the socialization of caring may occur. Peer groups can provide students with a forum for support and validation. In a peer group setting, expertise does not rely on one individual, but is shared. It is a way to connect to others with similar needs, to develop as an individual, and to decrease feelings of isolation.

Nursing scholarship has embraced the value of caring communities within the educational environment. The enacted curriculum of group process as it relates to practice encompasses theory from both nursing and education. It supports constructed knowing and brings the concepts of community and caring together. Models of leadership based on caring will ultimately benefit nursing practice. Nurses who demonstrate caring leadership understand the value of human relationships in the practice setting, are able to create caring environments, and work toward fulfilling mutual visions (Felgen, 2003; Hardt, 2001; Watson, 2000). Research on student leaders who exhibit caring behaviors can begin to answer our questions and provide pedagogical models for learning. Concepts of leadership experienced during educational programs will find students ready at graduation to practice in settings requiring characteristics of collaboration, self-confidence, vision, and caring.

MODEL FOR CARING LEADERSHIP IN GROUPS

Realizing the significance of peer-to-peer interaction as a learning methodology, Southern Connecticut State University's baccalaureate nursing program began a course entitled Group Process. This one-credit course integrated sophomore, junior, and senior nursing students in small group interaction. Each semester, nursing students registered for a group process section that fit their schedule. The groups met for 1 hour a week during the semester. They received 0.5 credits/semester for the course, graded as pass/fail.

Faculty decided that trust and confidentiality would be enhanced if they were not present during group sessions. As a way to expose senior nursing students to a leadership role, they were assigned as group facilitators. The seniors met initially for an orientation to group dynamics and an introduction to the role of facilitator. Two to three seniors were assigned to each group, and each group had a faculty preceptor. Each week after the groups finished, the seniors would check in with their assigned faculty preceptor to submit attendance sheets and discuss any issues of conflict or problems that arose during group sessions. Confidentiality was maintained at all times.

The course emphasized gaining trust within a group setting; sharing feelings, thoughts, and experiences with other students; and learning and applying group process skills. When this course was initially developed, there was no task or outcome for the group to accomplish. My dissertation research became the vehicle for exploring concepts of caring and leadership from the peer perspective of students in these groups. Consequently, senior nursing students were interviewed, and all sophomore, junior and senior nursing students kept journals that were analyzed as part of the research.

Outcomes of using a group process course in an undergraduate nursing program are based on findings from the dissertation study (Wagner, 1997). One outcome of the course was gaining an understanding of how to work in groups. As group cohesion developed, senior facilitators felt more confident in their ability to facilitate their groups and were amazed at their ability to provide sophomore and junior students with knowledge and advice and be positive role models

(Wagner). For example, during the fall semester when sophomore students were studying math for their medication administration test, the juniors and seniors all worked together to help the sophomore students review the problems.

Senior nursing students who functioned as group facilitators fostered group cohesion by instilling confidence in group members, empowering individual students, and confronting issues of group conflict. The leadership of senior students was supported in a reciprocal manner as sophomores and juniors acknowledged the role of the facilitator as leader (Wagner, 1997). The ability to sustain leadership was strengthened through a socialization process that included reflection, sharing of clinical practice stories, and ethical dilemmas. Storytelling and sharing led to a greater understanding of the perspectives of others perspectives and diversity. As the semester progressed, seniors felt more confident sharing concerns from their clinical experience, and sophomores, who had not yet started clinical, gained a better understanding of what nursing is and received support that they can be successful from juniors and seniors.

Several factors in these nursing students' education fostered a sense of community in the classroom, and supported and internalized aspects of care and leadership (Wagner, 1997). When initially asked to define leadership, many of the seniors interviewed answered with traditional definitions mainly associated with management skills. When asked how they practiced leadership in-group, their responses were more reflective of caring leadership. Though the senior students might not have been able to articulate the connections between caring and leadership, their practice demonstrated otherwise. Listening, letting the group make decisions, getting others to participate, building on relationships, being sensitive to others, and focusing on positive qualities were all examples the senior facilitators gave as ways that they practiced leadership. This attests to the fact that caring leadership is more than what one knows; it is internalized and expressed as a way of being.

A context that is responsive and that facilitates the development of caring leadership is consistent with being humane, process oriented, dialogic, reflective, and developmental. The group socialization process allowed for the development and support of caring leadership in a manner that involved reciprocity, a flow of energy, and ultimately growth. The outcomes of the small group approach support a conceptual framework that values relationships based on connection rather than hierarchy. Using a web as a metaphor for the caring group, with caring and leadership as a component, implies that all strands are important and that all points are interconnected. These strands are identified in the circle of caring leadership as respect, sensitivity, listening, empowerment, support, trust, and personal knowing (Figure 11.1).

Leadership continues to be associated with administrative positions and with power. Instead of preparing nursing students to be future leaders, the group process course allows students to be leaders now. The confidence that faculty instilled in senior students through group facilitation demonstrated that they graduated feeling more confident, assertive, and respectful of others. This behavior in turn provides positive role models for the sophomore and junior students.

For caring leadership to be sustained, a caring environment that fosters the development of community is essential. As Hall and Allan (1994) commented, "Before empowering relationships can be formed, healers and clients require a caring community that supports and defines the importance of giving in inter-relationships" (p. 115). Students in this course felt that a caring environment comprised of safety, confidentiality, and a sense of belonging was important to establish at the outset.

PROS AND CONS OF USING GROUP PROCESS TO DEVELOP LEADERSHIP SKILLS

Research suggests that group process with multiple levels of nursing students supports the development of students as caring leaders (Wagner, 1997). There are many positive aspects of this course. Most important is the concept of respect and trust. The fact that students found this to be essential in caring relationships suggests that they will in turn treat colleagues with respect and try to establish trust within groups. Students felt that their confidence increased, they learned how to be better listeners, and they shared a commonality of experience. Learning how to work in groups will also prove beneficial after graduation as students assume leadership roles on teams and committees.

Seniors commented on several aspects of group. For example, many remarked on the difficulty of scheduling the class. They also mentioned that it was difficult to establish lasting relationships when groups changed from semester to semester. They perceived that it was important for faculty to continue to provide support and guidance to

FIGURE 11.1. Framework for caring leadership.

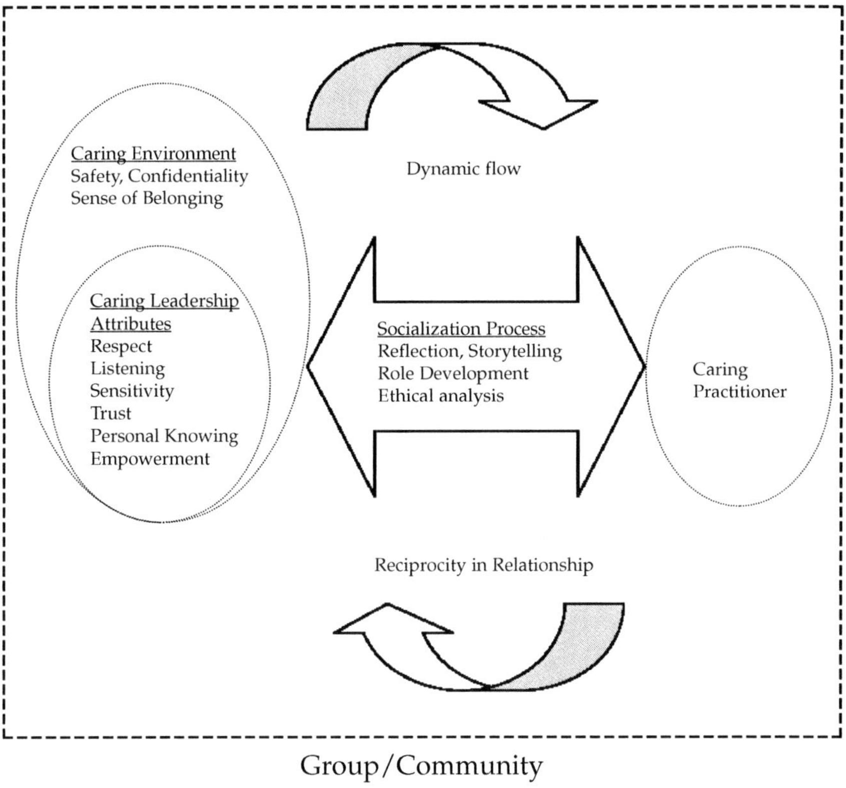

Group/Community

the group facilitators. To facilitate success in this type of course, faculty have to mentor and guide the senior facilitators so that they understand the purpose of the group and can function as caring leaders. One complaint from participants was that without effective facilitators, the groups were prone to become gripe sessions.

In subsequent semesters, the course was changed to reflect student concerns. Besides arranging for groups to meet over the full year, students took on a service-learning component as facilitators, for example, organizing baby showers for pregnant women in shelters and holding food drives and Easter egg hunts. Although leadership skill content was not the focus of this particular experience, a leadership seminar occurred simultaneously during the spring semester, strengthening the experience.

According to Margaret Wheatley (1994), "Leadership is *always* dependent on the context, but the context is established by the *relationships* we value" (p. 144). Values based on relational caring that are experienced during students' education will assist them as they participate in transforming health care systems that require a commitment to a caring-based value system. Providing students with an opportunity to demonstrate leadership skills in a supportive environment will facilitate development of the qualities of a caring leader: respect, trust, listening, support, and reassurance. As nurses they will carry the leadership practice of caring with them into whatever role they assume. If caring and leadership can be taught in this nontraditional way, the merits of a group process course will ultimately be measured by the care that patients receive and by the team building that occurs where these students practice.

REFERENCES

Allen, D. (1998). How nurses become leaders: Perceptions and beliefs about leadership development. *Journal of Nursing Administration, 28*(9), 15–20.

Beck, C. (1992). Caring among nursing students. *Nurse Educator, 17*(6), 22–27.

Bishop, A.H., & Scudder, J. R. (1991). *Nursing: The practice of caring.* New York: NLN.

Bolman, L., & Deal, T. (1995). *Leading with soul: An uncommon journey of spirit.* San Francisco: Jossey-Bass.

Bondas, T. (2003). Caritative leadership: Ministering to the patients. *Nursing Administration Quarterly, 27,* 249–253.

Boykin, A., & Schoenhofer, S. (2001). The role of nursing leadership in creating caring environments in health care delivery systems. *Nursing Administration Quarterly, 25,* 1–7.

De Pree, M. (1992) *Leadership jazz.* New York: Dell.

Dirks, K., & Ferrin, D. (2002). Trust in leadership: Meta-analytic findings and implications for research and practice. *Journal of Applied Psychology, 87,* 611–628.

Felgen, J. (2003). Caring: Core value, currency and commodity. Isn't it time to get tough about 'soft'? *Nursing Administration Quarterly, 27*(3), 208–214.

Gilligan, C. (1982). *In a different voice: Psychological theory and women's development.* Cambridge, MA: Harvard University Press.

Grams, K., Kosowski, M., & Wilson, C. (1997). Creating a caring community in nursing education. *Nurse Educator, 22*(3), 10–16.

Hall, J., & Allan, J. (1994). Self in relation: A prolegomenon for holistic nursing. *Nursing Outlook, 42*(3), 110–116.

Hardt, M. (2001). Core then care: The nurse leader's role in "caring." *Nursing Administration Quarterly, 25*(3), 37–45.

Helgesen, S. (1990). *The female advantage: Women's ways of leadership.* New York: Doubleday.

Jung, D., & Sosik, J. (2002). Transformational leadership in work groups: The role of empowerment, cohesiveness, and collective-efficacy on perceived group performance. *Small Group Research, 33,* 313–336.

Kouzes, J., & Posner, B. (1993). *Credibility.* San Francisco: Jossey-Bass.

Mayeroff, M. (1971). *On caring.* New York: Harper Perennial.

Nye, J. (2002). The eye of the follower: Information processing effects on attributions regarding leaders of small groups. *Small Group Research, 33,* 337–360.

Roach, S. M. (1991). The call to consciousness: Compassion in today's health world. In D. A. Gaut & M. M. Leininger (Eds.), *Caring: The compassionate healer* (pp.7–18). New York: NLN.

Senge, P. (1990). *The fifth discipline.* New York: Doubleday.

Wagner, L. (1997). Caring and leadership in female undergraduate nursing students: A group process experience. Unpublished doctoral dissertation, University of Hartford, CT.

Watson, J. (1988). *Nursing: Human science and human care: a theory of nursing.* NY: NLN.

Watson, J. (2000). Leading via caring-healing: The fourfold way toward transformative leadership. *Nursing Administration Quarterly, 25*(1), 1–6.

Wheatley, M. (1994*). Leadership and the new science: Learning about organizations from an orderly universe.* San Francisco: Berrett-Koehler.

White, N., & Rice, R. (2001). Collaboration to nurture the nursing work environment: The colleagues in caring practice task force. *Journal of Nursing Administration, 31*(2), 63–66.

CHAPTER TWELVE

Using Parse's Theory to Educate for Leadership

Sandra L. Ramey
Sandra Bunkers

Leadership is about who we are—as well as about what we do.

> Leadership is about creating, day by day, a domain in which we and those around us continually deepen our understanding of reality and are able to participate in shaping the future. This then is the deeper territory of leadership—collectively "listening" to what is wanting to emerge in the world and then having the courage to do what is required. (Jaworski, 1998, p.182)

Nurse theorist Rosemarie Rizzo Parse writes of courage, suggesting that a leader "is one who guides by blazing a path" (1997, p. 109). In "blazing a path" for nursing education, we decided that nursing theory should be the framework for developing a leadership course for students of the discipline. In this chapter we present the results of our efforts.

Parse's theory of human becoming, which addresses how persons structure meaning and come to know, how persons relate with others and the world, and how persons move beyond in situations, is a framework for discussing leadership concepts that create a fundamental shift in the way we think about the world. Parse (1997) identifies three essentials of leading: *commitment to a vision, willingness to risk,* and *reverence for others"* (p. 109). Content in the course is presented under at least one of each of these concepts. The concepts are reiterated with each activity. *Commitment to a vision* concerns itself with imagining what can be. "The vision offers hope and enlivens others to move in a particular direction" (p. 109). By creating scenarios and through role-play, students participate in imagining what can be. *Willingness to risk* involves facing challenges and making choices where the outcomes are not known. It involves trying out new ideas that have not been tried before. "Opposition, then, is an inevitable companion of spearheading new ideas or programs. Living with opposition is risking being challenged by others" (p. 109). Throughout the entire course, students are willing to risk within the context of group work and dialog. *Reverence for others* is valuing each individual whether she or he embraces or opposes the leader's vision. This valuing of others is noted in the way a leader treats the ideas and experiences of others. "In honoring others, the leader shows respect for the followers who cocreate the evolution of the vision" (p. 109). Reverence for others is embedded in the concept of connected knowing. Parse defines health as the living of value priorities. Leaders must constantly assess their living of value priorities in the context of commitment to a vision, willingness to risk, and reverence for others.

TEACHING STRATEGIES

Parse's essentials of leadership can be utilized to frame leadership content conceptually in undergraduate and graduate nursing programs. Students in both programs need time to develop a sense of self within a leadership role. At Marquette University, a Jesuit Catholic institution located in Milwaukee, Wisconsin, the educational leadership experience stems from the university's mission, which encompasses and emphasizes excellence, leadership, faith, and the development of leadership in service to others. When developing the content for the senior leadership course, these constructs were considered and provided the underpinnings for the leadership experience. Because these principles are congruent with Parse's essentials for leadership and the writings of Jaworski in *Synchronicity: The Inner Path of Leadership* (1998), the course format reflects a tapestry woven from the conceptualization of leadership framed with the concept of transformation. The linchpin for the course is the teacher-student relationship, and includes teaching and learning processes that focus on valuing the other's lived experience and knowledge.

In valuing each other's lived experience and knowledge, students within the leadership course are assigned to a team the first day of class. This team becomes the venue for exploring group process (including relationship building) throughout the semester, utilizing the principles of connected and constructed knowing (Belenky, Clinchy, Goldberger & Tarule, 1986). Each class commences with an overview and brief synopsis of information pertinent to the day's topic. Using the principles of guided design (Kemp, 1987), group focus is on developing decision-making skills as well as learning specific leadership concepts and principles.

Guided design is an instructional method developed in the 1970s by Charles Wales (Kemp, 1987). The method emphasizes working with other students in small groups to problem solve. Problem solving is facilitated by looking closely at each step of the decision-making process and applying the subject matter (p. 121). In this course, guided design is applied to traditional topics that include delegation, conflict management, and change. An application of the guided design technique is exemplified as follows. While assuming a leadership role in nursing, students are given a scenario in which an employee is found sleeping on the job. Initially, the small groups discuss what is most important in the situation and collectively explore possible options for action. At each step in the process the facilitator encourages the groups to a) analyze, synthesize, and evaluate the situation; b) role-play both sides of the hypothetical situation within their groups; and c) consider the ramifications of the chosen actions. Ultimately, students are asked to derive a plan to rectify the situation. Subsequently, each group shares with the larger class how and why they decided on their individual plans to deal with the situation, including what they experienced during role-play. In addition to guided design, the following teaching and learning strategies perpetuate self-exploration and facilitate growth for the student and contextually are linked to Parse's essentials for leadership.

COMMITMENT TO A VISION

Imagining what can be begins the process of moving in a new direction. An important component of moving in a new direction is creativity.

Creativity is inherent in problem solving. A film entitled *Everyday Creativity* (Jones, 1999) provides an excellent template for students to recognize that an infinite number of solutions can be applied to any situation. The film artistically uses photography from *National Geographic* magazine to illustrate how we use different lenses to view situations. The narrator emphasizes the value of creative thinking and espouses the premise that there are no wrong answers.

Companion pieces to the film include a CD-ROM, workbook, and PowerPoint with suggested activities for classroom use. One such activity is asking students to go into the hallway (or a similar open space) prior to viewing the film and then physically position themselves on a "creativity scale." The class facilitator gives only the instruction that a position of 10 represents the most creativity and 0 connotes the least. Soon, students autonomously decide which locations depict the benchmarks of most and least creativity on the scale and stand at that point in the hall. Not only is this a physical activity that students really enjoy, but also an excellent way to allow them to focus on their self-perception of creativity. Although most students assume a position at approximately the 5–7 range on the scale (indicating moderate creativity), others perceive themselves as a 9 or even a 0 on occasion. Before returning to class, students are asked to take note of where they stood in the hall. After the film and ensuing class discussion about the different ways classmates define creativity in everyday life, students are again asked to return to the hall and assume a place they now feel reflects their creative capacity. Almost always, individual perception of creativity has changed as students broaden their definitions of creativity and come to know and understand that they are much more creative than previously realized.

Part of becoming a leader is recognizing that leadership involves creatively identifying and evaluating resources. One such resource is technology. Electronic portfolios are useful to acquaint students with Web-based communication. Using electronic portfolios as a teaching and assessment strategy encourages students to experience technological communication firsthand. The process by which portfolios are constructed and developed (Ramey & Hay, 2002) is depicted in Figure 12.1. This model was created after thorough synthesis of the literature on electronic portfolio development and is based on our personal experience in not only developing our own electronic portfolios, but also in assisting numerous students with the process. Portfolios address the integrity of academic programs (Sorrell, Brown, Silva, &

FIGURE 12.1 Electronic portfolio construction for leadership development.

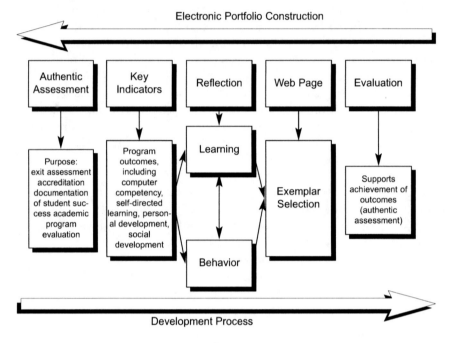

Kohlenberg, 1997) while actualizing the concept of "learning by doing" (Papert, 1993). Portfolios are viewed as reflective tools to document students' academic progress and as organized digests of artifacts documenting professional development. Portfolios include artifacts that support evidence of personal reflection on, and embodiment of program outcomes. Leadership students are asked to "reflect" (Schon, 1987) on their achievements and select exemplars that best showcase to others their development as professional nurses. The process is evaluated by assessing the students' ability to demonstrate achievement of program outcomes with the selected artifacts.

Electronic portfolios include the students' résumés, but they are much more than a vita. In addition, with the increasing prevalence of tele-health education methods, future leaders are expected to acquaint themselves with state-of-the-art technology during their careers. Electronic portfolios are a way to acquaint students with communication via technological methods. All creative endeavors call forth a willingness to risk.

WILLINGNESS TO RISK

When discussing a willingness to risk, Parse (1997) suggests that "leaders make decisions without fully knowing how the decision will be received or whether the outcomes will be successful" (p. 109). In a current journal article entitled "Engaging the Abyss: A Mis-take of Opportunity?" Mitchell and Bunkers (2003) suggest that nurses are constantly in situations working with others who are living intense experiences involving pain and suffering. The willingness to risks— involves "risking being present to the explicit-tacit truth of a situation" (Mitchell & Bunkers, 2003, p. 123). Leadership in nursing is risking being present with others in all kinds of patient care situations as well as in management and education settings that require one to address "the truth of the situation." One such situation is the role nurses play in today's response to bioterrorism.

When thinking about the threshold of when to act and when to withdraw, this premise is nowhere more apparent in leadership today than when addressing the complexity of disaster and bioterrorism preparedness. Ever since the reality that is September 11th, nursing leaders have attempted to address the safety and well-being of clients in institutions and in the community without really knowing how these strategies will play out in reality. Our leadership course addresses preparedness by including a Web-based discussion about preparedness framed by the leadership competences developed at Columbia University by Dr. Kristine Gebbie. In conjunction with the Centers for Disease Control and Prevention, the Columbia Center for Health Policy developed competencies for public health leaders (Leadership Competencies, 2003). These competencies help nurses understand their role in addressing bioterrorism (BT) and emergency preparedness. After viewing the Web site, students are asked in class to consider the ramifications of BT and emergency readiness, including fiscal aspects, ethical implications such as patient confidentiality, and their role in interdisciplinary collaboration imposed by the issue of preparedness.

REVERENCE FOR OTHERS

Honoring the experiences of others is part of being present for them as a nurse leader.

> Just being able to be there for others and to listen to them is one of the most important capacities a leader can have. It calls forth the best in people by allowing them to express what is in them. If someone listens to what I say, what I am feeling, then my feelings are given substance and direction and I can act. (Jaworski, 1998, p. 66)

In preparing for direction and action in caring for and serving others, students must recognize the importance and value of self-care. Role modeling reverence for others must begin with showing reverence for self.

In the leadership course, Silverstein's *The Giving Tree* (1964) and Sherwood's (1992) work help students understand and embrace the importance of self-care. Reverence for self and others is evidenced in Bunkers' (2000) book entitled *Simple Things,* which students are also asked to read. Comprised of poems based on Parse's theory of human becoming, Bunkers' book helps students understand the multidimensionality that is the reality of our nursing practice as well as our personal becoming. The book also acquaints students with the principles that constitute Parse's theory. The poems and aesthetically pleasing portraits encompassed in the book assist students with dialogue about unique possibilities (as they apply to leadership), including the concept of mentorship. Bunkers writes in a poem entitled "My Mentor":

> My mentor stands stronger than most, standing often for difference
> Difference means forging a new way in a mutual process of discovering
> the familiar-unfamiliar in shifting possibilities. (p. 23)

The concept of mentoring suggests to students the possibility of transforming in relationships. Classic literature also provides valuable perspectives embracing the concept of transforming in relationships. A classic piece of children's literature that connotes this concept is *The Velveteen Rabbit* (Williams, 1986), which provides a template for discussing what it means to be "real and genuine." Parse (1997) acknowledges, "Being dependable requires strength and integrity" (p.109); becoming real and genuine, with reverence for others, is part of passionate presence and an important component of transformational leadership.

PROS AND CONS OF USING PARSE'S THEORY TO EDUCATE FOR LEADERSHIP

The positive aspects of using the strategies discussed are that they are a creative synthesis of techniques to address different learning styles, different levels of computer proficiency, and other important topics, such as critical thinking and nursing theory. Creative synthesis also focuses attention on the aesthetics of learning with an emphasis on narrative and poetry as a way of cocreating knowledge. These strategies collectively help students refine and improve the quality of their writing as well as develop enhanced critical thinking skills. Most of the identified strategies use connected and constructed knowing in small groups; therefore, one limitation of using such a strategy may be that large numbers of students may not benefit equally from the learning experience and may even challenge their implementation in the leadership course.

SUMMARY

"Nothing will change in the future without fundamentally new ways of thinking; this is the real work of leadership" (Jaworski, 1998, p. 9). Using Parse's three essentials of leadership to frame a leadership course presents a new way of thinking about teaching and learning. Students need to have conversations about how they will handle and react to situations they will encounter in the reality that will be their practice. Classroom dialogue that focuses on commitment to a vision, willingness to risk, and reverence for others cocreates "a flow of meaning" (Jaworski, p. 13) with respect to the students' ability to be leaders within practice situations. Paraphrased from the Marquette University Vision Statement, this environment provides students with an educational experience that is genuinely transformational, so that they graduate better educated and as better people.

REFERENCES

Belenky, M. F., Clinchy, B. M., Goldberger, N. R., & Tarule, J. M. (1986). *Women's ways of knowing: The development of self, voice and mind.* New York: Basic Books.

Bunkers, S. (2002). *Simple things.* Sioux Falls, SD: Pine Hill Press.

Jaworski, J. (1998). *Synchronicity:The inner path of leadership.* San Francisco: Berret-Koehler.

Jones, D. (Director). (1999). *Everyday creativity* [Motion picture]. (Available from Star Thrower Distribution Corporation, 26 East Exchange Street, Suite 600, St. Paul, MN 55101)

Kemp, J. E. (1987). *The instructional design process.* New York: Harper & Row.

Leadership competencies recommended by the Centers for Disease Control and Prevention and Columbia University. (2003, March). Retrieved December 12,

2003, from http://www.nursing.hs.columbia.edu/institute-centers/chphsr/index.html

Mitchell, G., & Bunkers, S. (2003). Engaging the abyss: A mis-take of opportunity? *Nursing Science Quarterly, 16*(2), 121–125.

Papert, S. (1993). Situating constructionism. In I. Harel & S. Papert (Eds.), *Constructionism, research reports and essays, 1985–1990 (pp. 1–11).* Norwood, NJ: Ablex.

Parse, R. (1997). Leadership: The essentials. *Nursing Science Quarterly, 10*(3), 109.

Ramey, S., & Hay, L. (2002). Using electronic portfolios to measure student achievement and to assess curricular integrity. *Nurse Educator, 28*(1), 31–36.

Schon, D. A. (1987). *Educating the reflective practitioner.* San Francisco: Jossey-Bass.

Sherwood, G. (1992). The responses of caregivers to the experience of suffering. In P. Starck & J. McGovern, (Eds.) *The hidden dimension of illness: Human suffering* (pp. 105–113). New York: National League of Nursing, No. 15–2461.

Silverstein, J. (1964). *The giving tree.* New York: Harper & Row.

Sorrell, J., Brown, H., Silva, M., & Kohlenberg, E. (1997). Use of writing portfolios for interdisciplinary assessment of critical thinking outcomes of nursing students. *Nursing Forum, 32*(4), 1–18.

Williams, M. (1986). *The velveteen rabbit.* New York: Derrydale Books.

CHAPTER THIRTEEN

Educating Future Leaders Using Problem-Based Learning

Bev Williams

Educating nurses for leadership during an era of unprecedented world change is a challenge for nurse educators. Furthermore, with the health care system also in the midst of revolutionary change, nurses are increasingly expected to provide leadership within the context of interdisciplinary teams in day-to-day practice, in organizations, and in communities. This chapter highlights the use of problem-based learning in undergraduate baccalaureate nursing education as one way to facilitate the development of leadership competencies that will position nurses to influence legislation, nursing practice, and nursing education in a changing world.

PROBLEM-BASED LEARNING

Learners exposed to problem-based learning (PBL) as an instructional methodology acquire knowledge and skill in nursing by encountering authentic professional practice situations as the initial stimulus and focus of their learning activity (Barrows, 1986; Boud & Feletti, 1998). This varies from conventional instructional methodology, which relies on the use of professional practice situations as a culminating activity following faculty presentation of nursing content. Typically, a PBL nursing course in a baccalaureate program would consist of several real nursing practice situations. In small groups of 8 to 15, guided by a faculty tutor, learners grapple with the complexities of each practice situation, searching for connections across disciplines, using existing and newly acquired knowledge to generate possible outcomes of each situation. After identifying possible outcomes, learners present, justify, and debate each possibility, searching for the best possible outcome for the particular situation. Through collaborative investigation with classmates, learners refine and enhance their disciplinary knowledge and leadership competencies.

THEORETICAL FOUNDATIONS OF PBL

Recognizing that conventional classroom instruction was not completely preparing medical students to transfer the knowledge and skills learned in school to the demands of medical practice, McMaster Medical School faculty designed a PBL curriculum (Barrows, 1986). Although this endeavor was based more on ramifications for professional practice than on a specific, existing theoretical support, it did reflect the theoretical perspectives of such cognitive scientists as Dewey, Bruner, and Piaget (Norman & Schmidt, 1992; Schmidt, 1983, 1993; Wilkerson & Feletti, 1989). Within the cognitive science domain, PBL reflects both the rationalist (Albanese & Mitchell, 1993; Norman & Schmidt, 1992; Schmidt, 1983, 1993) and constructivist views of learning (Savery & Duffy, 1995).

Rationalist Perspective

A rationalist perspective of learning assumes that knowledge acquisition is primarily a result of individual cognitive activity in processing information (Schmidt, 1993). As early as 1938, Dewey suggested that knowledge could not be simply transferred from one individual to another. It could only be acquired through active cognitive engagement. Accordingly, existing cognitive structures within the individual influence the extent to which new information will be understood. In 1961, Bruner suggested that material organized according to an individual's own interests and cognitive structures has the best chance of being accessible to the individual's memory. This information processing perspective also reflects Piaget's description of cognition and the notion that thinking skills can be directly taught (Slavin, 1994).

Schmidt (1983, 1993) described several principles of PBL instructional methodology that reflect a rationalist perspective. According to

Schmidt (1993), a PBL activity employs the following instructional strategies and tactics:

1. Relevant prior knowledge is activated by engaging students in practical situational analysis initiated with articulation about what they do and do not know about the situation.
2. Elaboration on prior knowledge occurs through engagement of students in small group discussion, generation and critique of hypotheses, and peer teaching. During the review process that occurs at the completion of each practical situation discussion, students elaborate further on the relationship of new knowledge to prior knowledge.
3. Because the practical situation drives the learning of content and skills, students are continuously restructuring their knowledge as they work towards the best outcome.
4. Authentic practical situations that reflect the types of situations students will face as professionals serve as the framework for storing contextual cues and improving students' abilities to retrieve relevant knowledge when faced with similar situations in the future.
5. Students are motivated and spend more time processing information when they are discussing authentic practical situations that they perceive as relevant and meaningful. Increased time spent processing information results in a more complete cognitive structure from which to retrieve information.

From a rationalist perspective of learning, PBL utilizes instructional strategies to assist students in processing and storing knowledge in such a way that it can be easily retrieved when required in the future. By helping students to activate prior knowledge, connect new knowledge to prior knowledge, elaborate on knowledge to create strong multiple connections in memory, and structure knowledge with contextual cues, PBL addresses the issue of inert knowledge and enables students to apply what they have learned to similar situations that they might encounter in the future.

Constructivist Perspective

The constructivist perspective of learning assumes that knowledge acquisition is a continuous process of building and reshaping understanding as a natural consequence of experience in the world (Savery & Duffy, 1995). Learning is not about the acquisition of new knowledge but the constant reconstruction of what an individual already knows. The stimulus for learning is a cognitive conflict or puzzle (Dewey, 1938; Savery & Duffy). Learners must constantly check new information against existing information and adjust accordingly. In addition to being a continuous process, learning is described as a collaborative process in which individual understanding is rooted in social interaction. Knowledge acquisition is firmly embedded in the social and emotional context in which learning takes place. Conceptual growth arises from sharing perspectives and testing ideas with others. Such negotiation culminates in modifications in cognitive structure.

Savery and Duffy (1995) present principles that govern the design of PBL based on the constructivist perspective of cognition. The principles are based on the constructivist concepts of cognitive conflict, understanding through interaction, and social negotiation. Based on the assumptions of a constructivist perspective of cognition and learning, PBL activity employs the following instructional strategies and tactics:

1. Learning is essentially an act of active construction on the part of the student (Savery & Duffy, 1995). By requiring students to assume the role of professional and engage in self-directed learning, students experience the knowledge construction process.

2. Through collaborative group work and accessing a wide variety of resources, students experience and develop an appreciation for multiple perspectives.

3. Learning is embedded in authentic contexts so students acquire content and skills through the discussion of actual professional practice situations. This strategy enhances the retrievability of knowledge and skill when it is needed.

4. Students assume responsibility for their own learning and practice through self directed learning and leadership activities inherent in every PBL activity.

5. Self-awareness of knowledge construction and skill acquisition processes is encouraged during the reflective activities embedded in each PBL activity and during the review process that occurs with the completion of the situation.

From a constructivist perspective, PBL prepares students for professional practice by engaging them in authentic activities during their learning for that practice. Knowledge and skills are learned within a context that reflects the professional context within which they will practice as professionals. Contextualization of learning and the social support and interaction during learning help prepare students to transfer what they have learned to new situations and to avoid the pitfalls of inert knowledge. Specific instructional strategies proposed by proponents of both rationalist and constructivist perspectives include aspects of student self-awareness, autonomy and responsibility, interaction and collaboration, reflection and review, and leadership.

LEADERSHIP

Leadership is a complex and multidimensional concept that includes intrapersonal, interpersonal, and situational variables related to social, ethical and theoretical components. The social nature of leadership entails the interpersonal skills necessary to be effective in a variety of situations, whereas the ethical nature of leadership involves the inherent power to benefit the common good (Grohar-Murray & DiCroce, 2003). The authority of leadership is derived from the ability of the leader to visualize creatively in order to energize others to adapt to change.

The theoretical nature of leadership has evolved over time. Initially, leadership was considered to be a birthright, and it was believed that individuals in formal leadership roles were born with the ability to lead, influence, and direct others. This trait approach to leadership precludes the notion that individuals could develop into leaders. When it became clear that traits were insufficient to explain leadership, examination of leadership style (autocratic, democratic, laissez-faire) and behavior (telling, selling, testing, consulting, and joining) became the focus (Schmitt & Tannebaum, 1964). Though styles and behaviors are the means by which leadership is exercised, learning to use the behaviors in the right set of circumstances determines success as a leader. Through study of leadership effectiveness, the conceptualization of situational theory emerged (Prenkert & Ehnfors, 1997; Stogdill, 1948). Situational theory suggests that the behaviors required of the leader differ according to the situation.

Modern theorists continue to struggle with the elusive nature of leadership, identifying leadership as either transactional (one person taking the initiative) or transformational (all persons involved raising one another to higher levels of performance) (Burns, 1978; Dunham & Klafehn, 1990; McDaniel & Wolf, 1992). At this point, there seems to be general agreement on several aspects of leadership (Gergen, 2000). It is clear that leadership begins within the individual with self-knowledge, self-confidence, and reflection. Leaders must have a sense of timing, be able to articulate clearly a vision and creative ideas to achieve the vision, have the ability to persuade others, and be able to recognize others as sources of ideas and information. In addition, they must be able to work with others within an organized system. Finally, leaders should be able to inspire others to assume the leadership role.

PROCESS MODEL OF LEADERSHIP

For beginning nursing graduates, a process model of leadership (Grohar-Murray & DiCroce, 2003) is proposed, encompassing those elements that a leader should consider in order to engage in effective leadership. The process model is comprised of three stages: analysis of event, determination of action, and evaluation of action.

Analysis of the event includes consideration of the following variables: the event, the participants and their perceptions, organizational structure and climate, interpersonal processes, and controlling forces and limiting factors. After consideration of the factors that contribute to the situation, a course of action is determined. *Determination of action* includes generation of ideas for action to accomplish desired outcomes, weighing each alternative, and selecting the best alternative. At this point it is important to identify any barriers to the selected action and ways of managing any conflict. Finally, the results must be evaluated in terms of the actual outcome, even if unexpected. Criteria used to *evaluate the action* should reflect the immediate and the long-range effect of the action and should include the acceptability of the action and the direct and indirect impact on quality of care. The process model of leadership is one approach that highlights the forces in situations, leaders, and followers that influence actions in achieving desired outcomes.

FACILITATING LEADERSHIP THROUGH PBL

The development of leadership competencies is an essential educational outcome of PBL. During each phase of the PBL process, the development of leadership skills and abilities is emphasized. Working collaboratively, identifying and resolving conflicts, and expressing a well supported point of view in an assertive manner are just some of the leadership skills that are learned during the PBL process. The PBL graduate is most likely to engage in a process model of leadership because the phases of the PBL process are very similar to the stages of the process model of leadership.

Phases of PBL

In phase 1, before any preparation or study has occurred, a small group of learners and a faculty tutor discuss an authentic nursing practice situation that has been generated by practicing nurses. The situation may be presented as a video, an audiotape, or a written scenario complete with photos. Learners begin by reasoning aloud with an analysis of the situation, identifying what they do know based on their previous knowledge, what they do not know, and what they need to know in order to be the nurse in that particular situation. Using their own thinking processes with accompanying tutor coaching, learners develop the self-assessment skills necessary to identify learning needs through articulation of their internal thought processes. Learners formulate explanations, clarify understanding through negotiation, critique classmates' comments, establish learning goals, and create an action plan to meet those goals. These skills contribute to the learners' development of leadership competency in analyzing events.

During the second phase of PBL, learners activate their plans by engaging in self-directed study away from the group. Learners determine how they will learn the knowledge and skills they have identified and what resources they will use to assist them. This process assists learners in developing the reflective and self-directed learning skills that are critical components of professional practice and leadership competency in determining action.

In phase three, learners apply the information acquired during self-study to the discussion of the nursing situation, and accept, modify, or reject previous explanations. Learners mutually critique the quality of shared information as well as resources and research methods utilized during self-study. Through critiquing information, methods, and resources for value and effectiveness, learners consider alterations to their choices. Continuous evaluation of information, methods, and resources is critical to the process of reflective practice and leadership effectiveness.

During the final phase, learners summarize what they have learned and discuss how their knowledge and skills might be used in future practice. Learners consciously recall and reflect on learning that occurred, elaborate on the learning, and integrate it into their existing cognitive structures (Barrows, 1986). Ultimately, learners should feel confident interacting in this or a similar nursing practice situation in the future.

According to Barrows (1986), this process of situational analysis, determination of learning, needs self-study, application of knowledge, critiquing of resources and personal problem solving processes, and reflection of what was learned during the activity develops the students' abilities to become self directed learners. The PBL process engages students in activities that reveal their thinking processes so that they can monitor the effectiveness of their ability to analyze, reason, and acquire knowledge; this enables them to assume increasing responsibility for their own learning and that of their peers.

PBL AND LEADERSHIP COMPETENCY

There are several critical components of the PBL process that contribute to the development of leadership competency. Initially, group members need to negotiate group norms related to member expectations, participation, and decision making. Member expectations usually relate to responsibility, accountability, active listening, tolerance of diversity, accurate and honest feedback, and promotion of collegiality. The consequences of not fulfilling group expectations are usually discussed at this time.

In any effective group, participation and leadership are equally distributed among members so that decision making is flexible and conflicts are managed constructively. All groups have to contend with issues of power. Each learner generally has the opportunity to assume the leadership role of the group for some designated period of time. To assist learners in developing leadership skills, it is useful to specify course outcomes that guide learners to explore group process in depth. Because evaluation methods often determine the amount of energy learners commit to any activity, one way to ensure commitment to learning specific skills is to allot a portion of the course grade to the quality of participation and leadership in tutorial sessions.

Conflict is considered a normal stage of group development and should not necessarily be eliminated. In fact, conflict is often indicative of liveliness and innovation within a group. Initially, the tutor has a pivotal role in moderating tensions within the group. By following tutor modeling of the collaborating strategy of conflict resolution, individual group members eventually assume this role.

Evaluation of the group and individual member contributions to the group occur on a regular basis. At least once during the discussion of each practice situation and using specific evaluation criteria, learners provide constructive criticism to each other about individual contributions to group learning and group process. Verbal and written comments are expected to be both descriptive and evaluative in nature. Throughout the PBL process, learners learn to develop and critically reflect on their communicative, collaborative, and leadership skills and abilities.

BARRIERS TO PBL

Learners coming from conventional learning environments and those who tend to be quiet may find it difficult to adjust to PBL. They may find small-group learning, particularly the interpersonal and evaluative aspects, intimidating. Learners may also have different experiences in the PBL classroom depending on how the individual faculty member has interpreted the role of tutor in PBL.

In PBL the learning model rather than the teaching model is emphasized. This generally means that traditional faculty evaluation methods and faculty rewards will need to be restructured. The construction of real world problems is often time-consuming and learning to become a tutor is challenging. Faculty need assurance of rewards for their innovations, particularly during transition phases when learner evaluations may reflect challenges in both tutor and learner adjustment to PBL.

EVIDENCE FOR PBL

Small-group learning has intrapersonal, interpersonal, and intra-group benefits. Because learners are actively involved in learning, they are able to identify their own learning needs and goals. By sharing ideas, learners are exposed to different perspectives and may begin to examine analytically their own beliefs, values, and assumptions. Although working in small groups creates issues, learning how to deal with the issues contributes to learning leadership and team building skills.

Research Evidence

Research studies indicate that both PBL learners and their faculty have substantially more positive attitudes toward the learning environment (Allen, 1996; Lieux, 1996). PBL has also been associated with enhanced affective outcomes and academic performance levels (Hmelo, Gotterer & Bransford, 1997; Vernon & Blake, 1993). Employers increasingly report higher levels of satisfaction with PBL graduates (Alavi, Cooke & Crowe, 1997; Woods, 1996). Their effectiveness in the workplace does depend on the quality of coaching, modeling, and authentic evaluations used as part of their education (Krynock & Robb, 1999). Only one study provides specific documented evidence that PBL contributes to the development of leadership skills and abilities.

As part of a larger study exploring the relationship between PBL and self-directed learning, Williams (2002) held focus group interviews with learners at the end of their first and fourth years in a PBL undergraduate nursing program. One of the four themes inductively derived from the learners' descriptions of their experience in PBL was "confident and responsible." In relation to this theme, learners acknowledged learning a variety of skills, attitudes, and abilities commonly associated with competent and effective leadership.

Learners described themselves as self-aware and confident. At the end of first year, learner comments included: "If you are a good facilitator, you gain confidence and others look at you as if you know what you are doing and they feel like you know what is going on" and "It comes out in the way I relate to people—the way I think and the way I deal with people is completely different now." By the end of fourth year, comments included: "This program gives you confidence," "You learn to examine yourself and learn how your actions impact others," and "Before I came into nursing, I was really quiet but you have to speak up in this learning format and that gives me confidence." Learners also indicated that they had developed the ability to work effectively with others. At the end of the first year, learner comments included: "In my group, we are starting to question each other and when we do that, we help each other out. We question our own work and that helps us understand it better." By the end of fourth year, learners' comments included: "If you have a problem with someone and it is affecting the group then it needs to be dealt with—it doesn't work well if you wait."

Dealing with ambiguity and diversity was another skill that learners felt they had developed. At the end of first year, they indicated that "people do have different opinions and I do learn different ways of thinking" and "I am adapting and that is good, because everything is not going to be perfect all of the time." By the end of fourth year, learners were saying, "Being in PBL with critical thinking and listening to other peoples' points of view, you learn that everybody in most situations is always kinda right" and "The ambiguity thing—I've learned to deal with ever changing situations."

Valuing continuing competence was evident in learner comments. At the end of the first year, learners said, "You have to learn how to learn—that's what university is all about," while graduating learners said, "We've learned how to be responsible for our own learning" and "We know how to find resources quickly, how to research and pick out useful information."

Developing leadership competency was a specific quality that PBL learners mentioned. At the end of first year, learners commented that "one of the reasons we are in small groups is that we are able to practice communication skills and develop leadership qualities," while graduating learners indicated that "I definitely feel comfortable in the leadership role. I don't think that through a traditional program I would be able to question older, more senior, nurses" and "I never really classified myself as a leader before I came into this program and now I think I have that skill." At the end of 4 years, these learners clearly described themselves as leaders. They indicated that they had developed many of the skills and abilities required of nurses in leadership positions.

SUMMARY

Nurses must be prepared as leaders who are competent, flexible, and able to energize others to adapt to change. Using the process model of leadership is one way of identifying the forces in the situation and leaders and followers who influence decisions for the effective outcomes. Interpersonal relationships significantly influence the possible alternatives that might be generated to make effective decisions and reach resolution. With similarities to the process model of leadership and emphasis on situational analysis based on well-researched knowledge, generation of alternatives, evaluation of outcomes, conflict management, and self and peer evaluation, PBL is an effective way to educate future leaders in nursing.

REFERENCES

Alavi, C., Cooke, M., & Crowe, M. (1997). Becoming a registered nurse. *Nurse Education Today, 17,* 473–480.

Albanese, M., & Mitchell, S. (1993). Problem based learning: A review of literature on its outcomes and implementation issues. *Academic Medicine, 68*(1), 52–81.

Allen, D. (1996). Teaching with tutors: Can undergraduates effectively guide student problem based learning groups? *About Teaching, 50,* 12–13.

Barrows, H. (1986). A taxonomy of problem based learning methods. *Medical Education, 20,* 481–486.

Boud, D., & Feletti, G. (Eds.) (1998). *The challenge of problem based learning* (Introduction). London: Kogan Press.

Burns, J. (1978). *Leadership.* New York: Harper & Row.

Dewey, J. (1938). *Experience and education.* London: Collier Macmillan.

Dunham, J., & Klafehn, K. (1990). Transformational leadership and the nurse executive. *Journal of Nursing Administration, 20*(4), 28–34

Gergen, D. (2000). *Eyewitness to power.* New York: Simon & Schuster.

Grohar-Murray, M., & DiCroce, H. (2003). *Leadership and management in nursing.* Upper Saddle River, NJ: Prentice-Hall.

Hmelo, C., Gotterer, G., & Bransford, J. (1997). A theory-driven approach to assessing the cognitive effects of PBL. *Instructional Science, 25,* 387–408.

Krynock, K., & Robb, L. (1999). Problem solved: How to coach cognition. *Educational Leadership, 57*(3), 29–32.

Lieux, E. (1996). A comparative study of learning in lecture versus problem based format. *About Teaching, 50,* 25–27.

McDaniel, C., & Wolf, G. (1992). Transformational leadership and the nurse executive. *Journal of Nursing Administration, 22*(2), 60–65.

Norman, G., & Schmidt, H. (1992). The psychological basis of problem based learning. *Academic Medicine, 67,* 557–565.

Prenkert, F., & Ehnfors, M. (1997). A measure of organizational effectiveness in nursing management in relation to transactional and transformational leadership: A study in a Swedish cancer hospital. *Journal of Nursing Management, 5,* 279–287.

Savery, J., & Duffy, T. (1995). Problem based learning: An instructional model and its constructivist framework. *Educational Technology, 35*(5), 31–38.

Schmidt, H. (1993). Foundations of problem based learning: Some explanatory notes. *Medical Education, 27,* 422–432.

Schmidt, H. (1983). Problem based learning: Rationale and description. *Medical Education, 17,* 11–16.

Schmitt, W., & Tannenbaum, R. (1964). How to choose a leadership pattern: Skills that build executive success. *Harvard Business Review, 6,* 116.

Slavin, R. (1994). *Educational psychology.* Boston: Allyn & Bacon.

Stogdill, R. (1948). Personal factors associated with leadership in a survey of the literature. *Journal of Psychology, 25,* 35–71.

Vernon, D., & Blake, R. (1993). Does problem based learning work? A meta-analysis of evaluative research. *Academic Medicine, 70,* 216–223.

Wilkerson, L., & Feletti, G. (1989). Problem based learning: One approach to increasing student participation. In A. Lucus (Ed.), The department chairperson's role in enhancing college teaching. *New directions for teaching and learning, 37* (pp. 51–60). San Francisco: Jossey-Bass.

Williams, B. (2002). *The self directed learning readiness of baccalaureate nursing students and faculty after one year in a PBL undergraduate nursing program.* Unpublished Dissertation, University of Alberta, Edmonton, Canada.

Woods, D. (1996). Problem based learning for large classes in chemical engineering. In J. L. Ratcliff (Ed.), *New directions for higher education, 68* (pp. 91–99). San Francisco: Jossey-Bass.

CHAPTER FOURTEEN

Using Online Clinical Scenarios to Build Leadership Skills

Connie Wilson

A strategy that has been found useful to assess and promote critical thinking is the use of clinical scenarios and case studies (Malloy & DeNatale, 2001; Oermann, 1999; Tomey, 2003). Case studies and scenarios have often been used interchangeably in the literature; however, case studies are a more in-depth view of a real or simulated clinical situation (Jeffries, n.d.). Clinical scenarios are real events or problem-focused events that reflect two criteria for fostering critical thinking: the introduction of new information and the provision of feedback on the thought process of the response (Oermann). The online clinical scenarios created for BSN and RN-BSN courses at the University of Indianapolis meet these two criteria and are described in this chapter.

The use of online clinical scenario discussions is an educational strategy that can enhance skill application in leadership. Skills that include critical thinking and problem solving, peer review, and written communication are developed through each of the discussions. More specific leadership skills, such as understanding and applying concepts of change theory, motivation, ethical principles, use of leadership Web resources, and managed care principles, are addressed through individual discussions.

Each BSN and RN-BSN course at the University of Indianapolis required an outcome related to critical thinking. Faculty were challenged to determine how critical thinking would be implemented and measured. Course-related examinations that contained a few short essays were one way, but they were often found to be inadequate to measure the specific components of critical thinking. Further, they had other limitations, such as time constraints (Oermann, 1999; Teaching Today, 2003).

ONLINE DISCUSSIONS OF CLINICAL SCENARIOS

Online discussions using clinical scenarios were incorporated into the BSN and RN-BSN leadership courses in 1999. The decision to create leadership-based clinical scenarios in a discussion format was for three primary reasons. First, it was a way to provide a measurement of critical thinking and support the critical-thinking outcome. Critical thinking can be defined as reasonable, rational, reflective, autonomous thinking that inspires an attitude of inquiry. As described by Facione (1990; Facione, Facione, & Sanchez, 1994), the components usually identified with critical thinking include analysis, evaluation, inference, explanation, and self-regulation. The online discussions engaged students in these elements of thinking. The discussion guidelines and integration of the critical-thinking components are shown in the accompanying box.

Guidelines for Online Discussion

1. Include at least one reference from the course text to support the discussion

2. Include a theory base or principle to support your discussion

3. Discussions must be thorough with evidence of critical thinking:
   - Identify the problem
   - Analyze components involved
   - Synthesize information from the text (or other sources as needed) and relate it to the problem
   - Discuss a solution
   - Identify the implications/consequences based on your problem solving/decision making

---

Second, as the clinical settings for leadership and management experiences have become more complex, with increased work demands on the staff nurses and increased patient acuity, students tended to receive less support in time and attention by the nurse manager, charge nurse, and team leader for addressing their clinical objectives. Opportunities for student experiences, such as team leading on an inpatient nursing unit, became more difficult to obtain as a result of the clinical climate. In answer to the changes in the clinical setting and the decline in experiential learning, discussions based on specific clinical scenarios were created. Key concepts covered in the scenarios could be encountered in a clinical setting but unfortunately not by all students, as each clinical experience varied. The discussions were used to fill the gap in clinical experiences so that each student had an opportunity to address key concepts of leadership and management.

Finally, the didactic time for covering the leadership/management content through small and large group discussions, lecture, and brief case studies was limited. No didactic time was available for individual students to process critically a scenario with adequate depth while connecting theory to problem analysis and implementation of a solution. Online discussions again filled the gap for students to individually process clinical scenarios with the application of critical thinking criteria and didactic theory (Malloy & DeNatale, 2001).

Online discussions consisted of seven leadership and management scenarios and one Web critique that required students to think critically through the situation or activity and integrate learned content and clinical experiences to arrive at a solution. The discussions represented eight critical areas of leadership identified by the faculty: planned change, fiscal planning, motivation, communication and managed care, delegation, conflict management, Web-site critique of leadership information, and staffing. Active engagement through scenarios allowed application of content to actual clinical situations and encouraged students to draw upon their own experiences.

Students had 5 days following the presentation of content to complete the online discussion through Discussion Board on Blackboard, the learning platform used by the University of Indianapolis. Once a student posted her or his discussion, other students participated in peer review of their discussion. Students had an additional 2 days to select one student response to critique. No more than two students were permitted to critique any one student's discussion. Nursing faculty had the opportunity to respond to the discussions and the replies. The nursing informatics discussion is the only one that requires no student reply. The following guidelines applied to the critique:

1. Critically analyze the discussion response of another student.
2. Offer insights or additional information that will challenge the author to rethink his or her response
3. Communicate your reply in an assertive, respectful manner

Each of the discussion responses and replies had a designated number of points assigned. Full or partial points were given based on the guidelines as a simple rubric for scoring. A rubric is a set of descriptive statements used to assess a student's work and "typically employed when a judgment of quality is required." (Moskal, 2000, p. 1). Moskal further describes the benefits of a rubric as a way to determine the extent to which the criteria have been met and to provide feedback to the student on how to improve.

For example, faculty may assign 10 points for each discussion and use the rubric to designate a point value for each of the guideline components. A behavioral statement derived from number three in the guidelines might be: "The problem is clearly described and all components in the scenario are listed correctly." If included in the discussion, this statement would indicate that the student adequately met two of the components identified in the critical-thinking guideline; the student would achieve the number of points corresponding to the guideline components. If the problem was not clearly addressed or not all components were listed, the student would not receive assigned points. Along with assignment of the score, students are provided specific feedback on ways to improve their discussions based on the rubric. The following exemplify two of the discussions:

Isn't It Freezing?
Hospital X is changing its patient documentation from paper to computerized charting. Your critical-care unit has been selected as a trial site for the new computerized documentation and you make recommendations about its use. As the nurse manager, how would you proceed in this change process when your staff openly expresses concerns about using computers for documentation?

Nursing Informatics

Locate one Web site pertaining to nursing leadership/management. Provide the URL (Web location/address) and summarize the following: (1) what the site contains; (2) how the site can be used by practicing nurse leaders/managers; (3) a critique of the quality of the site; (3a) when the document was written; (3b) who the author(s) are and do their qualifications support writing on this topic; (3c) what the links from this site tell you about authenticity; (3d) why you think the author created this Web document.

Written communication is another leadership skill developed through online discussions. Students strive to present an organized and logical discussion that leads to a solution and is supported by theory from the course text. Written communication needs to be clear and professional (Marquis & Huston, 2003). Grammatical and spelling errors are noted with student feedback as well as problems with how the discussion was constructed. Students have the opportunity to make one revision and resubmission of the discussion, making for more thoughtful and accurate responses.

EVALUATION OF THE ONLINE DISCUSSION FORMAT

One strength of online education is that it is learner-focused. Students become actively engaged in discussions and formulate their own ideas while drawing on course theory and personal experiences. Online discussions can be used to "create a more democratic, participatory learning environment" (Michigan State University, n.d., p.1). These kinds of discussions are important to the development of leadership behaviors. Billings and Connors (n.d.) suggest that Web-based or Web-enhanced courses provide access, flexibility, and convenience for learners. They refer to evidence gathered by Chickering and Ehrmann in 1996 on best practices related to technology-based education to suggest that it "promotes productive use of teaching and learning time" (Billings & Connors, p. 3).

Student responses to the online discussions have consistently been rated very positive. Based on their experience using this format, faculty concluded that the activity meets the intended outcomes. First, the discussions clearly apply principles of leadership covered in the didactic class. Second, the online format allows students to access the discussions at their convenience within a set time period. Third, the criteria provide a rubric for grading and assisting students to meet the faculty expectations for discussion, response, and reply. Finally, students find the application of knowledge from the discussions transferable to application exam questions and new clinical experiences.

Students have expressed concern over the amount of time required for discussions and the corresponding point value assigned to this activity. All discussions are completed outside of class time. There is also a time factor involved for faculty who provide students with feedback and award points for the discussions. Additionally, time is needed on the part of faculty to create realistic scenarios for discussion.

Intended outcomes from the learning activity include the development of critical thinking and problem-solving skills, improved written communication, and an ability to engage constructively in peer review. Other outcomes that have been observed include the ability to appreciate divergent views from other students and to accept constructive feedback from others. A serendipitous outcome is that students have learned to value knowledge from peers when they respond to a critique of their own discussion that is not part of the required assignment. Evaluation of the online discussions by students and faculty showed positive results in meeting the intended outcomes of developing leadership skills in BSN and RN-BSN students over the years that this strategy was used.

CONCLUSION

Online clinical scenario discussions are a useful teaching strategy to provide enhanced understanding and application of leadership skills in a realistic context for student learning. Clinical scenarios are presented and feedback from peers and faculty result in further development of key leadership skills. Finally, this teaching-learning approach draws upon learner-focused education and concepts of critical thinking to enhance leadership development in clinical practice.

REFERENCES

Billings, D., & Connors, H. (n.d.). Best practices in online learning. In *Living Book* (chap. 2) National League for Nursing. Retrieved December 28, 2003, from http://electronicvision.com/nln/chapter02/chapter_02.htm.

Facione, P. (1990). *Critical thinking: A statement of expert consensus for purposes of educational assessment and instruction.* Newark, DE: American Philosophical Association.

Facione, N., Facione, P., & Sanchez, C. (1994). Critical thinking dispositions as a measure of competent clinical judgment: The development of the California Critical Thinking Dispositions Inventory. *Journal of Nursing Education, 33,* 345–350.

Jeffries, P. (n.d.). How to write a case study for online education (Sigma Theta Tau International). Retrieved December 28, 2003, from http://www.nursingsociety.org/education/online_howto.pdf.

Malloy, S., & DeNatale, M. (2001). Online critical thinking: A case study analysis. *Nurse Educator, 26*(4), 191–197.

Marquis, B., & Huston, C. (2003). *Leadership roles and management functions in nursing* (4th ed.). Philadelphia: Lippincott.

Michigan State University (n.d.). Pedagogy and techniques: Class discussion. Retrieved December 28, 2003, from http://teachvu.vu.msu.edu/public/pedagogy/class_discussion/index.php?page_num=3.

Moskal, B. (2000). Scoring rubrics: What, when and how? *Practical Assessment, Research and Evaluation, 7*(3). Retrieved December 22, 2003, from http://PAREonline.net/getvn.asp?v=7&n=3.

Oermann, M. (1999). Critical thinking, critical practice. *Nursing Management, 30* (4). Retrieved December 28, 2003, from http://www.nursingmanagement.com.

Teaching Today Post-Secondary (2003, March). *Assessment in higher education: Education up close.* Retrieved December 22, 2003, from http://www.glencoe.com/ps/teachingtoday/educationupclose.phtml/print/9.

Tomey, A. (2003). Learning with cases. *Journal of Continuing Education in Nursing, 34* (1), 34–38.

CHAPTER FIFTEEN

Team Building Through Quilting

Martha J. Greenberg
Paula Scharf
Jane Romm

Movement from the Scientific Age—with its emphasis on following bureaucratic structure, procedures, and policies to accomplish tasks—toward a New Science Age stressing empowerment, collaboration, and team building requires professional nurses to enact leadership in a new way (Grossman & Valiga, 2000). Transformational leadership is considered essential for contemporary organizations and these leaders must focus on relationships and possess abilities to build networks and coalitions (Marelli, 2004).

Nursing faculty must design educational experiences that ensure students have opportunities to practice the behaviors and skills underpinning these and other important leadership-management concepts. This chapter details how the educational experience of a quilting project was incorporated into a nursing leadership and management course.

Leadership and management courses in baccalaureate curricula have long presented traditional concepts of leadership or management, such as theories, styles, motivation, "followership," team building, ethical issues, finance, and budgeting. Depending upon the readiness, motivation, goals, and experience of the nursing student, this type of course can be scintillating and relevant or dry as dust, perhaps having some future usefulness to the student years after graduation and additional clinical experience. Generic baccalaureate senior level students' priorities are often focused on postgraduation employment and success in passing the NCLEX-RN and this was the case with the senior class scheduled to take their leadership course at Pace University in the fall of their senior year.

Recent changes in the health care system toward a community orientation prompted faculty of Pace University Lienhard School of Nursing to design an integrated community-based undergraduate curriculum. The philosophic basis of this curriculum is to prepare students for holistic, relationship-centered practice with a focus on partnering with the community to provide care to individuals, families, and groups. Rolling out the new 4-year curriculum, faculty noted that even through junior year students were not cohesive, interacted little with each other, and lacked an esprit de corps. Cliques and outcasts were easily identifiable within the class of students who had spent nearly 3 years together. Several students even commented that they never spoke with, and knew little about, other class members, a few preferring to remain isolated from their peers and be anonymous. This was extremely troublesome to the faculty who were planning the senior level course and clinical experiences, because it was an outcome that totally conflicted with the relationship-centered emphasis of the curriculum. Traditional methods to build student partnerships and foster group cohesion, such as encouraging students to form study groups or including group assignments in class, failed to achieve their goals. A direct faculty attempt to mix up clinical group membership also failed to resolve the problem. The visionary purposes of the quilting project were to assist students to learn and understand leadership concepts and to provide an environment where they could practice and implement leadership behaviors. In the process it was hoped that they would develop a sense of commitment and caring toward and about each other.

THINKING OUTSIDE THE BOX

Two faculty teaching the senior level course in the new curriculum decided they needed to think outside the box, brainstorming about strategies that could foster a sense of community and partnerships among students. At the same time, they wanted to engage students actively in understanding and experiencing leadership and management concepts. Two of the course faculty were hobby quilters, who found that quilting provided a source of stress reduction and personal expression for them. Quilting in groups also introduced them to new persons previously unknown to them who shared stories and personal feelings during the process of either sewing together or sharing completed projects. One of the faculty was an avid walker and mentioned to her walking friend (who happened to be a fiber artist and quilter) the concerns that she faced in teaching this new course. After a mile walk, the two thought that a quilting project might be an innovative solution to building relations among students and promote unity.

The plan for the class was to present current concepts, knowledge, and theories of leadership and management using this creative tool and other traditional teaching-learning methods. Course requirements included participating in a group and completing a quilt, writing a journal about the process, and traditional written examinations. Because this first class admitted to the new curriculum had experienced many of the pains associated with curriculum change and were approaching their senior year, they were feeling a lot of stress. Therefore, it was the hope of the faculty that group quilting would also serve to decrease students' anxiety.

CLASS MEETINGS AND THE QUILTING PROCESS

The senior class of 24 students were assigned numbers (1–5) and then divided into 5 groups (numbers one, two, three, etc.; each became one group). This method of group assignment was intended to give students the opportunity to interact with other students they did not usually sit with and know as friends and peers. Jane, the visiting home and careers teacher and artist/walking friend of Martha, was the lead classroom instructor, and attended the first class meeting. She described the history of quilting, including the functional purpose of quilts (warmth) and the social outcomes of quilting bees, for example, camaraderie, exchange of ideas, and political and social conversation (Horton, 1994). Jane also demonstrated the basic techniques of building an appliqué quilt. She brought in photographs and samples of quilts that were previously completed by senior citizens and grade-school children in courses she taught, enabling the nursing class to see finished results. The quilts were made according to the guidelines of a charitable organization, ABC Quilts.[1] The mission of ABC Quilts is to send love and comfort to at-risk children in the form of handmade baby quilts and to use the process of creating quilts that promote awareness, informed choices, and community service. Students were instructed while they were creating the quilts to consciously direct unconditional love and caring thoughts to these unknown children who would receive the quilts.

Course faculty members Martha and Paula donated fabric and fusible bond for the appliqués. The associate dean donated a rainbow assortment of thread that she had preserved from childhood, as her family had been in the upholstery business. Students selected fabric for the squares they would create and they were given an 8½-inch square piece of fabric that would serve as the background of their individual patch. Jane drafted pattern pieces that depicted nursing images, for example, a stethoscope, figures of people, and crutches. Students were given instructions about use of the fusible bond material to make templates of the patterns they would use for their quilt blocks. The design of each block was executed using an appliqué sewing technique, whereby the shapes and figures were appliquéd to the background fabric square. The planned finished quilt size was 48 by 48 inches. Four of the quilts were formed with 16 blocks, and one quilt contained 20 blocks.

Each week, time for the project was allotted to the latter part of the class period. A major concern for some students was their inability to sew. Several students did not even know how to thread a needle. The students who had some sewing skills patiently taught the basic stitches to those without sewing skills. One student said, "Oh, lord, I am clueless about quilting. I have never quilted before. How am I going to do it?"

Students finished their individual quilt blocks outside of class and then brought them to the fourth class to build the quilt with their group members. After each group planned its quilt, the group made a diagram of the order of the blocks to ensure that the quilt was sewn according to their wishes. Martha brought each quilt home, studied the diagram, and sized and pieced all of the blocks, referring to the illustrations that the students created for placement of the blocks. Sashing strips were added to separate each block. Finally, borders, batting, and backing were added and the quilts were bound to finish the quilts prior to hand quilting. Time spent on this part of the process was about 3 hours per quilt. Fortunately, the five groups completed their blocks at different times with all five quilts completed and ready for quilting by the fifth week of the semester.

A ritual evolved as each quilt was put together. Each group stood before the class and presented its finished quilts, and Martha photographed each. Amazement and pride were obvious in the students' faces as they viewed their quilts. Classmates demonstrated their approval with cheering and applause! After seeing the first quilt that was put together, one student wrote in her journal, "When I saw the quilt I thought of Martha Rogers saying that the whole is greater than the sum of its parts and I began to think of the power that each of our groups has. . . that our class has."

DEVELOPING TEST TAKING SKILLS

In order to justify the time spent on an aesthetic project, which some students initially resented as use of their tuition dollars and lecture time, the quilting time allotted during the final hour of class time also focused on test-taking strategies. While each group formed a quilting circle, a review of NCLEX-RN type questions took place. Test questions were viewed on an overhead projector and students were instructed to choose the correct answer. Martha purposely chose test questions that were out of her realm of expertise so that the class could hear her critical-thinking analysis of questions and distractors when the class could not answer the question correctly. One student commented in her journal entry, "When we use this group time to practice board questions as a class, the rationale we give for our answers is remarkable! I don't think anyone of us has realized before this how much applicable knowledge we have acquired."

Each student also had the opportunity to socialize with group members as questions were viewed and they sewed. In fact, sometimes it was difficult to concentrate on test taking because of the raucousness. At one point the faculty was concerned about the lack of "crowd control" in the classroom, but recognized that a major goal of stress reduction was met, evidenced by the apparent high spirits of the class. One student said, "It felt so good to be working on something in which I could just relax and not have to think about passing exams and papers due for other classes. It was a good mechanism for alleviating stress."

JOURNAL ENTRIES

Students were required to write a weekly journal that constituted 10% of the course grade. The purpose of the journal was to demonstrate synthesis of class readings and experiences on leadership, management, team building behaviors, and their individual and peer leadership development in writing about the semester-long quilting process. The journal was submitted at two points in the semester, at midterm and at the final class meeting.

Learning outcomes of the quilting project were apparent in the students' journals and included enhanced communication and conflict-management skills, relationship building, and working in teams and groups. Communicating effectively began on the first day as the groups chose fabric and, in some cases, decided on a theme. One student said, "I felt all along that communication was key. We had to negotiate effectively to decide on our arrangement. We are all so different with different backgrounds, values, and beliefs. We never totally disagree with each other. You don't want to overstep your boundaries."

Students also felt free to express feelings in their journals that described less positive group dynamics and behavior. They were encouraged by the faculty to practice conflict-resolution techniques to deal with discord. Humor can be an effective way to deal with conflict, break the tension in stressful situations, and build relationships. Humor is a very desirable behavior in a leader-manager (Kelly-Heidenthal, 2003; Marriner-Tomey, 2000; Marrelli, 2004). At week nine, one student writing in her journal practiced this technique: "Working in groups is not always a positive experience. This week, one group member 'A' started to instigate a fight with another member. I started to laugh and make jokes and luckily that calmed everyone down. I have to admit being forced to work with 'A' is definitely a learning experience. Though I think it would be easier working with my friends, working with such an array of different people is really teaching me a lot."

CONCLUSION

With the exception of one comment criticizing the quilting project ("More time should have been spent practicing NCLEX-RN type questions; the quilting took up too much class time"), the end-of-semester students' course evaluations were positive. The quilting experience instilled in students the basis for team building, helped them to enact leadership behaviors, and had positive stress relieving outcomes. One student dubbed quilting as a metaphor for the students' senior year:

> In the sub-groups of our quilting, we have discussions about managerial principles, but we also have connected through the quilting itself. I think the quilting is our metaphor. We are really learning to put all the pieces together, ever so slowly yet with so much care to create the bigger picture. In the beginning 99.9% of the class really didn't think quilting had much to do with nursing; however, maybe it IS nursing.

At the end of the 13-week course, there were tangible results never before experienced in any other nursing course in the curriculum: five quilts sewn with love and caring. Writing in her journal, one student said, "We are finished with the quilt. With great effort the quilt looks beautiful and I hope that the child who gets the quilt understands that hard work and love made the quilt what it is."

Contact information for ABC Quilts is info@abcquilts.org.

REFERENCES

Grossman, S., & Valiga, T. (2000). *The new leadership challenge: Creating the future of nursing.* Philadelphia: F. A. Davis.

Horton, L. (1994). *Quiltmaking in America: Beyond the myths.* Nashville, TN: Rutledgehill Press.

Kelly-Heidenthal, (2003). *Nursing leadership and management.* Clifton Park, NY: Delmar.

Marriner-Tomey, A. (2000). *Guide to nursing management* (6th ed.). St. Louis, MO: Mosby.

Marrelli, T. M. (2004). *The nurse manager's survival guide* (3rd ed.). St. Louis, MO: Mosby.

CHAPTER SIXTEEN

Using Art, Literature, and Music to Teach Leadership

Jacqueline A. Dienemann
Betsy Frank
Margaret M. Patton

A ll nursing students, whether they are prelicensure or returning students getting baccalaureate or higher degrees, can bring knowledge they have gleaned from life experiences to the classroom. One way to help students build on what they already know is to integrate knowledge from art, literature, and music into many of their learning experiences through the use of metaphor. This chapter focuses on the use of metaphor as a way to awaken students to what they already know about leadership. The teaching strategies described can be used in a variety of courses where leadership concepts are taught, for leadership is not learned solely in a specific didactic course. It is learned throughout the curriculum when students are asked to envision change, develop expertise, communicate, critically analyze situations, achieve outcomes, and mentor others (Lemire, 2002).

Why use metaphors? Certainly other teaching strategies can help students call forth what they already know and apply the familiar to newly learned subject matter. Metaphors, or symbolic images, however, are uniquely suited to generate a range of complementary and competing insights about the nature of a concept, such as leadership, and how that concept can be demonstrated (Morgan, 1997). Metaphors that use art, literature, and music capture a way to encompass a concept through an alternative to empirical or scientific knowing (Carper, 1978; Chinn & Kramer, 1999). Making use of a metaphor for learning content in the classroom setting is challenging to all participants. Students are challenged not only to receive the intended message, but also to participate in establishing the symbolism of the learning situation. The development of this symbolism is what is offered by the use of the metaphor. The whole intent and purpose in using a metaphor in teaching leadership, therefore, is not to make the acquisition of the knowledge more difficult, but rather to put it into a frame of reference that is pertinent to the point where the student is today.

Using a variety of metaphors allows faculty to show that leadership is multifaceted and that no one theory will totally explain it. At first, one metaphor may be very persuasive and may obscure other aspects of the complexity of the leadership concept. Upon further exploration, using literature, art, and music, students can come to know just how complex leadership is.

TEACHING STRATEGY TEMPLATE

When using a metaphor, begin by telling the students what topic the metaphor is meant to parallel. Second, provide a rich description of the metaphor with images or facts that can be translated to leadership. Third, ask students as a group to translate the metaphor to the topic. Using a white board, overhead, or projected computer screen, the faculty or a student then summarizes the parallels found. This visually assists students to build a set of parallels. Fourth, discuss what the metaphor emphasizes about the topic and what it ignores or minimizes. Fifth, assign students to write a guided essay of a paragraph or two, reflecting (in class or in an e-mail), about a personal application of this metaphor or what they learned from using this metaphor or linking the metaphor to a reading, musical composition, or work of art.

The discussion of metaphors, however, can be more open. Students could simply be asked to do free writing about what a piece of music, literature, or art says about leadership.

LITERATURE AS METAPHOR

Many students enter the classroom accepting the theory that leadership is an inborn trait (Bower, 2000). In fact they may say such things as, "I am not a born leader. I like to sit back and let others take the lead." Using widely available leadership assessments might help students discover that they do, indeed, have some leadership capabilities. But using literature as metaphor may point out this lesson in a more dramatic and enduring way. For instance, leadership may be examined using biographies of great historical or fictional leaders (Stowe & Igo 1996; Valiga & Bruderle, 1997). Choosing a book many have read allows immediate discussion. For instance, the fictional character Harry Potter is a born leader. What traits of leadership identified in research did he demonstrate? Further discussion reveals that when taken to the extreme, this offers a serious distortion of reality, as does any one theory. Leadership is more than a destiny or trait; at times Harry is not a leader at all and has to be taught to lead by his mentor. A discussion like this leads directly to reviewing the development of leadership theories from traits, to power, to situations, to transformation, to servant leadership in learning organizations. Students can be asked to brainstorm other fictional characters who demonstrate each of these theories. These discussions open students to the idea of examining multiple theories about leadership and struggling with the fact that leadership is paradoxical and may be a time limited phenomenon.

Movies can be used as well (Cannon & Hofman, 2000; Kirkpatrick, Brown, Atkins & Vance, 2001). (For a more thorough discussion of the use of movies, see chapters 17 and18). A valuable resource for literature and movies to use, and guides for classroom discussion and analysis is Hartwick Leadership Cases (Hartwick Humanities in Management Institute, 2003).

MUSIC AS METAPHOR

The use of music as metaphor provides a rich context within which to explore leadership. Leadership has been described by Frank (1997) as symphony, with the leader as the conductor. Faculty can use this metaphor to lead a discussion of how one evaluates a concert performance. Different stakeholders (management, musicians, audience) will assess the success of a concert using different measures, such as box office revenues, artistic merit, or personal pleasure. If the stakeholder is management, for example, students could be asked to translate the metaphor into an analysis of the functions of a nurse executive as leader of a home health agency. As a manager, what does the leader need to plan, organize, direct, or control? Regarding followers, who does the leader need to coach, guide, communicate, motivate, develop, and delegate to? What stakeholders will assess the success or failure of the nurse's leadership? What measures will they use? How may they conflict?

Popular music as metaphor can also be used to help students examine opportunities for emergent leadership that arise when the structures of an organization are in the process of dramatic change. In the past, popular music was controlled by access to recording and air time by major studios and radio networks. Most of American popular music was developed and performed by Americans. Today, popular music has global influences of innovative sounds and rhythms. There are multiple sources shaping popularity, much like the many stakeholders involved in shaping health care. No longer is there one authority of how music should sound, but it is judged by new criteria such as the number of followers, aesthetics of a niche or if it crosses over to multiple groups, longevity of performers, and sales. Audiences are more assertive and knowledgeable about what they desire. There are many opportunities for musicians to perform at small venues and on the Internet, sell CDs of their work, and build a following. The breakdown of the rigid hierarchy controlling access to recording due to innovations such as the Internet has led to more opportunities to have a hit song and be a leader in popular music. After this or another rich description of the chosen metaphor, the instructor guides students to see how this reflects the current health care system and what new opportunities have emerged for nurses as leaders during chaotic change. Students could then do a short essay in class on what new insights into situations and leadership in health care they learned from using this novel viewpoint.

Music metaphors can also be used as a mechanism to brainstorm and see old information with new eyes. A way to examine today's health care delivery system is to discuss types of music and their performances as metaphors for different health care services. Examples of metaphors are given below, followed by possible answers by students in italics.

- Classical music by an orchestra follows strict rules of design and requires harmony among many experts. *In health care, it is a good metaphor for inpatient surgery whose goal is to be as close to perfection as possible.*
- Neoclassical music by a local ensemble is less strict in its design, but still requires many years of training in classical music for musicians, much like . . . *elective, ambulatory surgery whose goal often is patient quality of life.*
- Jazz music in a club is improvisational, but performed by trained musicians, like . . . *primary care where the goal is adaptation to the needs of the presenting patient.*
- Country music in a barn uses a limited number of instruments, and tells stories of life, like . . . *hospice, where the goal is acceptance of life as it has been lived.*
- Reggae music at a festival uses a limited number of instruments and presents one cultural perspective, like . . . *culturally sensitive changes in care for specific populations such as children, Chinese immigrants, etc.*
- Marching band music is uniform and in step. It is very stylized music with a crisp, even tempo . . . *like the routine, everyday work in urgent care where one goal is efficiency.*
- Blues music is emotionally provoking, heavily toned, and performed differently each time it is played. It reminds us of . . . *psychiatric care with a goal of evoking buried emotions.*

Offer a metaphor and ask them to identify a type of health care delivery that it reflects and why. There is no right answer, only the relevance of the rationale is important.

Music along with dance metaphors may be used to discuss how the relationship between leaders and followers is changing. Historically the head of a hospital or health system chooses the music and the dance. Middle managers, clinicians, and support people follow the steps. The health care world was once stable and everyone knew the dance and their part. This is no longer so clear. Leadership has evolved as the health care delivery system has become a place of uncertainty and change. New dances are constantly evolving. We began with solo dancing by the leader (exhibited leadership traits), then a ballet (the dances are known but the story changed with the situation), then square dancing (transformational, where the caller changed the moves during the dance guided by a vision of the future), and now modern dance (the choreographer shares power with the dancers who improvise to the music). Yet at times it seems as if leaders and followers are asked to do two dances at once, due to the discontinuous, incremental way that change occurs. Ask students to give examples of times when they were a leader or observed a leader who was expected to provide clear decisions and expectations while simultaneously sharing decision making and flexibly developing others who may be resisting change.

In addition to analyzing musical compositions, students can engage in a hands-on music production experience that can help them to understand the four styles of leadership. By way of example, in two different classes, each consisting of about 50 senior baccalaureate nursing students studying leadership and advanced roles in nursing practice, the discussion for the next class day was to be the four styles of leadership, that is, democratic, autocratic, bureaucratic, and laissez-faire. Because these terms as simple words or word phrases were not entirely new to the students, their initial reaction to learning more about the styles held little enthusiasm. It was plain and simple, "Oh, well, heard this before." These senior students had undoubtedly heard these terms before and perhaps could have even presented a definition for each; however, awareness of knowing what something is provides little testimony as to how it works. Therefore, rather than focusing on the traditional definitions, students were challenged to apply the terms to the leadership and advanced practice roles of the educated nurse, where most of them will undoubtedly find themselves someday.

With some guidance from the teacher, the class divided itself into four relatively equal sections. Each section was handed a piece of paper with directions about what they were going to be doing and what the desired outcome was. The directions on the paper simply said that group members would become a music-producing group. Each music-producing group had to demonstrate a specific leadership style through a musical presentation. The presentations had to be adequately clear to the audience (the remainder of the class) so they could understand what kind of music they were listening to. The type of group leadership was determined and exemplified, therefore, by the interaction within the group and the product of the type of music played. The group's music and the way it was presented made it clear to the listeners whether this was a democratic, autocratic, bureaucratic, or laissez-faire group.

The first group represented the *autocratic* organizational style. The group assumed the position of a musical ensemble with a leader who told them what to do and how to do it, with no consideration of input by the group. Each played an instrument, that is, children's musical instruments, precisely as commanded without dereliction, while the leader barked orders. The class responded within about 3 minutes that it was autocratic style. The second group presented laissez-faire leadership style. No one seemed to have any control here, until finally one of the members of the group declared that he would like to play something with his instrument. (These were improvised instruments from the classroom supplies that the students had each brought with them, e.g., a book "drum" with pencil drumsticks). After he played his piece, the other musicians went back to jammin' to their own sense of control. The audience recognized this style immediately and identified it. This continued with a variety of presentations in both classes until all groups had presented and the audience identified each organizational leadership style.

The class discussion of this exercise was very positive. Students did admit that at first they thought the assignment was a "pretty dumb" thing to do; however, preparing the musical composition, identifying a leader, and actually performing truly cemented in their minds the identified organizational leadership style of work, not just as it is defined in the text, but also how it can look in action. Both classes agreed that music was an excellent metaphorical medium because everyone at least understood it and had experience with it. Students also said they never really seemed to have much opportunity to be creative and that this exercise permitted and even encouraged them to think and act using creativity. By itself, that made the exercise more fun than anticipated. One group even decided that they were going to sing their next assignment!

ART AS METAPHOR

Using art as metaphor provides a rich format within in which to explore leadership concepts, for art is sculpture, painting, drawing, cooking, and a whole host of other craft media. Images of works of art can illustrate the difference in people's expectations and perceptions of quality, and that perception is the truth to that viewer. Classical art is representational and uses cultural symbols for the person's power, wealth, and influence. Impressionist art is best seen as a whole from a short distance; its focus is on nature and everyday life. Modern art is interpreted in a unique manner by each artist. A discussion of these movements in art can lead to a whole exploration of what quality care is, because each type of art appeals to each person differently. Students can then ponder whether quality, like beauty, is in the eye of the beholder or whether quality is something that can be judged solely by objective criteria.

Another way to use art is to have students go to the university art gallery or another gallery or view a painting online or in their art history texts. Ask them to reflect upon what this painting says about nursing leadership within today's health care environment. Will students view the scene as chaotic like the images in Picasso's Guernica, or more bold and vivacious like the colors in a Goya painting? This more open-ended assignment allows students to reflect on a wide range of contexts within which one can view nursing leadership within health care systems. Response to an assignment such as this has been overwhelmingly positive. In-class and online students have commented that they have never been asked to do such an assignment and they truly enjoyed their art-as-metaphor exploration.

Faculty can also use art to direct the discussion toward a specific leadership topic. For example, faculty can assign students to create a metaphor for how leaders and followers interact using a type of leadership defined in their text. In order to do this, students are asked to bring an object or picture to class and describe how it is a metaphor for leadership. Students have brought in lasagna and discussed how the interaction of ingredients creates a laissez-faire intermingling of tastes; a basket to show transactional leadership in the structured pattern of weaving, resulting in a well-designed or poor quality basket; and a flowerpot with a single Gerbera daisy to demonstrate transformational leadership, having a tall stem of ethics, vision shown by the flower, many follower leaves that are interdependent with the stem, and a strong root system of competencies.

Personal expressions of art also can help students learn about what it entails to be a leader. Using Aroian (2002) as framework for discussion about the leader as visionary, students working in groups can express their visions for quality nursing care. One person is blindfolded and the others help that person to draw the group's vision of quality care (J. Aroian, personal communication, January 20, 2000). Having students use solely nonverbal communication further solidifies the need for teamwork in developing a vision for an organization. Following one such exercise, a student asked if the faculty member would display the drawing on the faculty's refrigerator. The faculty responded by saying all the drawings would be displayed on the course bulletin board in one of the school's hallways.

LEARNING OUTCOMES

Metaphors drawn from art, music, and literature are a rich resource for teaching the aesthetic knowing that helps one come to understand what leadership is. Metaphors ask students to go beyond empirical outcomes to reexamine the processes that led to the outcomes, and they also inject fun and enjoyment by touching on students' creative abilities. Students learn that aesthetic experiences contribute to knowing a subject more deeply and these experiences should be sought out as a mechanism to offer new perspectives when new solutions are sought. Metaphors provide a fresh perspective that can engage a class in lively discussions that can link seemingly disconnected topics. For some students, metaphors may seem an absurd attempt to fill class time. They may not have an experiential background in the arts, literature, or music to draw from or may have compartmentalized this aspect in their life as not relevant to scientific health care. Before students can be open to utilizing this strategy to learn about leadership, the instructor must overcome this resistance. One approach is to begin with short exercises and consistently assist students in linking metaphor to theory and research on leadership. For example, begin with more concrete references using universally known characters from literature, such as comparing the leadership competencies of Peter Pan and Captain Hook, before moving to more abstract metaphors. Ask them to propose other metaphors as you discuss topics. Frequently solicit feedback so that students perceive the connections and purpose of the exercises. This can be verbal; short, guided essays based on reflection about the metaphor and its links to leadership theory or research; or personal experiences. Also ask students to describe how metaphors enhanced their learning about leadership behaviors in challenging situations. In sum, the use of metaphors can transform an often dry topic into an exciting discussion that opens students' eyes to a whole new world of nursing leadership opportunities. Students who never saw themselves as leaders begin to know that everyone has the capacity for leadership development.

REFERENCES

Aroian, J. (2002). Leader as visionary: Leadership education model. *Nursing Leadership Forum, 7*(2), 53–56.

Bower, F. L. (2000). *Nurses taking the lead: Personal qualities of effective leadership.* Philadelphia: Saunders.

Carper, B. (1978). Fundamental ways of knowing in nursing. *Advances in Nursing Science, 1*(1)13–23.

Chinn, P. L., & Kramer, M. K. (1999). *Theory and knowledge: Integrated knowledge development.* St. Louis, MO: Mosby.

Frank, B. (1997). Quality care. What makes the difference? *Journal of Nursing Administration, 25*(5), 13–14.

Hartwick Humanities in Management Institute, (2003). *Hartwick classic leadership cases and Hartwick classic film leadership cases academic case study catalog.* Oneonta, NY: Author. Web site: www.hartwick.edu/hhmi/

Hofman, M. (2000, March). Everything I know about leadership, I learned from the movies [electronic version] *http://pf.inc.com/magazine/20000301/17290.html*

Kirkpatrick, M. K., Brown, S. T., Atkins, A., & Vance, A. (2001) Using popular culture to teach nursing leadership. *Journal of Nursing Education, 40,* 90–92.

Lemire, J. A. (2002) Preparing nurse leaders: A leadership education model. *Nursing Leadership Forum, 7*(2), 47–52.

Morgan, G. (1997) *Images of organization* (2nd ed.). Thousand Oaks, CA: Sage.

Stowe, A .C., & Igo, L. C. (1996). Learning from literature: Novels, plays, short stories, and poems in nursing education. *Nurse Educator, 21*(5), 16–19.

Valiga, T. M., & Bruderle, E. R. (1997). *Using the arts and humanities to teach nursing: A creative approach.* New York: Springer

CHAPTER SEVENTEEN

Using Popular Films to Measure Student Understanding of Leadership

Mary S. Tilbury

The need for strong and effective leadership in nursing has never been greater. Change, challenge, and opportunity are the order of the day in the health care system. As the largest group of health care providers, nurses and nursing are well positioned to make a substantial difference in the outcomes of professional and organizational life.

Baccalaureate educational priorities traditionally stress the development of knowledge, skills, and competencies in the provision and management of client care. Concomitantly, they emphasize growth in critical thinking skills, the exercise of independent judgment, and the transmission of the profession's values, attitudes, and beliefs. Educational programs also seek to provide students with the ability to participate actively and effectively in organizational systems, the setting in which the majority of their practice life will be located.

Student learning priorities, however, are understandably focused on curriculum content that will help them excel academically and develop beginning expertise in meeting the needs of the clients they seek to serve. Students also recognize that clinical courses provide the principal means by which the practice license is secured. Program content not directly related to these goals is not infrequently referred to as "nonclinical" or "support" courses, one means of denoting a sort of second class status. These realities present instructional faculty with a unique challenge. This chapter details how cinematic paradigms are used in traditional and online applications of a capstone leadership course to address these and other teaching and learning student needs.

AN INNOVATIVE APPROACH

A strategic objective of the University of Maryland School of Nursing—to offer the baccalaureate completion program for registered nurses (RN/BSN) option online—required course faculty to examine closely accepted classroom teaching and learning methods that were used in a capstone leadership course. In the generic curriculum, leadership content was conveyed in a two-course sequence, the first course offered early in the program and the second, close to completion. Both generic and RN/BSN curricula required this second course, which primarily focused on fundamental leadership and management concepts and theories, such as strategic and operational planning, structural and fiscal systems, organizationally based legal principles, power and authority, motivation and conflict management theories, decision making, performance management, and leadership styles.

Clear innovative and creative teaching and learning strategies were indicated, creating an opportunity to capture more effectively the student's interest in a nonclinical area of study, challenge and enhance critical-thinking skills, and develop an appreciation as to how leadership knowledge, skills, and competencies could enrich professional practice.

After considerable faculty discussion, a decision was made to use popular cinema as a primary means of evaluating, through examinations, the student's ability to analyze and synthesize course concepts and theories. The use of cinematic paradigms of leadership provided two additional advantages. First, faculty was challenged to develop equivalent course requirements between the traditional classroom application and the online offering, and cinema could be used in each without difficulty. Faculty was also striving to formulate evaluation mechanisms that could address academic integrity issues proactively, and the variety of popular cinema available for adaptation was seemingly endless. Finally, group mini-case studies that focused on creating and describing real-world leadership challenges were selected as the means by which students could use theory to analyze and solve simulated problems. The remainder of this chapter details how cinema was used to evaluate established course objectives, the film selection process, the procedure used in developing examination items, a review of selected student processing procedures, and the keying and grading of exams.

THE FILM ADAPTATION PROCESS

Two examinations were required in the course, one at midterm and a cumulative evaluation at the end of the semester. The film selection process for the midterm began shortly after the beginning of the semester. Typically, faculty reviewed films that are readily available at video stores, focusing on those that are available for 5 to 7 days. This process may require the screening of several films, so as to select one that best relates to the content covered during the first half of the semester. Priority consideration is given to films that are organizationally based, such as *Jerry McGuire, John Q,* or *Remember the Titans.*

Course faculty review and discuss potential selections and a final decision about the examination film is reached, as a rule, without difficulty. Two members of the instructional faculty develop items based on a generic test blueprint of key theories, concepts, and principles. For example, students may be referred to particular scenes in the movie, and then questioned as to whether the scene represents specific theoretical content.

Students might be asked to apply a legal standard, such as the Fair Labor Standards Act to film content, or a legal principle, such as employment at will. Bureaucratic characteristics, for example, line and staff positions, provide the foundation to question whether a particular character's role reflects one or the other, and the application of power source theory (Tomey, 2000) is readily available for the development of test items in the vast majority of films reviewed.

Although some films are better than others, there has been little or no difficulty finding cinematic material for the application of course content. Once completed, the draft examination is submitted to other instructional faculty and test items are finalized. During this aspect of the process, items may be accepted, modified, or deleted.

The emphasis is placed on developing items that are clearly stated and that accurately reflect content validity.

A representative exam may contain 20 to 25 items, with individually assigned point values, and questions are developed as short answer, multiple choice, or a combination thereof (see box 1). Concurrently or immediately after formulation, the faculty uses a similar group review process to develop the exam key used in grading. After a film has been used as an examination vehicle, short segments may be used to illustrate and anchor theoretical content in selected classes or online course modules. It is rare that a film is used a second time for testing purposes, and if so, the interval is characteristically no less than four semesters in length.

Multiple-Choice Questions

Sample question from the movie *John Q:*
At one point in the film, an emotional discussion takes place between John Q and Dr. Turner in the hallway leading to the Emergency Room. John Q pleads with the surgeon to give his son a new heart and when this approach is unsuccessful he produces a gun and holds Dr. Turner and ER staff hostage. Which of the following sources/types of power did John Q use in his plea and in occupying the ER?

      a. legitimate power
      b. referent power
      c. expert power
      d. reward power
      e. coercive power

  1. a and b only
  2. b, d and e only
  3. a and e only
  4. a, c and e only

Sample question from the movie *Jerry McGuire:*
At the beginning of the film, Jerry writes a mission statement for his firm. Shortly thereafter, he is fired. Briefly explain why Jerry's employment is terminated so abruptly.

EXAMINATION PROCEDURES

An announcement regarding the film selected for an examination is posted online or made in class a minimum of 2 weeks prior to the exam. If a student finds the film objectionable due to its rating, use of language, or violent content, for example, they are given the option of notifying faculty within a set time frame. Students raising objections receive an exam based on a previously used G-rated film. This occurrence is rare, but the option is offered prior to objections or concerns being expressed about a particular film.

A copy of the film is also placed in the school's media center so that rental is not the only access option, and particularly since the online application of the course has been expanded to include generic students who are frequently on campus. The actual exam is made available online or distributed in class 1 week after the film announcement has been made. Students have 1 week to complete the exam. Using this film acquisition process, any copyright infringement concerns are avoided.

Students may elect to complete the exam in partnership with another student in their course section. This option is based on the faculty's belief that consultation between and among professionals should be modeled, particularly when dealing with leadership and/or management issues. Exams include specific directions and expectations as to the date and time that they are due, and penalties are established for exams that are submitted late. A course policy is also in effect regarding any exam that is outstanding 1 week after the due date. Students who do not submit an exam within the established time frame are required to complete an exam based on another film, since the faculty grade and return student exams 1 week following submission.

Onsite or traditional classroom sections of the course review their exams in class. The exam key is posted for online students and it may be expanded or modified to include explanatory information that is generated after online instructors have analyzed individual items. Sometimes faculty will post an announcement or use e-mail to inform online students as to item rationale, if indicated. Thereafter, if students have questions, individual contact and online discussion with the instructor is encouraged.

CINEMATIC APPLICATIONS AND ILLUSTRATIONS

A variety of films have been used over time for examination development—*Twelve Angry Men, Harry Potter, Maid in Manhattan, Jerry McGuire, The Hunt for Red October, America's Sweethearts,* and *John Q,* to name a few. Selected illustrations of item development are provided to students to clarify and enhance an understanding of cinematic applications. These and other films offer multiple opportunities to apply cinematic paradigms of leadership. Examples are as follows:

John Q is a film starring Denzel Washington and Robert Duvall. John Q, the lead character, finds that his only child needs a heart transplant, and he has no insurance to cover the procedure. He has recently been reduced to part-time status at the factory where he is employed, because business is poor, and he is anxious about raising enough money to cover the cost of surgery. One of John Q's many strategies for raising the money is to work as much overtime as he can get. The question developed, on the basis of these cinematic circumstances, requires the student to apply Fair Labor Standards Act provisions regarding overtime eligibility.

The Hunt for Red October is an action-packed film that focuses on a Russian submarine captain, played by Sean Connery, who is intent on defecting and bringing an innovative class of submarine with him to the United States. The film offers multiple opportunities to apply: planning principles at the strategic and operational level; conflict-management strategies; characteristics of a bureaucratic structure, power, and authority; and leadership theory. For example, using planning theory students can be asked to differentiate between the boat's strategic assignment and orders and the captain's operational plans for defection. The identification of characters that serve in line versus staff positions can be discerned and the leadership styles of Captain Ramius and the CIA operative, Jack Ryan, played by Alec Baldwin, can be evaluated from a theoretical perspective.

The film *Remember the Titans* tells the dramatic, true story of a high-school football team's racial integration experience. The film follows the team's new coach, played by Denzel Washington, who strives to provide leadership in this challenging situation and to build a winning team. In one dramatic scene during training camp, which is held in Gettysburg, Pennsylvania, the coach takes the team to the cemetery where those who fought for the North and the South were buried. He delivers an emotionally charged speech in which he appeals to the team's members for cooperation. This scene alone offers instructors the opportunity to probe the student's understanding and application of conflict management theory, as well as others, such as leadership and motivational theory.

The opening scenes of *Jerry McGuire* provide a rich source of material related to mission statements and the organizational concepts of vision and values. Tom Cruise plays the role of Jerry, a highly charged, type-A sports agent who finds his scruples. In a moment of conscience, he prepares a mission statement that emphasizes quality client service as an organizational priority, as opposed to profits, and circulates the document to his colleagues at the agency. Shortly thereafter, Jerry is fired. This cinematic material is used to query students as to why Jerry was fired. Based on class content and required readings, the students should be able to recognize the conflict between Jerry's vision and values and those of the organization and that his superiors consider his perspective as a threat that must be removed.

STUDENT RESPONSES AND EVALUATION

Students have responded positively to using cinema as a vehicle for course examinations. They report that while they initially felt pleased about an exam procedure that is essentially take-home and open-book, they found the exams surprisingly challenging. Students also expressed an appreciation for the creativity and innovation that the approach represents. In addition, they find that the exams not only further reinforce the synthesis and application of theory, but the film content also serves as a conceptual anchor. They are able to recall in their practice settings those scenes that reflect course content. Indeed, in this case a picture may be worth a thousand instructor words. Course evaluation comments, such as those that follow, are typical: "This course is a must!!!!!" "The movies made the content come alive for me." "Now when I go to the movies I keep looking for leadership concepts. Do you know how long that will last?" and "At first I thought that an open book, take-home exam would be a snap—using the movies really makes you think!"

In addition to holding the student's attention, there are other aspects of the examination process that have been reported as constructive. For example, watching the examination movie frequently becomes a family activity, bringing those who must often support the students with their demanding schedules closer to the educational process. Finally, students share that while working with a partner takes longer, they find that the process enriches the learning experience, thereby gaining a better understanding of the material.

SUMMARY

Cinema represents a creative and innovative approach to leadership education, one that captures the student's interest in a nonclinical area of study. Further, it challenges students to develop their critical thinking skills and offers them a conceptual anchor for leadership content that can be used in any organizational setting. Students and faculty at the University of Maryland School of Nursing have responded positively to the use of cinematic paradigms of leadership in a capstone leadership course.

This method for learning about leadership also has been successful in addressing academic integrity issues that frequently surround the repeated use of more traditional forms of testing. Use of cinema is compatible with conducting online examinations that do not require intricate student exam schedules or the use of proctoring resources. The greatest benefit, however, may be that the application of theory to popular cinema can be readily transferred to the "movie of professional practice."

REFERENCES

Tomey, A. M. (2000). *Guide to nursing management and leadership* (6th ed.). St. Louis, MO: Mosby.

CHAPTER EIGHTEEN

Teaching Leadership in Community-Based Settings Through Film

Joy E. Wachs
Joellen B. Edwards

L eadership skills are essential to nurses and other health professionals as they prepare to engage with community members to
improve health status. This chapter describes a unique strategy
used for teaching leadership to undergraduate nursing students and
interdisciplinary groups of health professions students including
nursing, public and allied health, and medical students. Although this
description was generated from experiences that have been successful
in rural, community-based settings, the strategy—teaching leadership
through film—is applicable to any nursing education setting.

SETTING

East Tennessee State University (ETSU) is a doctoral/research-inten-
sive regional university primarily serving the Southern Appalachian
region of northeast Tennessee, southwest Virginia, and western North
Carolina. The majority of its 12,000 students are regional residents, yet
the university welcomes learners from across the nation and the globe.
A major mission for ETSU is the preparation of a variety of health

professionals through the Division of Health Sciences, formed in 1989. The colleges of Nursing, Public and Allied Health, and Medicine, all members of the division, have been recognized nationally as experts in rural, community-based care and interdisciplinary health professions education.

The colleges, with support from a W. K. Kellogg Foundation grant (Community Partnerships for Health Professions Education) partnered in 1990 in a unique educational endeavor to educate undergraduate nursing, undergraduate public and allied health, and medical students in interdisciplinary groups in rural primary care and community settings. This innovation—rural primary care track—was conducted in full partnership with the rural communities hosting the educational programs. The long history of collaboration among disciplines and communities has yielded a curriculum from which self-selected nursing, medical, and public and allied health students study together in a set of interdisciplinary community-based classes and clinical experiences. The learning experiences have expanded to include seminars and projects for graduate nurse practitioner, public health students and family practice residents (Behringer, Bishop, Edwards, & Franks, 1999; Edwards, 2001; Edwards & Smith, 1998; Richards, 1996).

The success of the rural primary-care track influenced a revised undergraduate (BSN) curriculum that is community based (Edwards & Alley, 2002), promoted changes in the public health internship experiences, and supported significant alteration in the medical curriculum. Medical students enter clinical experiences in rural communities in their first year, concurrent with their basic science studies, and engage in longitudinal, community-based experiences in the family practice residency programs. The rural primary care track curriculum includes communication for health professionals, health assessment, rural health and community leadership courses.

Students learn to assess individuals and communities simultaneously, and by their third semester in the program are planning, implementing, and evaluating community programs in collaboration with local agencies and institutions. In the final semester, students implement in-depth health improvement projects, working closely with community members to meet needs identified by residents and organizations. Individual capstone experiences positively affect the lives of rural residents through the screening, intervention, and education provided or facilitated by the students.

EMERGING FOCUS ON LEADERSHIP

Over the years of curriculum development and with increasing experience in implementing community projects, faculty recognized that a focus on *community leadership* for interdisciplinary students was essential. They also recognized that effective leadership cannot be taught in one course or clinical experience, but rather must be integrated into every level of the curriculum. Understanding leadership strategies and experience in leadership situations are essential for all health professionals, but critical for those who intend to practice in community-based settings. Health professionals who choose to practice in small rural communities (Behringer, et al., 1999) must be willing to engage with their community, and when appropriate, assume active leadership positions to improve the community's health. They must also become competent and comfortable in their ability to work through state and national advocacy organizations to bring a systems-level approach to improving rural health. Leadership skills, such as visioning, strategic planning, embracing diversity, fostering interprofessional relationships, and networking, take on critical significance for the rural nurse, physician, or public health professional. These professionals are often alone or part of a small team of experts available within a geographic region. To succeed in improving health, professionals must be able to work together effectively and collaborate with community members in a meaningful way.

The community-based interdisciplinary aspects of the rural primary care track curriculum are particularly salient for developing leadership abilities in nursing students. Because of longstanding gender and professional bias, nurses have struggled to be accepted as leaders within the health system. As the delivery system continually evolves, they must be competent and confident in accepting their rightful leadership roles in interdisciplinary teams, the community, and health care organizations (Porter-O'Grady, 1994).

LEADERSHIP CONCEPTS IN THE CURRICULUM

The ETSU rural primary care track focuses on the principles of emotional intelligence (Goleman, 1994, 1998; Goleman, Boyatzis, & McKee,

2002), collaborative practice (Mattesich, Murray-Close, & Monsey, 2001; Sullivan, 1998), and the value of diversity in addressing community health issues (Katzenbach & Smith, 2003; LaFasto & Larson, 2001; Lencioni, 2002). Faculty use a variety of opportunities to integrate leadership in the curriculum. For example, the Helene Fuld Trust sponsored the Leadership in Nursing Education (LINE) program at the University of California-San Francisco. Its purpose was to provide an opportunity for ETSU faculty to explore the components of emotional intelligence and ways to offer interdisciplinary students opportunities to master the leadership competencies of self-awareness, self-management, social awareness, and relationship management. Faculty were trained in a variety of team-building activities, including Myers-Briggs preference inventory analysis (Myers, 1995), Mobile Team Challenge low ROPES course activities (Rainey & Torres, 2001), and strength and limitation awareness to help students better understand themselves and the gifts they bring to community-based projects. Students and faculty develop teams composed of individuals with diverse knowledge, attitudes, and skills with the idea that diverse teams can better meet the needs of the community than teams with a single set of strengths.

The curriculum is also predicated on an experiential model of learning and a service orientation. Thus, Greenleaf's (1970) model of servant leadership fits this curriculum well. Students are expected to learn the lessons of servant leadership, health care delivery, community organizing (Mattesich, Monsey & Roy, 1997; Minkler, 2002), and program planning and evaluation by working with community residents and groups to identify community strengths and needs, collaboratively plan programs to meet those needs, and evaluate the impact the programs have had on the health of the community.

Although students are aware of the importance of diversity in teams, they are often limited in their understanding of people with different backgrounds, belief systems, and ways of working within the community. The dilemma is how to assist students to learn about diversity in a safe environment and then offer them the ability to put that learning into action. Though leadership concepts can be learned in a variety of ways, contemporary film offers a strategy that allows students to grapple with difficult topics by looking at characters in film, and then moving beyond to applying the principles to their own lives and professional practice.

TEACHING LEADERSHIP THROUGH FILM:
AN INNOVATIVE STRATEGY

The film curriculum was developed based on the experience of one author in the W. K. Kellogg National Leadership Program. A cross-group seminar at Birmingham Southern College in 1999, entitled "Leadership in Film," allowed participants to view four films during the 4-day seminar: *Crimson Tide, Baby Boom, Amistad,* and *The Milagro Bean Field War.* After viewing each film, participants gathered for a 1- to 2-hour discussion, using questions designed by facilitators. Questions focused on leadership concepts such as transformational and transactional leadership (*Crimson Tide*), leadership during a historical racial event (*Amistad*), the personal aspects of leadership related to gender (*Baby Boom*), and the role of citizen leaders (*Milagro Bean Field War*). Discussions focused on the actual experience of watching the film and how to move beyond the film to discuss potentially difficult emotional issues.

This experience was brought back to the university and significantly revised to meet the needs of interdisciplinary-health-science students with the goal of creating a better understanding of interdisciplinary roles, leadership concepts, and the value of diversity, which are key aspects of successful leadership. Each semester, students were asked to view two films outside of class. Often, students elected to watch the films together on the weekends, thus finding another way to become better acquainted. It was inconsequential that some had already viewed the assigned films because the context became the most important variable. With the aid of study questions, students began to focus on issues rather than on plot or characters. For example, using *Erin Brockovich* and *Mr. Holland's Opus,* students were asked to identify the vision of the main character, obstacles the character encountered in trying to make the vision a reality, and the need for constructive relationships in moving oneself, a group, or a community toward a goal. Because the questions were centered on issues rather than plot, students could view different films and still have a meaningful discussion.

Choosing the films and designing the questions was difficult. Faculty had watched a myriad of films, and continue to do so, as they seek the best combination of relevance for students and substance for discussion. In the discussion of racial diversity, the original films chosen were *Amistad, Remember the Titans,* and *Barbershop.*

Although these films were certainly appropriate, it became clear through discussion that students had little appreciation for the struggle of African Americans in the United States and the events of the Civil Rights movement in American history. Therefore, films like *Malcolm X, Mississippi Burning, Rosewood,* and *The Ghosts of Mississippi* replaced some of the original films. Question design closely followed the choice of film. In face-to-face discussion, it was appropriate to spend time discussing the plot and characters so that everyone was aware of differences and similarities among the films. Then questions were framed to bring out issues rather than facts. For example, in discussing socioeconomic status and Appalachian culture, students were asked to discuss what it means to be poor or to live in poverty. How are people without resources treated by those with resources? How does living in Appalachia add another burden to people who already live in poverty? Why is it that people's culture is so important to them, often more important than money or employment? Facilitators often take students back to the films as a way of finding examples of these abstract notions. For example, students and faculty often discuss the need for rural Appalachian communities to preserve the beauty of their mountain home while allowing progress in terms of employment and connection with the outside world. What is the correct balance of preservation and progress?

As with many curricula, time is always a challenge. The Tennessee Board of Regents mandated that all undergraduate curricula across the state reduce their credit hours to 120, thus impinging on courses like Leadership in Film. Faculty responded to this challenge by moving the discussion portion of the learning to online (e-discussion) forums (Table 18.1). This required revamping the questions as there was no purpose in asking questions that had a single answer, such as "Describe the plot of the film." Rather, study questions had to focus more on critical thinking, controversy, and substantiation. Students were asked to answer each question and then return to the discussion forum in a few days to respond to at least two classmates' comments per question. Thus began training for online discussion. Within a semester, students began to understand the importance of their responses to others and often responded more frequently than required if discussions became heated or were particularly meaningful.

Positive outcomes of moving to the e-discussion forum included 100% participation (everyone viewed the film and contributed to the

TABLE 18.1. Tips for Developing Leadership E-discussions Based on Contemporary Film

E-discussion Development Tips

1. Choose films that are readily available to students for rental or purchase.

2. Faculty must review films every time assigned to grasp again the nuance of the issues to which the students are responding.

3. In the first semester of the curriculum, all students should view the same film. As the students become more accustomed to e-discussion, it is appropriate to offer them several films with related themes from which to choose.

4. Faculty need only write 3–5 questions per film. If there are too many questions students lose interest and find the assignment tedious rather than stimulating.

5. Questions must be open-ended, offering the opportunity for discussion, debate, and resolution.

6. Questions may begin with specifics about the film, especially early in the curriculum, but need to progress rapidly to applying insights to practice.

7. To generate e-discussion, ask students to respond to each question posed and then later return to the discussion forum and respond to the answers offered by at least two classmates.

8. Faculty need to comment or question regularly to demonstrate their involvement in the e-discussion process.

9. Faculty can post the e-discussion forum for 2–4 weeks depending on student schedule and class meetings.

10. The optimum e-discussion group size is 8–12.

discussion); students felt more inclined to disagree and sometimes demonstrated emotion that came through clearly to the reader; and faculty had a written record of the discussion to review and use for comment in class.

The current wisdom among educators is to leave the e-discussions alone, monitoring but not participating in order to keep students interested and not waiting to hear what the teacher has to say. This may be wise, but it is important to comment occasionally to let students know that faculty are reading their comments and value their opinions. Usually, beginning students need more supervision because they perceive participation as more risky. Later in the curriculum, especially if the group has had stable membership, students are freer with their thoughts and less faculty supervision is needed. In addition, faculty sometimes need to move the discussion back on topic. In one forum, first-semester students discussed at length the quality of the film and actors. Faculty were not interested in film critique for this course but rather in the issues that had been identified through study questions. A gentle reminder sufficed that though their angst about the quality of the film was appreciated, faculty needed to focus on the content assigned.

As students progress through the curriculum, they become more sophisticated in their comments and responses but often their biases remain intact. The results are lively discussions, deeper insight, and new learning. In a discussion on gender diversity, some students responded to their viewing of the film *GI Jane.* A male medical student was very clear that though he believed women could serve in the military, they should not try to be accepted into elite units like the Navy SEALS. A female nursing student took him to task. He soon learned that she was a longtime member of the Army Reserves and had fought in Operation Desert Storm. Other students joined the conversation and tried to explain their positions. This discussion might never have happened in traditional medical or nursing school classrooms but was fundamental to understanding divergent views of men and women. Students and faculty further discussed how providers treat men and women as they practice nursing and medicine. Do providers have similar expectations of men's versus women's behavior when they are sick or injured? Do providers prescribe or administer pain medications differently?

With appropriate e-discussion training, all students can benefit from film-based discussion. The further along students are in their education, the more complex the issues and resulting conversations can be. Students can then relate to a wider range of clients and are less likely to see issues as black and white. Students tell us everything "turns to gray." This approach has allowed both personal and professional perspectives to be examined and has assisted students and faculty in learning more about each other, their professional approaches to practice, and their leadership capabilities.

FILM AS A TEACHING TOOL:
POSITIVES AND NEGATIVES OF THE STRATEGY

Many positive learning experiences have emerged from the use of popular film as a teaching strategy. Fully engaged in a world of relentless media, students generally find the use of contemporary film to be a relevant and acceptable learning methodology. They are comfortable with the film medium and can relate to the characters portrayed. Students find the strategy efficient in terms of time and energy. There is some appeal to a homework assignment that allows them to gather with friends and food to accomplish their assigned task. Though students must focus on delving into perspectives presented in the film guides, they enjoy the opportunity to relax in a comfortable setting, choosing their own time, place, and company to view the film.

Faculty members find benefits to using film to promote and facilitate learning about leadership. Used as a springboard for e-discussion, this strategy ensures that each person contributes thoughts and perceptions to the group. The e-discussions also allow them to think through their positions on leadership issues, resulting in deeper, more meaningful face-to-face discussions and debates in the classroom. Engagement in the film and e-discussion also prepares students for the realities of leadership in interdisciplinary and community settings, leading to improved performance on project teams. Last, faculty can monitor students' progress as they think critically about the leadership ideas and examples presented in the films, and can guide them by posing further, individualized questions to stimulate analysis in needed areas.

Although appropriate technology eases the burden for faculty members, using film can have drawbacks; for example, it may be time-consuming. Care must be taken to use high-quality films that exemplify the leadership topic under discussion. Films must be viewed, rated, and categorized according to their best use in the curriculum. Keeping up with the new films available, though enjoyable, can take a significant amount of faculty time. Films often use stereotypes to portray their characters. A significant amount of faculty energy is needed to help students recognize stereotypes and facilitate discussion about the dangers and pitfalls of stereotypical thinking, particularly when related to gender and professional or racial and ethnic images. Few films present models of female nurses as strong leaders; faculty must help students to deal not only with stereotypes about nursing but also with the lack of critical roles for nurses in contemporary film. Sometimes students believe that films are superficial and not a legitimate method for learning. Students must learn that they are not critiquing the actors or the plot, but the leadership strategies and ideas offered in the film.

OUTCOMES OF USING FILM FOR COMMUNITY LEADERSHIP EDUCATION

Four areas have served as focal points for selecting films. Those are health care delivery systems, nursing, diversity, and vision.

Health Care Delivery Systems

Nurses implement a multitude of leadership roles, all linked through a common goal of improving the health care delivery system for patients, families, communities, and providers. The chaos and constant change occurring in the delivery system impacts them at every level. In many settings, nursing interactions take place when patients and families are at a point of personal crisis. Leadership in clinical and community settings in the face of crisis is part of the nursing role.

In one film exercise, *Regarding Henry*, students explore what can happen as a patient and family in crisis enter and navigate the health care system. Their e-discussion focused on what they perceived as effective and ineffective leadership strategies used by health professionals in the film at various points in the patient's journey (Table 18.2). Regardless of discipline, students were struck by the impersonality of the health care system and the callousness toward patients, families, and some staff members. The film evoked great emotion and personal sharing among students. Their conclusion was that beyond a basic level of professional competence, the health care system is "about relationships among people." They determined that their role as leaders in the system was to facilitate healing relationships that offered the best chance of improved outcomes for the patient or community.

Nursing

The profession of nursing has changed dramatically over the past 100 years. Yet many health provider colleagues still respond to nurses as they did at the turn of the 20th century rather than as the highly educated and skilled leaders they are today. Therefore, exploring the discipline of nursing with interdisciplinary health science students allows other health professions to reframe their notions about nursing and nurses while at the same time allowing nursing students to clearly articulate their leadership role in the health care system.

	Health Care System
TABLE 18.2. Leadership and Film Curriculum: Health Care System	
Film	*Regarding Henry (Paramount Pictures)*
Questions	1. Think about Henry before and after his injury. What were his measures of success before and after the injury? How did he have to reinvent himself?
	2. What did you see and feel in the emergency department after Henry was injured? How did the health care providers interact with Henry's wife? Compare this with the rehabilitation hospital. What techniques were used to help Henry and his family? What differences in approach to the patient and family were used?
	3. Based on the lessons from this film, how might you work best with clients in a clinical setting? How might you work best with the community as client?
Critical themes and insights on leadership generated in e-discussion	• Seek congruence and honesty in professional and personal self
	• Treat others as courteously as you wish to be treated yourself
	• Communicate concern
	• Tailor interventions to needs of client
	• Use personal strengths to promote interaction with client and family
	• Maintain professional competency
	• Take a comprehensive view of patient and whole family
	• Do "fair share" of hard work as part of team or team leader

As much as films with strong nurse characters are difficult to find, the discussions that have evolved from these films have captured the essence of nursing for both ETSU medical and nursing students (Table 18.3). Concepts such as holistic focus on clients, caring, advocacy, and evidence-based care have all come through film discussions. Students easily identified stereotypes, in particular those related to attire and gender, and realized that sometimes those stereotypes were related to the setting of the film, such as World War I or a mental health facility in the 1960s. Although stereotypes of nurses in white uniforms and

	Nursing
TABLE 18.3. Leadership and Film Curriculum: Nursing	
Films	*The English Patient* (Miramax Films) *Girl, Interrupted* (Columbia Pictures) *In Love and War* (New Line Cinema) *MASH* (Twentieth Century Fox) *One Flew Over the Cuckoo's Nest* (Fantasy Films) *Pearl Harbor* (Touchstone Pictures) *Wit* (HBO Films)
Questions	Focus on the nurse or nurses in the film. What was their motivation for providing nursing care? What tasks did they perform? What was the most important thing they did in the film? What characteristics did the nurse or nurses in the film display? Were these characteristics stereotypical? Were they accurate depictions of nurses and nursing as you know it today? In a brief statement or two, define what nursing is and why it is or is not a pivotal profession in the U.S. health care system.
Critical themes and insights on leadership generated in e-discussion	• Nurses are involved in physical care of clients but more important, in the emotional care of clients. • Nurses are competent in both high-tech procedures and expressions of caring. • Nurses are strong advocates for their clients. • In spite of paternalistic systems, nurses challenge authority for their patients' health. • Nurses are not effective if they are either too personally involved or are too distant from clients emotionally. • Nurses are the backbone of the health care system. • Nurses meet a wide variety of client needs. • Nurses provide holistic care. • Nurses have many opportunities to serve. • Nurses are the human face of health care. • Nurses have the respect of the public.

caps were portrayed as love interests to physicians and patients, students found positive images that nursing faculty have attempted to transmit to every generation of nursing students since Nightingale. Nurses are efficient, compassionate, competent, independent, dedicated, and confident. Both nursing and medical students were able to refine definitions of nursing and develop an appreciation for the role of nurses. Interdisciplinary students developed an understanding of how they can practice together to benefit clients in rural communities by better understanding each other's history and current roles.

Diversity

Maximizing the strengths of diverse members of the health care team or community is a critical aspect of leadership. Health team and community members come together from many religious faiths, cultures, and experiential backgrounds. Males and females, various professional groups, and persons of diverse racial and ethnic heritage are among the groups that nurses will serve as leaders. The ability to foster consensus and common understanding among diverse people is essential to successful leadership.

In one film exercise, racial diversity and discrimination was the backdrop for discussion. The student group was multidisciplinary, male and female, and of differing religious faiths and ethnic backgrounds. Questions were designed to raise awareness of both overt and subtle discrimination and its effects on both leaders and group members (Table 18.4). The film discussion became a springboard for students to explore their own biases and feelings and design strategies to employ in leadership roles. Students reacted strongly to the discrimination portrayed in the films and engaged in increasing self- and other-awareness as they explored diversity in leaders and followers. Although the films were centered on racial discrimination, the students identified other forms of discrimination and stereotyping.

Vision

In order to lead, nurses must have a vision of where they are going and what they will accomplish when they arrive. The ability to develop a vision of what could be rather than accepting the status quo is a gift bestowed on few leaders; however, all leaders can listen for the voice of vision and organize others to make that vision a reality.

	Racial Diversity
TABLE 18.4. Leadership and Film Curriculum: Racial Diversity	
Films	*Amistad* (Dreamworks Pictures) *Barbershop* (Metro-Goldwyn-Mayer) *The Color Purple* (Warner Bros.) *Ghosts of Mississippi* (Castle Rock Entertainment) *The Long Walk Home* (Artisan) *Malcolm X* (Warner Bros.) *Mississippi Burning* (Metro-Goldwyn-Mayer) *Remember the Titans* (Walt Disney Pictures) *Rosewood* (Warner Bros.) *White Man's Burden* (Rysher Entertainment)
Questions	What is racism? What basic assumptions are necessary for racism or any other ism to survive? Why are "isms" so prevalent in human society? What responses to discrimination were seen in the film? Who assumed leadership roles in the films? What were the strategies portrayed in the film used by the leaders to overcome the racism depicted? How have you or could you use the strategies portrayed?
Critical themes and insights on leadership generated in e-discussion	• Adapt leadership style to situation. • Person with appropriate skill set should take leadership role based on situation and need. • Continually reaffirm commitment to cause or goal. • Deal with persons, not stereotypes. • Acknowledge concerns and fears honestly. • Communicate clearly. • Foster alliances toward common goals. • Promote mutual respect. • Know when to give up leadership role to allow growth of group.

Without vision, leaders and followers are unable to find a direction and reach a common goal.

There are many films in which actors have a vision and try to bring that vision to fruition—sometimes with great difficulty (Table 18.5).

TABLE 18.5. Leadership and Film Curriculum: Visioning	
	Visioning
Films	*The American President* (Castle Rock Entertainment/Universal Pictures) *Contact* (Warner Bros.) *Dave* (Warner Bros.) *Erin Brockovich* (Universal Pictures/Columbia Pictures) *Ghandi* (Columbia Pictures) *Hoosiers* (Hemdale Film Corporation) *Mr. Holland's Opus* (Hollywood Pictures) *Music of the Heart* (Miramax Films) *Pay It Forward* (Warner Bros.) *Songcatcher* (Rigas Entertainment)
Questions	Think about the challenge the main character is facing and the vision that character has for the future. How does that vision collide with the visions of others? With reality? In what ways are relationships important to vision formation? Vision implementation? What sacrifices must be made in order to sustain a vision? In today's world, post 9/11, what vision do you have for America and the world? What is your role in seeing that vision to reality?
Critical themes and insights on leadership generated in e-discussion	• Believe in self and believe in cause. • One person can create change and make a difference. • Nontraditional change agents are often underestimated by others. • Sometimes we have to sacrifice in the short term to achieve a long-term goal. • Persistence and commitment are essential to community change. • Relationships are foundational to turning a vision into reality. • It takes time to change. • Accept the challenge and assume success.

Beginning the process of turning a vision into reality requires the "hero" to believe in both self and the cause. In this film exercise, students explore the passion of vision and strategies that different people use to turn vision into reality and translate their insights to visionary leadership. They discover that developing and implementing a vision requires passion, perseverance, and supportive relationships. Though every person can make a difference, it is easier to make sacrifices to accomplish a goal in collaboration with supportive friends and colleagues.

SUMMARY

Teaching leadership through film is a strategy that can be used with nursing and interdisciplinary groups of learners. Students find the experience valuable, and the insights they display are highly appropriate to the study of leadership. Films must be selected carefully and faculty must guide e-discussion or classroom debate in a sensitive manner. The potential for personal and professional growth among students can be realized, and students leave the experience having benefited from its richness.

REFERENCES

Behringer, B., Bishop, W., Edwards, J., & Franks, R. (1999). A model for partnerships among communities, disciplines, and institutions. In D. Holmes and M. Osterweiss (Eds.), *Catalysts in interdisciplinary education: Innovation by academic health centers.* Washington, DC: Association of Academic Health Centers.

Edwards, J. (2001). Collaboration between medical and nursing education in community-based settings. In J. McCloskey-Doughterman and H. Grace (Eds.), *Current issues in nursing (6th ed.).* St. Louis, MO: Mosby.

Edwards, J., & Alley, N. (2002). Transition to community-based nursing curriculum: Processes and outcomes. *Journal of Professional Nursing, 18(2),* 78–84.

Edwards, J., & Smith, P. (1998). Impact of interdisciplinary education in underserved areas: Health professions collaboration in Tennessee. *Journal of Professional Nursing, 19(2),* 144–149.

Goleman, D. (1994). *Emotional intelligence.* New York: Bantam Books.

Goleman, D. (1998). *Working with emotional intelligence.* New York: Bantam Books.

Goleman, D., Boyatzis, R., & McKee, A. (2002). *Primal leadership. Realizing the power of emotional intelligence.* Boston, MA: Harvard Business School Press.

Greenleaf, R. K. (1970). *The servant as leader.* Indianapolis, IN: Robert K. Greenleaf Center for Servant-Leadership.

Katzenbach, J. R., & Smith, D. K. (2003). *The wisdom of teams.* New York: HarperBusiness Essentials.

LaFasto, F., & Larson, C. (2001). *When teams work best.* Thousand Oaks, CA: Sage.

Lencioni, P. (2002). *The five dysfunctions of a team.* San Francisco: Jossey-Bass

Mattessich, P. W., Monsey, B., & Roy, C. (1997). *Community building: What makes it work?* St. Paul, MN: Amherst Wilder Foundation.

Mattessich, P. W., Murray-Close, M., & Monsey, B. (2001). *Collaboration: What makes it work.* St. Paul, MN: Amherst Wilder Foundation.

Minkler, M. (2002). *Community organizing and community building for health.* New Brunswick, NJ: Rutgers University Press.

Myers, I. B. (1995). *Gifts differing. Understanding personality type.* Palo Alto, CA: Davies-Black.

Porter-O'Grady, T. (1994). Building partnerships in health care: Creating whole systems change. *Nursing & Health Care, 15(1),* 34–38.

Rainey, C. A., & Torres, C. B. (2001). *Mobile team challenge. Low ROPES course facilitator's manual.* Maryville, TN: MTC.

Richards, R. (Ed.) (1996). *Building partnerships: Educating health professionals for the communities they serve.* San Francisco: Jossey-Bass.

Sullivan, T. J. (1998). *Collaboration. A health care imperative.* New York: McGraw-Hill.

CHAPTER NINETEEN

Leadership Education for the Common Good: A Pilot Program

Nelda S. Godfrey

In *Leadership Reconsidered: Engaging Higher Education in Social Change,* the W. K. Kellogg Foundation challenges colleges and universities to "empower students by helping them develop those special talents and attitudes that will enable them to become effective social change agents" (Leadership Reconsidered, 1999, p. 2). In response to this challenge, the Department of Nursing at William Jewell College piloted the Pryor Leadership Studies Program in Nursing (PLSP-N) for all undergraduate nursing students. This chapter describes the PLSP-N initiative.

The Pryor Leadership Studies Program (PLSP) at William Jewell College has a 10-year history of effectively combining strong academic leadership theory with outstanding experiential learning opportunities. Students from all majors can apply to the four-semester certificate program. The more than 200 graduates of the PLSP program have helped to articulate the program's importance and potential impact on students' lives. Listed as one of the college's "distinctives," the PLSP is a premier program of the college whose mission is to "provide a superior liberal arts education in a distinctively Christian environment" (William Jewell College Catalog, 2003–2005).

Modeled after the highly selective Pryor Leadership Studies Program (PLSP) at William Jewell, this program is specifically designed to integrate nursing leadership research and theory within an experiential learning methodology. Principles of self-leadership, situational leadership, servant leadership, and shared leadership are studied in the second semester of the first five semesters of the nursing program, and then reinforced and applied in the remaining three semesters (Figure 19.1).

Nursing students participate as a cohort in classroom and leadership learning lab activities, yielding opportunities to use team building and leadership skills over a period of time, thereby mirroring the nursing work environment. Each student participates in a vocational internship, a service leadership project, and a leadership legacy initiative. In addition, each student also develops a personal mission statement and a leadership growth plan.

A variety of experiential learning experiences occur on and off campus. PLSP-N graduate outcomes include a strong theoretical base in leadership and healthcare, presentation skills and the ability to articulate a position, flexibility and the capacity to shift leadership styles as needed, an awareness of diversity issues and the capability of dealing with ambiguity, and a values framework that includes concern for the common good.

GROUNDED IN THEORY

The PLSP-N Leadership for the Common Good program is based on the theoretical foundations of *experiential learning* (Dewey, 1938/1997; Kolb, 1984) and *servant leadership* (Gardner, 1990). Experiential learning ensures that students are not only thinking about something, but also doing something. Claxton and Murrell (1987) describe the four parts of the experiential learning cycle as (a) concrete experiences, (b) reflective observations, (c) generalizations about experiences, and (d) active experimentations. Each of these areas is then associated with an area of development, that is, affective, perceptual, symbolic, and behavioral, leading the student to learn best when learning is grounded in experience (Claxton & Murrell, 1987).

The PLSP-N takes the experiential learning theory a step further in applying Burton's Outward Bound model of "What? So what? Now what?" in two 3-day Outward Bound Alternative retreats. Classroom and learning lab experiences precede the retreats, providing theory and practice before more concentrated application.

FIGURE 19.1. Leadership for the common good.

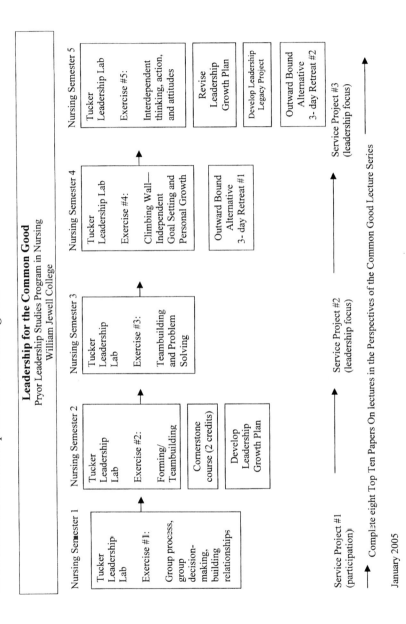

Leadership for the Common Good
Pryor Leadership Studies Program in Nursing
William Jewell College

Nursing Semester 1	Nursing Semester 2	Nursing Semester 3	Nursing Semester 4	Nursing Semester 5
Tucker Leadership Lab	Tucker Leadership Lab	Tucker Leadership Lab	Tucker Leadership Lab	Tucker Leadership Lab
Exercise #1: Group process, group decision-making, building relationships	Exercise #2: Forming/Teambuilding	Exercise #3: Teambuilding and Problem Solving	Exercise #4: Climbing Wall—Independent Goal Setting and Personal Growth	Exercise #5: Interdependent thinking, action, and attitudes
	Cornerstone course (2 credits)			Revise Leadership Growth Plan
	Develop Leadership Growth Plan		Outward Bound Alternative 3- day Retreat #1	Develop Leadership Legacy Project
				Outward Bound Alternative 3- day Retreat #2

Service Project #1 (participation)

Service Project #2 (leadership focus)

Service Project #3 (leadership focus)

Complete eight Top Ten Papers On lectures in the Perspectives of the Common Good Lecture Series

January 2005

209

The theoretical notion of servant leadership has particular application in the Pryor Leadership Studies Program in Nursing at William
Jewell College. A historical Baptist institution, William Jewell College
professes to follow the ideals of Christ as it provides a superior liberal arts education in service to the community and the world. Serving
others *for the good of others* is inherent within the structure and function
of the educational institution.

John Gardner (Gardner, 1990), a central figure in leadership literature and author of *On Leadership*, speaks of the common good:

> As long as we accept the idea of pluralism (and we cannot abandon it),
> we let ourselves in for the consequences. . . . But a society in which plu-
> ralism is not undergirded by some shared values and held together by
> some measure of mutual trust simply cannot survive. *Pluralism that*
> *reflects no commitment whatever to the common good is pluralism gone*
> *berserk.* (author's italics) (Gardner, 1990, p. 97)

Gardner then operationalizes the pursuit of the common good as a
central function of leadership:

> A primary task of our dispersed leadership is to achieve a workable
> level of unity within the society. It is well to specify a workable level
> because the last thing we want is unqualified or oppressive unity. Our
> freedom, our pluralism, our dispersion of power all invite healthy con-
> flict as various groups and individuals pursue their diverse purposes.
> The reconciling of such divergent purposes is one of the tasks of the
> leader. (Gardner, 1990, p. 97)

The single, simply stated program goal of the PLSP-N is *to develop stu-*
dents as leaders. It should be noted, however, that this occurs within the
context of the four S's—self-leadership, situational leadership, servant
leadership, and shared leadership. In the PLSP-N, the fundamental
reason one develops as a leader is to serve others more ably.
Experiential learning and servant leadership form the theoretical
foundations for success in the PLSP-N.

STRUCTURE OF THE PROGRAM

The notion of the common good is infused throughout the curriculum
of the five-semester Pryor Leadership Studies Program in Nursing.

Using the college's Tucker Leadership Lab, beginning nursing students participate in a 4-hour low elements experiential learning exercise during the first week of the nursing program. In this activity they learn to recognize group process and practice group decision making, and begin to build relationships. Leadership as one of seven curricular concepts in the Department of Nursing curricular model is also discussed in the didactic setting.

In the second semester, students are introduced to leadership theory and application in a 2-credit-hour Leadership Studies Cornerstone course. This class is designed to introduce students to leadership theory and engage them in a variety of self-discovery exercises, and provides them with individual and collaborative leadership experiences. A variety of teaching methodologies are used, including role-playing, small group work, case studies, student presentations, experiential learning in the Tucker Leadership Lab, and a service activity such as working on a Habitat for Humanity house for a Saturday. A final and important component of the course is the development of the student's leadership growth plan. An example of a student's mission statement section of the leadership growth plan follows:

> My Mission Statement: I will always take time for my family and then for myself. I will always remember that it is not if you succeed or fail but what you learn along the way. I will remember that life is precious and that it is fragile and should never be taken for granted. I will always look to God when I'm troubled as well as the good times, too, and remember that if it were not for him then I would not be here. I will always do what I think is right even if it goes against the tide. I will always remember everyone's life that I touch and keep the experience in my heart always. I will strive to be the best nurse I can be and to never stop learning, for when that happens I need to stop being a nurse. I will always love my family no matter how much we argue. I know that they will always be there for me in good times and bad. I will always remember when life becomes troubled to look at a child and see things the way they are seen. And finally, I will remember life is a dance and to always keep dancing and not sit it out.

Students in the third semester of the PLSP-N program participate in a daylong team building and relationship building exercise in the outdoor Tucker Leadership Lab. They also complete a leadership based service project of their choosing, constructing a proposal containing goals and objectives prior to the event, and a formalized written evaluation after the experience. Finally, students progress in their efforts to complete eight "Top Ten" papers, assignments where students summarize in narrative form the top ten points made by a speaker in the Perspectives of the Common Good lecture series at William Jewell College. The PLSP-N requires that eight papers be completed during the five-semester program.

Fourth semester PLSP-N students complete another leadership service opportunity of their choosing, submitting written proposals and evaluations as before. The Tucker Leadership Lab experience this semester includes the climbing wall in a challenge-by-choice situation, highlighting independent goal setting and personal growth. It is during this semester that students complete the first of two 3-day Outward Bound Alternative retreats.

In the final semester, students take a 4-credit leadership course within the nursing curriculum. As part of the course requirements, students revisit their Leadership Growth Plan and revise it accordingly, and they develop a Leadership Legacy project that they present in PowerPoint and paper formats. The purpose of the Leadership Legacy project is to instill the notion that leaving a leadership legacy is a lifelong responsibility, and that leadership growth is a lifelong process. The Tucker Leadership Lab Cardinal Crossing is a high-ropes activity designed to foster interdependent thinking, action, and attitudes, and it provides a capstone experiential learning activity. Students also complete the final 3-day retreat during this semester and participate in an intensive final debrief event prior to graduation. The debriefing gives students an opportunity to reflect on their expanded notion of leadership that was shaped by the previous five semesters, and to plan ways to incorporate these leadership skills in their new work environments.

BENEFITS OF THE PLSP-N PROGRAM

Though the first graduates of the PLSP-N have only been in the workforce less than a year as of this writing, a number of benefits have already accrued. The first cohort was a voluntary one, with 47% ($N = 15$; 7 participated) of the graduating class participating. All PLSP-N students successfully passed NCLEX-RN on the first attempt. All have employment in the unit and institution of their choice. In addition, two of the students were chosen to present their research at national or international conferences during their senior year, while a third participated in a statewide leadership conference for nursing students.

Faculty from both the Leadership Studies Program and the Department of Nursing also identified advantages to the PLSP-N. They cite the opportunity to get to know the students on a different level and the excitement of seeing a sense of lifelong learning develop as two of the most important outcomes of the experience. Disadvantages associated with the program include a heightened level of attention to detail on the part of assigned faculty and the need to deal with the positive and negative results of change. Despite difficulties, however, faculty members involved in the PLSP-N have embraced the concept and its application in the program and are enthusiastic about its continuation.

OUTCOMES

The PLSP-N would not be possible without the interest and commitment of William Jewell College. Individual talent development is a central institutional value and as such the PLSP-N clearly reflects the college ethos. Fortunately, the PLSP-N's viability from an institutional standpoint is stable for the foreseeable future.

A number of expected outcomes have occurred during the program's short 2-year history. First, students move more deliberately from a dependent to an interdependent mode of functioning with their peers. Second, there is a greater sense of "giving back" at all levels within the program. Third, there seems to be a greater sense of emotional toughness, or resilience, among the students who embrace what the PLSP-N has to offer. They convey a strong sense of being able to handle whatever comes along when interacting with peers and teachers, and as a result function as effective problem solvers in a variety of settings. These outcomes are desired in the workplace, and one hopes, positive results will continue in the future.

From an administrative standpoint, students are much more skilled in problem solving and stress management as a result of the 2-credit cornerstone course in the junior year. "Naming the problem" in the work they do in the course has made a substantial difference in helping students mobilize and become more proactive. Students at this level in the curriculum determined that a mentor program was needed for incoming nursing students. As a result of the leadership course, students developed and implemented the mentoring program because they saw the need. This is especially remarkable because it was not part of a class assignment or extra credit. Their ability to see a need and meet it yielded a 7.2% first-semester attrition rate for the class they mentored, compared with a mean 5-year first semester attrition rate of 23%. Their efforts made a difference in the incoming students' adjustment to the William Jewell nursing program.

Perhaps, though, the most important commentary on the outcomes of the program comes from students. One student said, "It helped me realize my own strengths and weaknesses and gave me a 'safe haven' of people that understood where I was at and was able to be supportive." Another responded about the Leadership Cornerstone class:

> Yes, this course fit well within the curriculum. Although this is probably the hardest semester I have had so far in terms of workload and mental stress, that is probably exactly the reason why this was a good time for the class. The leadership and self-improvement activities of the class helped immensely.

A third student remarked, "It was beneficial because I got to know my class better and developed better support."

CONCLUSION

The Pryor Leadership Studies Program in Nursing at William Jewell College was designed to use experiential learning and servant leadership as the foundation for a comprehensive, multi-semester leadership program for undergraduate nursing students. Though the program is still new, both students and faculty have identified a number of positive outcomes. A focus on self-leadership, situational leadership, servant leadership, and shared leadership provided the building blocks for instilling the notion of leadership as a lifelong pursuit.

REFERENCES

Claxton, C., & Murrell, P. (1987). *Learning styles: Implications for improving educational practices.* Washington, DC: George Washington University Graduate School of Higher Education.

Dewey, J. (1938/1997). *Experience and education.* New York: Simon and Schuster.

Gardner, J. (1990). *On leadership.* New York: The Free Press.

Kolb, D. A. (1984). *Experiential learning: Experience as the source of learning and development.* Englewood Cliffs, NJ: Prentice-Hall.

Leadership reconsidered: Engaging higher education in social change. (1999). Battle Creek, MI: W. K. Kellogg Foundation.

William Jewell College Catalog (2003–2005). Liberty, MO: Author.

ACKNOWLEDGMENT

The author would like to thank Sylvia Nadler and Kevin Shaffstall for their assistance in preparing this manuscript.

PART THREE

Leadership Education
in the Clinical Setting

CHAPTER TWENTY

Practice-Oriented Leadership Education

Jane Aroian
Jacqueline A. Dienemann

In light of the expanding role of professional nurses in health care settings today, it is imperative that they acquire the leadership skills necessary to influence positively this dynamic and uncertain environment. These skills are vital for them to make an impact, considering the powerful relationship between leadership strength and influence. One characteristic of effective leaders is attainment of formal preparation and educational credentials in addition to work and life experience. The American Association of Colleges of Nursing (AACN) and the Council on Graduate Education for Administration in Nursing (AACN, 1996; Dienemann & Aroian, 1995) operationally define the professional nurse as one who has been prepared with a minimum of a baccalaureate or higher degree in nursing. When this definition is applied to the workplace, it sets a baccalaureate in nursing as the minimum for nursing management and specialized clinical positions across the continuum of health care. For RNs without a baccalaureate degree, access to attaining this credential has been increased through distance learning, outreach programs, and tuition support by many health care employers. This chapter describes practice-oriented education, an innovative approach to developing leadership skills in practicing nurses.

LEADERSHIP DEFINED

Leadership in healthcare is defined by the World Health Organization (WHO) as moving people, services, and systems toward the health for all strategy. The purpose and skills of leaders are defined as follows:

> Persons in posts of leadership should have a comprehensive grasp of the processes involved in developing and implementing the Global Strategy of Health for All. They should have a concern for social justice, ability to communicate, courage to take risks and make bold decisions, and faith in people's ability to contribute to the improvement of their own health. They should be in a position to motivate others and direct the national health development effort toward health for all. (WHO, 1998, p. 4)

Leaders include those who demonstrate these behaviors regardless of formal position in an organization. In fact, leadership is needed by nurses in all types of positions to improve health care systems and the outcomes of patient care at the institutional, community, state, national, and international levels. Nurse leaders working in different settings and positions utilize a different mix of leadership skills to fit their context, but capability is needed in all skills (Henry, Lorensen & Hirschfeld, 1992).

Leadership differs from management in that it may be applied separately from positional authority in an organization. Each nurse may be an emergent leader on issues affecting professional practice and patient care. Nurses in administrative positions are expected to also be leaders and use their positional authority to shape health care systems to improve health for all. Management functions for nurse administrators throughout the globe include: determining organizational structure, formulating policy, planning for resources and programs, setting standards for quality improvement, administering resources, ensuring information flow, budgeting and accounting, administration and supervision of personnel, training and developing others, monitoring work processes and evaluating outcomes, and coordinating networks to secure resources to accomplish goals (Henry, 1996).

Practice-oriented education (POE) is an educational approach that energizes the connections among workplace experience, professional education, and the liberal arts and sciences. For the last two years, *U.S. News & World Report* (2003) has recognized Northeastern University as the top innovator in POE programs that combine higher education with real world experiences. This chapter addresses how Northeastern University prepares nurse and health care administrators for advanced practice using a POE environment.

POE teaches leadership development with integrated, progressive learning intermixing experiential life-based and formal classroom-based knowledge and skills. Using the academic setting as a crucible, faculty and preceptors model, facilitate, and guide the learning of leadership. The Leadership Education Model (Lemire, 2003) (described in Part I) designed specifically for nursing emphasizes that leadership is not encapsulated in one academic course, but that learning should be integrated throughout the curriculum in order to build leadership capacity and comfort in enacting leadership roles.

Northeastern University uses POE for graduate education in nursing in the Master's program in Nursing Administration (MSN) and the joint Master's program in Nursing and Business Administration (MS/MBA). Students in the joint program take additional courses in business. In both programs students are challenged to synthesize knowledge derived from theories, research evidence, and experience regarding nursing and health administration. The primary goal is for students to learn to use their clinical knowledge and administrative skills to provide leadership through resolving problems in innovative ways while developing others.

The program is front-loaded with theory courses completed before the yearlong practicum or integrated in an individualized program plan. Students choose to focus their practicum in administration of community health or health care organizations. The required and elective courses for the administration specialization are offered through the general rubrics of (a) community health, health policy, and epidemiology; (b) health care organizations and professional role; (c) finance and budgeting; (d) human resources and operations management and; (e) advanced nursing practice.

Students are exposed to leadership theories throughout their curriculum with more in depth study in one course. Theories are examined for their ability to explain behavior seen in the workplace. No grand theory is accepted as comprehensive. The history of leadership theory is traced by describing what has prevailed through the tests of time, using varied social perspectives and research. Students move from the great man model, to contingency, to situational leadership, to transitional leadership, to transformational leadership and finally, administrative conservatorship (Haller, 1998).

MANAGER/LEADER AS DEVELOPER MODEL

The framework for the program is the manager/leader as developer model (Bradford & Cohen, 1984/1997). The strength of the model lies in its research base and behavioral orientation. This administrative conservatorship model uses concepts further developed by Senge (1990). The emphasis is on applying systems thinking as a leader in a complex, constantly changing interconnected environment. Leaders have two primary functions: to eradicate purposely those structures and processes that produce disconnection and fragmentation in health services and to coach others to view themselves as leaders in constant interaction with new services, new competitors, new partners, new regulations, and new technology (Kreuger-Wilson & Porter-O'Grady, 1999). This model views uncertainty as "normal" and states that a key leadership function is to choose strategies that effectively guide decision making during times of uncertainty rather than those that seek to eliminate it.

The model has seven major concepts that are the focus of practicum seminars: *overarching goals/vision*, or the ability to set common goals among a group in an organization; *staff development*, the recognition of strengths and limitations in individual practitioners and the skill to stimulate their growth; *team development*, the matching of talents of individuals who make up a group and work toward common goals; *group decision making*, empowering a group to accountably make decisions; *staff autonomy*, respect for individual practice and the professional need to retain a defined scope of responsibility; *two-way communication*, listening to what is said and what you say in an effort to understand the views of others; and *external influence*, exploring the outside environment and being alert to and striving to influence events outside of the health care setting. For a more comprehensive explanation of this model as used in nursing administration education, see Aroian, Meservey, and Gilbert-Crockett (1996a, 1996b).

LEARNING TO UTILIZE THE
MANAGER/LEADER AS DEVELOPER MODEL

Students come to the practicum knowing the theory. They are assigned to keep a journal about what transpires at their practicum. This is the basis for seminar discussions that are focused on identifying and analyzing applications of the major theoretical concepts in the model. For example, a student recently identified the concept of "over-arching goal/vision" as a focus for analyzing the activities surrounding preparing for a magnet hospital application at their practicum site. The application had grown out of a vision and value statement created by the nursing administrators and staff to articulate staff nurse work in their institution. As part of the student's orientation to the agency she viewed a video of the chief nurse executive (CNE). The CNE began by welcoming the new staff member to the institution and then spoke of how we, the nurses, created a vision that articulated our belief in the importance of nursing work. Next she shared that they were "on a journey toward magnet hospital certification." She gave the examples, always emphasizing how the nurses created and developed the center for professional development, a professional practice model, a collaborating governance structure, and a clinical recognition program. In the student's analysis of the video, she connected the concept of "overarching goal/vision" to the vision and value statement of this agency. She discussed her insights and the magnet recognition program in seminar and answered her fellow students' many questions. Over the year, she continued to analyze how the value and vision statement did and did not guide the magnet journey and the relationships of practicum experiences with the other six major concepts of the model.

ETHICS TRAINING

The program utilizes the World Health Organization's (WHO) definition of leadership that emphasizes ethical behavior, rooted in an abiding concern for the welfare of those who receive care, as well as the moral shape of society (WHO, 1998). We link that to nursing ethics and a distinguished history of concern encompassing both the individual and the context of care. This is explicated through the nursing code of ethics (American Nurses Association [ANA], 2001) and its interpretive statements, nursing theories and postmodern ethical theories, such as the ethic of care and feminist ethics. These resources are introduced in the Health System and Role course taken early in the program. We are fortunate to have a faculty member teaching that course who is an ethicist, an advanced practice nurse, and a supervisor of a neighborhood health center.

In her introductory remarks she invites each student to share their responses to questions on the pre-course ethics assessment where they are to specify two areas of ethical concern in nursing practice and to summarize the ethical concerns that nurse leaders/managers confront. She writes the students' responses on the blackboard and engages them in a lively discussion relating the nursing code to their responses. She also reviews changes in the code and their theory base. She notes that the code now explicitly expands its definition of patient to individual, family group, or community and that the code also now addresses duties of the nurse to self.

Students discuss how the advocate role includes being an authentic moral agent and how that is a duty to self. This is grounded in reflections on instances of treating others with and without respect within the health care system, and reflections on other instances of patients having insufficient knowledge to make informed treatment choices. Students discuss what they could have done to prevent these situations. A third area of reflective discussion is the moral duty to participate in shaping the profession and health policy and the collective participation of professional organizations in this process.

In the practicum courses, students use the Standards of Professional Performance from the ANA *Scope and Standards of Nursing Administration Practice* (2003) to guide the analysis in their log each time they encounter an ethical decision-making situation during a practicum day. At the next seminar, students lead a discussion about the situation. If students are not bringing ethical dilemmas to the seminar, the faculty probe the group to review their experiences. They emphasize the importance of leaders making a constant effort to reflect and act with a well-grounded foundation in ethics in order to be successful change agents. Moreover, using this practice they will become well prepared to address any serious challenge to ethical practice faced by nurses today (Daly, 2002).

HONING POLITICAL AND EMOTIONAL INTELLIGENCE SKILLS

In POE courses, students are continuously asked to hone their political and emotional intelligence skills (Goleman, 2000). In doing so, nurses are taught how to take creative risks within organizations to remove traditional, legal, and regulatory barriers that disallow their full scope of practice in the best interest of consumers. They also learn the importance of professional organizations for political action to advance the profession. Professional practice includes educating the public and policy makers about the scope of practice of registered nurses and advanced practice nurses, nurse's extensive training and competencies, and the relationship between registered nursing care and positive outcomes for patients. It also includes leadership to advance the shift of costs and services from acute, remedial care, and cure to prevention, early detection, and disease and disability management (AACN, 1999).

Students' theory base for learning their political and emotional skills can be found primarily within courses in epidemiology, community health, health policy, health law, human resources, and operations management. An example of learning to apply political and emotional intelligence arose out of the sudden announcement of a major reorganization of the health department when a student was completing her practicum there. Staff had 4 days to relocate to different offices and locations as part of a reorganization to facilitate interdisciplinary planning and streamline management during a time of budget cuts. Most staff members were disgruntled by this announcement; however, the student's preceptor saw it as an opportunity to advocate for continuous funding for priority programs. She pointed out that reorganization would destabilize relationships and could open up opportunities to push for positive changes for patients.

The student wrote in her log and shared in seminar her subsequent assignment to review community health centers. She was to compare scope of services, billing revenues, costs, and health outcomes for the target area for each community health center. Her preceptor helped her identify sources and access data. The preceptor planned to use the information to advocate for community health centers and possible realignment of resources to target areas of greatest need.

The student related in seminar that the emotional intelligence of her preceptor taught her how to remain calm and see the value of quickly arming oneself with data. She learned how the reorganization could be used as an opportunity to influence decisions on priorities when difficult resource allocation decisions were being made. The student became an advocate herself, by requesting her peers and faculty to bombard the governor's administration and state legislature with letters and e-mails about local priority programs and health care initiatives for patients, families, and the communities.

THE PRACTICUM EXPERIENCE

Students and faculty begin planning for the practicum at least six months prior to actual placement. The practicum is a major commitment of time and involvement by student and preceptor and is the equivalent of eight hours per week for one academic year. The first step in preparation is a meeting between the clinical placement director and the student to review the student's work experience, history, and career goals. A three-way meeting follows, where the faculty member leads brainstorming to determine possible placements. Fortunately, Boston is a center of multiple major health systems and community health organizations with outstanding nurse leaders. A tentative choice and one option is identified, and the clinical placement director forwards a request to a potential preceptor along with the student's résumé and summary of career goals. The nurse leader then either declines or agrees and suggests possible cost containment or process improvement projects. The student then assesses possible fit and either sends a letter declining or accepting, with a copy to the placement coordinator. Acceptance letters are written as if the student were applying for a project position and explaining why he or she should be chosen. After accepting, the student schedules a formal interview with the nurse leader. As in an employment interview for an advanced practice position, the student and nurse leader discuss the student's qualifications, the project needs, and course objectives. Afterward, if the leader offers the student placement, a formal contract is initiated between the university and health care setting, clarifying expectations and work commitment for both the student and preceptor. Students and nursing administration faculty are informed when the contract is signed.

One major shift in nursing education is the change in emphasis from teaching processes to student outcomes (McBride, 1999; Pesut & Herman, 1999). For the practicum, a portfolio is used to demonstrate learning outcomes. All course documents are included in the portfolio. The first entry is the student's letter, followed by individual and course practicum objectives and a planned timeline for the project. Thereafter, students add weekly logs of time spent at the practicum, a graded written critique of an article on the weekly topic in the syllabus, and a weekly situation analysis.

Throughout their experiences students are encouraged to have discussions with their preceptors at the end of each day about the dynamics they see and how the preceptor learned their skills. The weekly analysis provides an opportunity to apply one key concept from the manager/leader as developer model. The analysis includes responses to the following questions: What was the leader doing? Why? What was accomplished? How does this reflect the concept? How did the leader learn to handle this situation? How does this relate to my nursing administration practice? What are my learning needs relative to this situation?

The practicum project must focus either on cost containment or quality improvement. The goal of the first semester is validating the need for the project with a needs assessment that results in evidence-based, desired project outcomes (Dienemann, 1998). At the end of the first month, students lead meetings with the faculty supervisor and preceptor to report on their progress and summarize the meeting in their logs. At the end of the semester, students write self-evaluations using objectives and the timeline for reference, sharing it with the preceptor; both sign the document. Students then meet with faculty supervisors to discuss their performance.

The second semester portfolio differs in that student's weekly situational analysis may utilize the manager/leader as developer model, novice to expert model (Benner, 1999), or The Standards of Practice and Professional Performance for Nurse Administrators (ANA, 2003). The project is completed and outcomes evaluated. This evaluation and an updated résumé are included in the portfolio. Each week students participate in seminars that center on discussions of the week's situation analyses and the week's topic in the syllabus. Time is allotted for students to provide each other with written feedback.

SUMMARY

Increasingly, nurses are viewing nursing as a career and coming to value lifelong learning and periodic formal academic preparation for new roles. Simultaneously, new and nontraditional positions are developing that utilize nurse's professional values, experiences working in collaborative, multidisciplinary teams, training in critical thinking, and broad knowledge of the health care system (McBride, 1999). Nurses are emerging as leaders throughout the health care industry, demonstrating how nursing prepares people for many career paths.

POE is a valuable approach to use in all levels of nurse education. It is uniquely suited for work with those returning for higher degrees to capture the experiential learning that occurs at work. The intent of facilitating practice oriented leadership development is to increase the ability of nursing graduates to demonstrate systems thinking in daily practice to improve both nurse and patient outcomes.

REFERENCES

American Association of Colleges of Nursing. (1999). *A vision of baccalaureate and graduate nursing education: The next decade.* Washington, DC: Author

American Association of Colleges of Nursing. (1996). *The essentials of master's education for advanced practice nurses.* Washington, DC: Author.

American Nurses Association. (2003). *Scope and standards of nursing administration.* Washington, DC: Author.

American Nurses Association. (2001). *Code of ethics and interpretive statements.* Washington, DC: Author.

Aroian, J., Meservey, P., & Gilbert-Crockett, J. (1996a). Developing nurse leaders for today and tomorrow: P. 1 Foundations of leadership practice. *Journal of Nursing Administration, 26*(9), 18–26.

Aroian, J., Meservey, P., & Gilbert-Crockett J. (1996b). Developing nurse leaders for today and tomorrow: P. 2 Implementing a model of leadership. *Journal of Nursing Administration 26*(10), 29–33.

Benner, P.E., et al. (1999). *Clinical wisdom and interventions in critical care: A thinking-in-action approach.* Philadelphia: Saunders.

Bradford, D., & Cohen, A. (1997). *Managing for excellence (Rev. ed.).* New York: Wiley. (Original work published 1984).

Daly, B. (2002). Moving forward: A new code of ethics. *Nursing Outlook, 50* (3) 97–99.

Dienemann, J. (1998). Assessing organizations. In J. Dienemann (Ed.), *Nursing administration: Managing patient care* (2nd ed., pp. 267–271). Stamford, CT: Appleton and Lange, p. 267–271.

Dienemann, J., & Aroian, J. (1995). *Essentials of baccalaureate nursing education for nursing leadership and management and master's nursing education for nursing administration advance practice.* Unpublished document. Council of Graduate Education for Administration in Nursing.

Goleman, D. (2000). Leadership that gets results. *Harvard Business Review, 78*(2) 78–90.

Haller, K. (1998) Leadership and management in patient care delivery systems. In J. Dienemann (Ed.), *Nursing administration: Managing patient care* (2nd ed., pp. 405–416). Stamford, CT: Appleton and Lange.

Henry, B. (1996). Conference summary. *Themes issues and challenges. Reflection of needed competencies for executive nursing leadership in major teaching hospitals and academic health centers* (pp. 36–38). Boston: Harvard Nursing Research Institute.

Henry, B., Lorensen, M., & Hirschfeld, M. (1992). *Management of health services by nurses.* Geneva, Switzerland: World Health Organization.

Krueger-Wilson, C., & Porter-O'Grady, T. (1999). *Leading the revolution in health care: Advancing systems igniting performance* (2nd ed.). Gaithersburg, MD: Aspen.

Lemire, J. A. (2003). Preparing nurse leaders: A leadership education model. *Nursing Leadership Forum, 7*(2), 47–52.

McBride, A. (1999). Breakthroughs in nursing education: Looking back looking forward. *Nursing Outlook, 47*(3), 114–119.

Pesut, D., & Herman, J. (1999). *The art and science of critical and creative thinking.* New York: Delmar.

Senge, P. (1990). *The fifth discipline: The art and practice of learning organizations* (pp. 408–409). NY: Doubleday.

US & News & World Report (2003). Programs that really work. *America's best colleges,* Author.

World Health Organization (1998). *Health for all.* p. 4 Accessed from http://www.who.int/wha-1998/pdf98/ea5.pdf.

CHAPTER TWENTY-ONE

Using Shift Coordinators to Teach Leadership Skills Needed for the NCLEX-RN

Julia W. Aucoin
Susan Letvak

Rapidly changing health care environments, high patient acuity levels, and increasing use of nonprofessional staff have all placed increased leadership demands on new graduate nurses, especially baccalaureate prepared nurses. This chapter describes a clinical strategy for teaching leadership skills to senior year undergraduate students at the University of North Carolina at Greensboro.

Leadership is an essential component of baccalaureate nursing education. Nursing education has relied heavily on didactic and often passive approaches to learning (Demarco, Howard, & Lynch, 2002), but today innovative strategies are needed to enhance leadership training for our students. Graduates need to be able to teach, delegate, and supervise other staff with safety and competence. Strong leadership skills are necessary to achieve these core competencies. In addition, the National Council Licensure Examination for Registered Nurses (NCLEX-RN) places emphasis on priority setting, delegation, and decision making, which are all leadership skills. In the 2004 NCLEX-RN test plan, 13% to 19% of the questions are on management of patient care, an increase of 6% over the 2001 test plan. Of the 18 knowledge categories addressed by the NCLEX-RN, several encompass traditional concepts that are considered essential for leadership: principles of teaching and learning, quality management, communication skills, clinical decision making/critical thinking, ethics, scope of practice/professional roles, and care management/leadership. Specifically, the NCLEX-RN includes the following care management/leadership activities based on the 2002 Practice Analysis:

1. Make appropriate referrals to community resources.
2. Provide and receive report on assigned clients.
3. Collaborate with other disciplines in providing client care (physician, RT, PT, radiology, dietary, lab, etc.).
4. Supervise care provided by others, for example, LPN/VN, assistive personnel, and other RNs.
5. Initiate and update multidisciplinary care plan, care map, clinical pathway used to guide or evaluate client care.
6. Maintain continuity of care among care agencies.
7. Serve as a resource person to other staff.
8. Participate in educating staff. (Smith & Crawford, 2003, pp. 48–57).

Additional activities based on the Practice Analysis are also important to the nurse's leadership role and are linked to the knowledge categories listed above. They are as follows:

1. Check/verify accuracy of order.
2. Participate in maintaining the institution's security plan (i.e., newborn nursery security, bomb threats, fire emergency plan, etc.).
3. Participate in the performance improvement/quality assurance process (formally collect data or participate on a team).
4. Receive and transcribe health care provider orders.
5. Report unsafe practice of a health care provider.
6. Report error/event/occurrence per protocol (i.e., medication error, client fall, etc.)

A didactic course on nursing leadership and management is offered during the first semester of the senior year at the University of North Carolina at Greensboro, along with concurrent nursing courses in community health and gerontology. Students are required to demonstrate principles of leadership and management in coordinating groups of individuals, peers, and staff during an integrated 12 hour/week clinical. They work with charge nurses on a variety of clinical units over the course of the semester, which offers for students new and exciting opportunities.

THE EXPERIENCE

The idea for the experience came while observing charge nurses in a community hospital, during a student clinical experience. These nurses rarely took patient assignments, although they ended up spending their time in patient care, not on paperwork or at the desk where one would expect to see the charge nurse. They made rounds on all patients, participated in assessments, contributed to discharge planning, and functioned as resources for problem solving. Their decision-making skills were evident as they assigned patients to beds and staff to patients and organized other work tasks.

The students were then asked about their previous opportunities to work with a charge nurse. Because these were final semester senior students, they were expected to say that they had already had sufficient team leader or charge nurse opportunities. The students reported that it depended on the setting in which they had done their integrated clinical work and the comfort level of the instructor as to whether they had led a team, much less worked with the charge nurse. Thus it was clear that we needed a more effective method of providing leadership experiences.

The next step was to discuss the role of the charge nurse with the nurse manager and the idea of having students work directly with charge nurses. The nurse manager was excited about the opportunity to shape future graduates' leadership experiences and helped to facilitate a meeting with other nurse managers. The purpose was to develop a plan to carve out a portion of the integrated leadership, community, and gerontology clinical as a leadership experience with the charge nurses of this community hospital. The charge nurse within the hospital was called the "shift coordinator" and was clearly a patient care leader with responsibility to keep patient care safe and flowing.

Listed here are the most heavily weighted items from the facility's job description for the shift coordinator:

1. Creates positive work environment among coworkers by exhibiting leadership, and confidence in the shift coordinator role
2. Recognizes and effectively handles unit issues and patient concerns as they arise and renders appropriate actions
3. Sets a positive attitude and plans how to accomplish the work with the given amount of staff; talks frequently to team members to provide positive support and to redirect activities as needed
4. Serves as a clinical resource person for staff, role models advanced clinical skills, and practices standards of care
5. Coordinates activities safely and effectively in high acuity, emergency, and disaster situations
6. Collaborates with the supervisor/manager on possible solutions for attaining needed staff. Informs supervisor/manager of staffing solutions.

Additional standards of performance address bed/procedure assignment, communication, workflow, staffing, and clinical and leadership skills.

The nursing management team agreed to a rotation for eight students, one in each of eight locations in the hospital, with one clinical instructor making rounds among all students and locations. An introductory letter was drafted from the hospital's education department and course faculty to introduce the shift coordinators to the expectations for the experience. The units identified for participation were critical care, telemetry, oncology, surgical, medical, and PACU. Additionally, the nursing supervisor and the performance improvement coordinator agreed to take a student each day. In this facility, the nursing supervisor responds to all codes, deaths, and incidents, and helps to manage staff as well as problems on the units. Performance improvement staff actively participates in patient care improvement processes through data management and care map development.

Two clinical groups of eight students each were shared by two clinical faculty to yield a 2:16 ratio, rather than the traditional 1:8 ratio. As this was an integrated clinical course covering community, gerontology, and leadership skills, the experiences were separated so that the students had dedicated days for each. The intent of this was to help them focus on the specific skills that they were to attain. Yet, the order of these experiences varied with every student. A typical week would include a community or gerontology day plus a leadership day, or might include two community days depending on the rotation. A spreadsheet was used to plot the rotations to provide every student with comparable experiences. One faculty member agreed to handle all the leadership days (and gerontology days) to provide continuity for the agency and the students. The other faculty managed the community experiences. The students benefited from the experience of two faculty members during the rotation, and the agencies benefited from having consistent expectations from only dealing with one faculty.

Students were assigned 5- to 8-hour shifts for the leadership experience (40 of the total 180 clinical hours for the course), with no more than two shifts on the same hospital unit, in order to provide opportunities to see a variety of decision making styles and at the same time be able to try out methods learned on a second visit to the previous unit. This facility has both 8- and 12-hour shifts to accommodate mature nurses' physical needs through provision of flexible schedules.

The specific behaviors expected of shift coordinators were to:

- think aloud about problem solving
- share responsibility for decision making
- demonstrate communication techniques for working with peers
- make bed and staff assignments with students
- clarify when consultation is required with a supervisor

The specific behaviors expected of students were to:

- ask questions
- demonstrate initiative by offering responses to situations
- actively participate in decision making
- practice communication techniques for working with other nurses
- seek feedback from shift coordinator

Additionally, students could complete a wide variety of clinical activities for this course representing all course objectives. These activities included the following:

1. Select a theory of aging, epidemiology, or management and describe how it is demonstrated in the care of an individual or family unit in the clinical setting.

2. Find the theory of nursing that is described in the organization's (clinical setting) policy and procedure manual and critique its usefulness or effectiveness in the clinical setting.
3. Take one day's case load in one clinical setting and prioritize the order in which you would have seen patients had they all presented at the same time. Explain why.
4. Describe a management opportunity you've experienced in the clinical setting and how effective you were with it.
5. Describe the leadership style demonstrated during one day's leadership clinical setting and its effectiveness. Discuss what leadership improvement you recommend.
6. Investigate the management of an ethical situation encountered in the clinical setting.
7. Explore the need for an ethics committee in the clinical setting if one is not present.

OUTCOMES OF THE EXPERIENCE

Faculty have continually evaluated students' learning through direct observation, group post-conferences, and reading of weekly clinical journals. Students have demonstrated growth and increasing awareness of leadership principles and their own leadership skills throughout the semester. Students were able to compare and contrast the leadership styles of the different shift coordinators they have worked with, learning as much from "poor" leaders as from strong nurse leaders, as they worked with three to five different shift coordinators. Weekly reflective journals, electronic discussion board posts, and the end of semester seminar provided many opportunities for students to discuss their observations and obtain feedback from faculty and peers. An unexpected outcome has been students' awareness of changes in each other. During the final seminar, which serves as a forum for presentations on individual growth, numerous students have spoken of changes in themselves. For example, students who were once quiet and withdrawn are now more self-confident and willing to participate in group activities. Students also recognized self-growth; for example, they are no longer afraid to give orders to staff nurses. They have developed negotiating and conflict resolution skills. Most important, they are able to observe the theoretical principles of leadership and demonstrate them in actual clinical learning experiences.

The shift coordinators and the faculty feel positive about the experience, and several units have requested to be included in the rotation next year. As the semester progressed, the faculty needed to provide less guidance, suggesting that with experience the shift coordinators could manage the student relationship as a fully precepted experience with periodic feedback from the faculty. The nurse managers reported that the shift coordinators grew in their roles as they learned to articulate their functions and explain many of their decisions, encouraging them to share these thoughts more openly with their colleagues throughout their normal dealings. Specifically, shift coordinators were able to reflect on why they made the decisions they did. For example, when an admission came to the unit, one shift coordinator voiced that she chose the nurse who would give her the "least grief" and did not always consider other factors that might have determined which nurse should take the new patient. Several students wrote in their self-evaluation that they did not realize they had leadership potential, yet the experiences brought out skills they did not know they possessed. Almost all students reflected in journals that they have a new appreciation for the shift coordinator role, which will change how they function in the staff role during their employment. In the end, all parties involved felt that the experience was valuable and contributed to strengthening the leadership role of graduate nurses, and that the experience should be continued.

REFERENCES

DeMarco, R., Howard, L., & Lynch, M. (2002). Nursing students' experiences with and strategic approaches to case-based instruction: A replication and comparison study between two disciplines. *Journal of Nursing Education, 41*(4), 165–174.

Smith, J., & Crawford, L. (2003). *Report of findings from the 2002 RN practice analysis linking the NCLEX-RN to practice.* Chicago: National Council of State Boards of Nursing.

CHAPTER TWENTY-TWO

Teaching the Value of Evidence-Based Practice

Betsy Frank

The Institute of Medicine (2003) recently published a report stating that one of the key components of education for all health professions is to learn how to engage in evidence-based practice. The report further states that participating in research and other learning opportunities fosters the acquisition of this competency. Despite nursing's long history of including research courses as a part of baccalaureate and higher-degree programs (Ludemann, 2003), Buerhaus and Norman (2001) note that students need more experience in implementing quality improvement projects. To assist in achieving this competency, the focus of this Chapter is to introduce students to evidence-based practice and require that they complete projects that are of value to the institutions where they have their clinical experiences.

The leadership education model (LEM) is an evidence-based model that consists of six constructs that can be translated into a variety of teaching strategies to promote leadership education across the various undergraduate and graduate nursing programs (Lemire, 2002) (see Part I of this book). Not only is the model evidence-based, but the value of evidence-based practice fits well within the model's various constructs, particularly leader as expert (Frank, 2002) and leader as achiever (Dienemann, 2002).

Evidence-based practice is not just research application. It also takes into account clinical expertise and patient and provider values. When all these components are taken into account, quality improvement in patient care can occur. How, then, does the leadership education model guide faculty to help students understand the value of evidence-based practice? Two components of the model, leader as expert and leader as achiever, can give particular direction to faculty. The leader as expert (Frank, 2002) construct is organized around the four ways of knowing (Carper, 1978). Of particular interest for evidence-based practice are the empirical and ethical ways of knowing. In order for evidence-based practice to occur, students and practitioners alike must know the research in the area where quality improvement is needed. Students and practitioners must also have a strong grounding in ethics if the right quality improvements are to be made in the right way. The leader as achiever construct suggests (Dienemann, 2002) that in order for students and practitioners actually to implement needed quality improvement, a full understanding of the organizational change process is needed.

What follows is a description of a multistage process, grounded in the leadership education model that introduces undergraduate nursing students at Indiana State University College of Nursing (ISUCON) to the value of evidence-based practice. The LEM is built on the assumption that leadership education doesn't occur in one course alone, but across the curriculum. Being able to apply the various aspects of the model across the curriculum helps students to see how leadership is involved in various components of nursing practice, such as evidence-based practice. Thus, the value of research is introduced to students in beginning courses, wherein students are taught to differentiate between articles that are reports of research studies and clinical and opinion articles. Students are required to use research articles to support content presented in various written assignments. A more thorough examination of evidence-based practice occurs in the junior year when all students at ISUCON take an introduction to nursing research course.

Early on in the course, students are introduced to the concept of clinical scholarship (Sigma Theta Tau International, 1999). In the discussion of clinical scholarship, students delve into one of the cornerstones of clinical scholarship, evidence-based practice. This discussion focuses on the fact that evidence-based practice is more than just research utilization. Students are shown Web sites (see Table 22.1) where extant medical and nursing evidence-based practice recommendations are catalogued. Of course, students still learn the usual things taught in such a course, for instance, how to look for research and clinical literature and how to critique the research they read. The final assignment in the course is the evidence-based practice project. Students select a nursing care practice that may need changing and then they gather research and other literature such as published standards of practice and current policy manuals. Students may also survey practitioners informally regarding their topic. Once all the information has been gathered and analyzed, students make their own recommendations for needed practice changes.

Undergraduate students who are already registered nurses (RNBS) often choose topics from their worksites. For example, one student who was a nurse manager was involved in a quality improvement project on pain management. Patient satisfaction surveys on her unit showed that postoperative patients were less than satisfied with their pain management. For her project, this student gathered research and practice guidelines regarding management of acute pain and then made practice recommendations. Her ultimate goal was to educate her staff on current pain management guidelines and then track changes in patient satisfaction surveys and chart audits to evaluate whether or not practice changes were made. Although the student was involved in this particular quality improvement project prior to taking the research course, her newfound knowledge better enabled her to search the literature and subsequently design an educational program solidly grounded in the evidence available on acute pain management.

What about generic baccalaureate students? Can they also envision changes needed in clinical practice and make appropriate recommendations? Yes, they can. These students often have questions about clinical practices that may not conform to the standard of practice learned in the classroom. With guidance they can also make practice recommendations. Two such examples are pain management during circumcision and lifestyle changes to promote health in patients with irritable bowel disease. This project, then, provides a solid foundation for further knowledge and skill development in evidence-based practice.

As mentioned above, part of implementing evidence-based practice involves understanding how the change process impacts upon making those changes happen. Therefore, in the nursing leadership course, students complete another evidence-based practice project, but an additional component, the change process, is now added. Projects in this course arise from either a work setting or from the capstone clinical course. What is most important is that projects for all students, RNBS and generic, arise out of a real need within an organization. The prior project may or may not have arisen out of such a need, depending upon the students' experience to this point. Students may know the value of evidence-based practice, but now they come to know that it is not enough simply to understand standards of practice. They must also learn how organizations make many changes in order to implement standards that improve patient care processes and outcomes. For example, students must learn what the process is for making a policy change within an organization.

What is exciting for all students is that the organizations do use their projects to make needed changes. True enough, some students may have had this experience with their projects in the research course, but now these students really gain insight into how to implement changes in an organization by focusing on the facilitators and barriers to change. Students learn that it is not only the appointed leaders who can impact change, but that all in the organization have the potential to influence the change process. For example, one student was asked to investigate what a medical-surgical unit could do to decrease the incidence of postoperative deep vein thrombosis (DVT). In order to accomplish this project, the student had to learn what the standards of practice were for preventing DVT. Further, the student had to understand how she could introduce the information she had gathered to the unit in question. As evidence of the fact that the quest to learn about standards of care for preventing DVTs did make a difference, the student received an e-mail from a clinical nurse specialist who said the student's information was going to be presented at an in-service education program.

Another student was asked to look at ways to improve the nursing care of patients with congestive heart failure (CHF). The student learned not only the standard of practice for care of patients with CHF, but also the financial implications of care, an essential component of the skill set for leader as expert and achiever (Dienemann, 2002; Frank, 2002). This student further learned that a mundane task of installing an easy to reach receptacle to hold discharge instructions was essential to improving care delivery. Examples of other projects have included changes in care processes to verify placement of nasogastric tubes, the use of topical anesthesia for painful procedures performed on pediatric patients, and ways to improve overall patient satisfaction. In this instance the student analyzed patient satisfaction data and made specific recommendations on a particular inpatient unit for improvement.

Certainly students learn that empirical knowing is critical to evidence-based practice. But what about ethical knowing? For one student, ethical knowing was reinforced after she collected data and made practice recommendations to reduce back injuries in nursing and other health care personnel. As a result of the literature review for this project, the student learned that what is taught to personnel regarding lifting did not match current recommendations for no lift work environments (Nelson et al., 2003). The student was incensed. Why wasn't the organization following practice guidelines? On further exploration the student learned that the organization was moving toward a no lift environment. The student's project showed that the investment in equipment could offset the financial loss from health care expenses and workdays lost as a result of injuries. The student did learn, however, that making the right change doesn't come easily and the move to a no lift environment will take time.

One of the keys to promoting evidence-based practice is for educators to give students opportunities to demonstrate that they personally can gather evidence to change practice and improve the quality of patient care. Students learn that they, as nurses, can make a difference, and also that quality improvement is an interdisciplinary effort. In addition to developing evidence-based practice competencies, the Institute of Medicine (2003) recommends that students need to learn to work in interdisciplinary environments. Many of the projects that students work on, such as pain management, require them to understand the role of other members of the health care team to ensure the success of quality improvement efforts. In sum, they have real experience with the notion that leadership can be shared within a team.

Evidence-based practice is not an abstract concept to be taught in the classroom. Rather, using the leadership education model as a guide, educators can create opportunities where students can experience the successes and challenges of quality improvement that is grounded in the principles of evidence-based practice.

REFERENCES

Buerhaus, P. I., & Norman, L. (2001). It's time to require theory and methods of quality improvement in basic and graduate nursing education. *Nursing Outlook, 49*(1), 67–69.

Carper, B. (1978). Fundamental ways of knowing in nursing. *Advances in Nursing Science, 1*(1), 13–23.

Dienemann, J. (2002). Leader as achiever. *Nursing Leadership Forum, 7*(2), 63–68.

Frank, B. (2002). Leader as expert. *Nursing Leadership Forum, 7*(2), 57–62.

Institute of Medicine. (2003). *Health professions education: A bridge to quality.* Washington, DC: National Academy Press.

Lemire, J. (2002). Preparing nurse leaders: A leadership education model. *Nursing Leadership Forum, 7*(2), 47–52.

Ludemann, R. (2003). How time flies: Strategies for teaching nursing research. *Western Journal of Nursing Research, 25*, 929–931.

Nelson, A., Owen, B., Lloyd, J. D., Fragala, G., Matz, M. W., Amato, M., et al. (2003). Safe patient handling and moving. *American Journal of Nursing, 103*(3), 32–44.

Sigma Theta Tau International (1999). *Clinical scholarship white paper.* Retrieved January 9, 2004 from the Sigma Theta Tau International Web site: http://www.nursingsociety.org/new/CSwhite_paper.pdf

TABLE 22.1. Evidence-Based Practice Web Sites

Web Site	URL	Site Description
Agency for Healthcare Quality and Research	*http://www.ahrq.gov/*	Federal government agency that contains evidence-based reports and practice recommendations
Joanna Briggs Institutue	*http://www.joannabriggs.edu/au/about/ home.php*	Australian site that focuses on evidence-based nursing practice. Some areas open to members only
Academic Center for Evidence-Based Nursing	*http://www.acestar.uthscsa.edu/*	University of Texas Health Science Center at San Antonio site that contains best practice recommendations done at the center and links to other practice sites
The Cochrane Collaboration	*http://www.cochrane.org/index0.htm*	Sponsors the Cochrane Library that gathers and regularly updates evidence-based literature reviews. Some areas open to members only

CHAPTER TWENTY-THREE

Developing Evidence-Based Practice Skills Through Experiential Learning

Kay Sackett
Janice M. Jones

The challenges of today's health care system have, by necessity, had an impact on the education of undergraduate students. Nurse educators need to prepare future leaders with academic and clinical experiences that give baccalaureate-prepared nurses ample skills in critical thinking, informatics, disease management, research, and publication. Experiential learning opportunities within the University at Buffalo School of Nursing that promote the development of leadership skills in evidence-based practice for RNBS and RNMS students are described in this chapter.

A generally accepted notion in the nursing profession is the existence of great variability in nursing practice and inadequate utilization of nursing research. Barriers to nursing research utilization have been well documented (Funk, Tornquist, & Champagne, 1995) and have focused on: the nurses' values, skills, and awareness of nursing research; organizational setting and its limitations; quality of the research; and presentation and accessibility of research findings.

Adopting a model of nursing practice based on evidence-based guidelines and research can improve patient outcomes, reduce errors, and yield a more consistent approach to patient care. This, in turn, can engender more efficient utilization of health care resources, which is especially valuable in an era of dramatic increases in the costs of these resources.

Managed care organizations (MCOs) have become the predominant means of health care coverage throughout the United States. Employing a disease management focus, MCOs have extensively implemented disease and wellness management programs that target outcomes, require the use of clinical information systems, and often extend across diverse settings and locales. One result of these programs is the existence of a huge amount of otherwise unutilized clinical data and information ripe for collaborative research initiatives. Large research data sets can be generated from computerized health care records and clinical information systems databases. There is tremendous potential for nurse researchers to collect and analyze these clinical and financial data for interventions, costs, member and provider satisfaction, and other outcome measures desirable to MCOs to facilitate evidence-based decision making.

There is ample support in the current literature to document the importance of evidence-based decision making. Rambur (1999) noted that the evaluation of practice outcomes is central to professional practice (providers) and a necessary foundation for new legislation, health policy, and third-party payers. This view is consistent with Valanis (2000), who describes the importance of outcomes analysis and evidence-based nursing research opportunities in MCO settings. Stone, Curran, and Bakken (2002) speak to the need for applying economic evidence to intervention-related costs. Goodwin, Iannacchione, Hammond, Crockett, Maher, and Schlitz (2001) discuss the potential to use MCO data repositories for data mining to identify more accurate predictors of preterm births. McNamara (2000) and McDaniel (1997) emphasize the significance of, and describe methodology for, extracting data sets from MCO databases of member and provider information usable in systematic research. Jones (1997) also speaks to the need for building and maintaining clinical information systems from which evidence can be produced to demonstrate contributions to cost control made by nurses in a managed care setting, through the pursuit and promotion of positive patient outcomes.

STRATEGIES

To illustrate the promotion of leadership skills development in evidence-based practice for baccalaureate students, experiential learning strategies from two courses—one didactic and one clinical—from the RNBS and RNMS curricula are described. A traditional management leadership course is required within these programs. Faculty who teach leadership courses believe it is the role of the nurse manager and clinical nurse to plan, develop, and implement evidence-based practices in the clinical environment. Students are required to complete projects that examine clinical challenges, using evidence-based research techniques that include best practice guidelines and reviews of research databases. Students must then provide evidence for selected best practices based on the accepted formats of meta-analysis, RCT studies, and general research.

EVIDENCE BASED PRACTICE
ASSIGNMENT—STRATEGY #1

NUR 440: CRITICAL ELEMENTS IN NURSING LEADERSHIP

Although students are exposed to the underpinnings of evidence-based practice in health care delivery perspectives and nursing research courses, they still are not fully grounded in the process of finding and evaluating evidence for clinical practices. Students are thus required to read a selection of articles to enhance their grasp of evidence-based practice basics.

Selecting a Clinical Problem

After completing the article review, each student must find a clinical problem to research. This may take the form of a policy or practice they wish to investigate. The student poses one of the following questions: What is the best way to conduct this practice? or What is the scientific basis for this practice?

Finding the Evidence

The search begins by consulting textbooks and conducting a literature review using MEDLINE, CINAHL, journals, and other general medical and nursing databases. Students are expected to search all of the databases listed in Figure 23.1 as well as selected databases from Figures 23.2 and 23.3.

Evaluating the Evidence

Data from the literature are then summarized. Students are not expected to conduct systematic reviews, as they have not been trained to do so. Students examine the evidence in terms of its hierarchy and appropriateness for the clinical setting in which they are practicing.

Conclusions are drawn based on the literature review and other relevant data. Students determine at what level they were able to draw conclusions. For example, Was a meta-analysis done? Were any systematic reviews found? They then determine at what level they were able to draw support for their conclusions. This includes citing the applicable articles found and describing those articles that were research-based versus clinical in nature. Students have often found national clinical guidelines to be the most reflective of evidence-based data and research.

Students are further required to determine what studies should be conducted based on the evidence reported to that point. For example, are a sufficient number of studies of adequate similarity reported such that meta-analyses would be appropriate, or is more empirical research indicated? If the latter, by whom should it be conducted and with what samples? Who should advocate for best practices for the policy, practice, or problem that is being examined? The advocacy question often elicits responses from students, such as whether the advocates should be staff nurses or physicians. Interestingly, it's rare that the nurse manager, clinical nurse specialist, or nurse practitioner is mentioned as a desirable or preferred best practice advocate. The report must conclude with a reference list in APA format, followed by peer evaluations of the other group members' contributions.

EVIDENCE BASED PRACTICE
ASSIGNMENT—STRATEGY #2

NUR 480L: HEALTH CARE MANAGEMENT IN THE COMMUNITY

The final clinical course that facilitates the development of an evidence-based leadership orientation within the RN student population focuses on community health care management. An education and service partnership with a local managed care organization, a research-based rehabilitation telephone triage company, and a Veterans Affairs tele-home-health primary care unit provides three Western New York clinical settings that illustrate the incorporation of evidence-based practice, case management, informatics, research, and publication skills. Additional learning strategies applied with these experiences include relevant negotiated assignments and e-journaling. Students complete negotiated assignments—for example, more extensive literature reviews, participation in a research/study protocol, or submission of an article or presentation for review—with preceptor and faculty supervision. E-journaling is completed each week, borrowing from health care informatics practices to describe the students' learning experiences. The e-journal is posted on a discussion board in a course management program. Subsequent discussion between the students, their peers, and the faculty and preceptors functions as an electronic conference when this format is used.

Negotiated Assignments

Negotiated assignments, completed by students along with their preceptors and/or faculty members, are elucidated below. Details are negotiated and described in the clinical log. Emphasis on evidence-based research is expected in all of the following.

1. Synthesize and present to the preceptor/faculty member a literature review on a clinical problem.
2. Develop and conduct for the preceptor/faculty member a segment of a research study/protocol on a clinical problem.
3. Develop and submit with the preceptor/faculty member an article for publication about this clinical experience.

4. Develop or pilot a survey on a clinical problem that has been identified by personnel at the organization or agency.

Population

This strategy is employed with our RNBS and RNMS student populations, as well as with our senior undergraduate nursing students. The principles are applicable to educating any nursing student population with an advanced practice focus, such as nurse practitioners, clinical nurse specialists, nurse midwives, and nurse anesthetists.

Evidence-Based Initiatives

The rationale for using evidence-based initiatives arose from a paradigm shift within the scientific community. The rigorous methodological requirements of scientific research revealed the value of data-based studies and research critiques. Evidence-based practice assumes that the best available evidence is applied to a specific clinical question. Members of the scientific community have espoused the use of a hierarchy of evidence that facilitates the adoption of evidence-based practice.

Canadian physician-epidemiologist Dr. Archie Cochrane championed the theoretical framework that drives evidence-based practice. In 1979, Cochrane called for the preparation, maintenance, and dissemination of systematic knowledge review in all divisions of the field of health care (Cochrane, 1979, 1989). Medicine was practiced with great variability throughout the world, largely based on experiential impressions, past practices, and hearsay. The Cochrane Database of Systematic Reviews offered the novel shift of focusing on the effectiveness of select, best practice interventions and treatments, as supported by tracked patient outcomes and, at times, consideration of cost. Cochrane's ideas spread first through the Commonwealth. Eventually, nine additional countries would collaborate to create the Cochrane collection and library.

It was not until 1996 that Sackett and colleagues (Sackett, Rosenberg, Muir Gray, Haynes, & Richardson) coined the term "evidence-based medicine." Evidence-based medicine (EBM) was a natural extension of the EBP initiative. Sackett et al. (1996) describes EBM as "the conscientious, explicit, and judicious use of current best evidence in making decisions about the care of individual patients. The practice of evidence-based medicine means integrating individual clinical expertise with the best available external clinical evidence from systematic research" (p. 71).

When nursing began to draw observably on the principles espoused by the evidence-based movement, evidence-based nursing practice was born (Cullum, Di Censo, & Ciliska, 1997; Pearson,Borbasi, Fitzgerald, Kowanko, & Walsh, 1997; Smith, 1997). Several nursing educators coined the term evidence-based learning (EBL) to describe the application of evidence-based activities in nursing education. Kessenich, Guyatt, and DiCenso (1997) describe EBL in nursing education as promoting students' skills development in problem definition, searching for evidence, evidence evaluation, and planning and conducting original research. In adopting this philosophy, faculty members guide undergraduate students in developing these skills to assist them in clinical decision making throughout their professional education and practice.

Evidence-based nursing (EBN) was a natural extension of the evidence-based initiatives. Stevens and Paugh (1999) describe EBN, consistent with the fundamental theme, as nursing practice that emphasizes reliance on information generated from the results of scientific research. Evans (2003), Jennings and Loan (2001) and McKenna, Cutcliffe, and McKenna (2001) support the hierarchy of best practice evidence in nursing. Components of best practice evidence include the following:

- Meta-analysis of randomized clinical trials (RCT) of adequate quality
- At least one well-designed RCT
- Well-designed clinical trials without randomization
- Well-conducted systematic reviews
- Well-conducted non-experimental studies
- Poorly controlled or uncontrolled studies
- Conflicting evidence, consensus reports, and published practice guidelines
- Qualitative studies and opinions from experts
- Clinical expertise, intuition, and anecdote

Nurse researchers, educators, and practitioners continue to build a body of science, based on the hierarchy of evidence. In terms of the hierarchy of evidence, Closs and Cheater (1994) support the idea of meta-analysis of RCTs of adequate quality and DiCenso and Cullum (1998) support the use of RCTs in nursing. There are however, few such meta-analyses that exist to clarify the status of knowledge and its relationship to defined areas of practice and theory development or randomized control studies designed for evaluating the effectiveness of a nursing intervention. As nursing becomes more sophisticated in conducting systematic reviews, intervention studies, and meta-analyses, a higher level of evidence in relation to nursing practice will be attained. Sackett et al. (1996), Sackett, Richardson, Rosenberg, and Haynes (1997), Sackett, Strauss, Richardson, Rosenberg, and Haynes (2000), and Driever (2002) remind us that clinical expertise is an important component of evidence-based practice. They do not, however, offer operational definitions for information gained from clinical expertise to be applied to evidence-based nursing practice or research. To date, funding agencies such as the Agency for Healthcare Research and Quality (AHRQ) and the National Institute for Nursing Research (NINR), and specialty organizations such as Oncology Nursing Society and American Association of Critical Care Nurses have given top priority to evidence-based nursing research studies.

ADVANTAGES AND DISADVANTAGES

Students come to realize that the basis for their nursing practice may take many forms from a highly sophisticated meta-analysis to a lower level of evidence, such as clinical expertise as found in popular clinical nursing journals, especially those geared to RN staff nurses. The database search takes much time and effort and students must employ good search strategies in order to uncover the evidence they seek. Computer literacy is a must if a search of sufficient depth is to be conducted. Enhanced writing skills, where clarity of information presented is crucial, are fostered. The conclusions drawn generally are easier to document and the final paper or negotiated assignment is relegated to only a few pages.

There has been a high level of student satisfaction in answering clinical questions rather than in spending an inordinate amount of time writing nursing care plans and determining rationale from a book. All students in each group are required to maintain a copy of the project or negotiated assignment and are urged to incorporate their projects into an "e-portfolio" or bring them to their interviews when seeking a nursing position. Employers have been most impressed with the students' work and have on some occasions hired them because of their evidence-based project. These students are looked at as highly desirable employees because of their ability to search for evidence in a scientific manner, draw conclusions, and evaluate the evidence in terms of implementation.

The ripple effect from this paradigm shift reached not only the health care delivery system, but also the education of future health care practitioners across disciplines. Inherent in this shift was the need to refocus faculty and student skill sets accordingly throughout the health care education, practice, and research arenas. This required new emphasis on such skills as literature retrieval, critical research appraisal, sophisticated techniques to synthesize dependable information, and the integration of point-of-entry information systems. Refocusing these skill sets fosters change and chaos in faculty, students, and preceptors involved with differing assignments; time for completing assignments, grading, writing, and rewriting; and encourages the education-practice partnerships that enhance evidence-based initiatives in nursing.

OUTCOMES

Outcomes from the didactic course are exemplified by selected samples of best clinical practice. Some examples of projects related to the acute care setting are as follows:

1. Best placement of a pulse oximeter (e.g., finger, toe, earlobe)
2. Use of music therapy: Does it work? In what settings? What types of music?
3. Pain control during circumcision.
4. Care of exit sites of peritoneal dialysis catheters.
5. Screening for depression on admission to an acute-care hospital facility.

The following negotiated assignments are examples of outcomes from the clinical course:

1. Diabetes and CHF questionnaires under development for use at the telephone triage center
2. Completed evidence-based literature reviews on
   a. Return on investment for a prenatal program
   b. Developing a nurse run telephone triage call center at a MCO
   c. Diabetes health risk assessment tools
   d. CHF health risk assessment tools
3. Submission of potential articles written by students, faculty and agency preceptors:
   a. Draft manuscript for *The Case Manager* journal titled "The Effects of Exercise and the Adolescent Cystic Fibrosis Patient: Demonstrating A Positive Return on Investment"
   b. Draft manuscript for *Home Health Care Management & Practice* titled "Students' Faculty and Preceptors Perspectives of Providing Tele-home Health Care"

Students, faculty, and clinical preceptors have all expressed great satisfaction in using these methods to engage RNBS and RNMS students and socialize them to the baccalaureate nurses' unique contribution to health care. Students are able to take back into the workplace the skills that they have learned in critical thinking, evidence-based practice, informatics, disease management, research, and publication. The students thus become the leaders and standard bearers for the use of evidence-based nursing practice in the clinical arena.

REFERENCES

Closs, S. J., & Cheater, F. M. (1994). Utilization of nursing research: Culture, interest and support. *Journal of Advanced Nursing, 19,* 762–773.

Cochrane, A. L. (1979). A critical review, with particular reference to the medical profession. *Medicines for the Year 2000* (pp. 1–11). London: Office of Health Economics.

Cochrane, A. (1989). Archie Cochrane in his own words. Selections arranged from his 1972 introduction to effectiveness and efficiency: Random reflections on the health service. *Controlled Clinical Trials, 10,* 428–433.

Cullum, N., DiCenso, A., & Ciliska, D. (1997). Evidence-based nursing: An introduction. *Nursing Standard, 11,* 30–33.

DiCenso, A., & Cullum, N. (1998). Implementing evidence-based nursing: Some misconceptions. *Evidence-Based Nursing, 1*(2), 38–40.

Driever, M. J. (2002). Are evidence-based practice and best practice the same? *Western Journal of Nursing Research, 24,* 591–597.

Evans, D. (2003). Hierarchy of evidence: A framework for ranking evidence evaluating healthcare interventions. *Journal of Clinical Nursing, 12*(1), 77–84.

Funk, S. G., Tornquist, E. M., & Champagne, M. T. (1995). Barriers and facilitators of research utilization. *Nursing Clinics of North America, 30,* 395–407.

Goodwin, L., Iannacchione, M., Hammond, W., Crockett, P., Maher, S., & Schlitz, K. (2001). Data mining methods find demographic predictors of preterm birth. *Nursing Research 50,* 340–345.

Jennings, B. M., & Loan, L. A. (2001). Misconceptions among nurses about evidence-based practice. *Journal of Nursing Scholarship, 33*(2), 121–127.

Jones, L. (1997). Building the information infrastructure required for managed care. *Image: Journal of Nursing Scholarship, 29,* 377–382.

Kessenich, C., Guyatt, G., & DiCenso, A. (1997). Teaching nursing students evidence-based nursing. *Nurse Educator, 22*(6), 25–29.

McDaniel, A. (1997). Developing and testing a prototype patient care database. *Computers in Nursing, 15*(3), 129–136.

McKenna, H., Cutcliffe, J., & McKenna, P. (2001). Evidence-based practice: Demolishing some myths. *Nursing Standard, 14*(16), 39–42.

McNamara, T. (2000). The net value of information in managed care. *Advances for Health Care Executives,* 69–72.

Pearson, A., Borbasi, S., Fitzgerald, M., Kowanko, I., & Walsh, K. (1997). *Evidence-based nursing: An examination of the role of nursing within the international evidence-based health care practice movement,* RCNA discussion paper no. 1, Deakin Act, Australia.

Rambur, B. (1999). Fostering evidence-based practice in nursing education. *Journal of Professional Nursing, 15,* 270–271.

Sackett, D. L., Rosenberg, W. M. C., Muir Gray, J. A., Haynes, R. B., & Richardson, W. S. (1996). Evidence-based medicine: What it is and what it isn't. *British Medical Journal, 312,* 71–72.

Sackett, D. L., Richardson, W. S., Rosenberg, W., & Haynes, R. B. (1997). *Evidence-based medicine: How to practice and teach evidence-based medicine.* New York: Churchill Livingston.

Sackett, D., Straus, S., Richardson, W., Rosenberg, W., & Haynes, R. (2000). *Evidence-based medicine: how to practice and teach EBM.* London: Churchill Livingstone.

Smith, C. (1997). Evidence-based nursing. *Nursing Management, 3,* 22–23.

Stevens, K., & Paugh, J. (1999). Evidence-based practice and perioperative nursing. *Seminars in Perioperative Nursing, 8*(3), 155–159.

Stone, P., Curran, C., & Bakken, S. (2002). Economic evidence for evidence-based practice. *Image: Journal of Nursing Scholarship, 34,* 277–282.

Valanis, B. (2000). Professional nursing practice in an HMO: The Future is Now. *Journal of Nursing Education, 39*(1), 13–20.

FIGURE 23.1 Evidence-based practice web sites—searching for the evidence.

Cochrane Library *http://www.cochrane.org*
Univeristy at Buffalo's Academic Databases: Evidence-Based Medicine Reviews (EBMR) *http://ublib.buffalo.edu/libraries*
National Library of Medicine—MEDLINE/PubMed *http://www.nlm.nih.gov*
Evidence-Based Health Care Resources at University of Rochester *http://www.urmc.rochester.edu/Miner/Links/ebmlinks.html*
The Joanna Briggs Institute for Evidence-Based Nursing and Midwifery *http://joannabriggs.edu/au/welcome.html*
Evidence-Based Nursing and Health Care Resources *http://ublib.buffalo.edu/libraries/units/hsl/internet/ebn.html*
Search CINAHL, MEDLINE, Health Reference Center—Academic, Journals@OVID and other databases that would be pertinent (e.g. CancerLit, AIDSline, PsycINFO).

FIGURE 23.2 Other web sites of interest.

Agency for Healthcare Research and Quality—Best Practice Standards *http://www.ahrq.gov*
Centers for Disease Control and Prevention *http://www.cdc.gov*
National Guideline Clearinghouse (NGC) *http://www.guideline.gov/index.asp*
Canadian Medical Association INFOBASE: Clinical Practice Guidelines *http://www.cma.ca.cpgs*
Healthy People *http://www.healthypeople.gov*
Health People 2010 Information Access Project—Partners in Information Access for Public Health Professionals *http://nnlm.gov/partners/hp*
Web sites for federal departments and agencies *http://www.health.gov*
Medscape *http://www.medscape.com*
National Heart, Lung, & Blood Institute *http://www.nhlbi.nih.gov/index.htm*
Oncology Nursing Society—Search: Clinical Practice *http://onsecom.ons.org*
NOAH: New York Online Access to Health *http://www.noah.cuny.edu*
Web sites of other professional organizations are also useful, e.g., AACN, AORN

FIGURE 23.3. Article recommendations for establishing basic EBP understanding.

Brown, S. J. (2001). Managing the complexity of best practice health care. *Journal of Nursing Care Quality, 15*(2), 1–8.

Closs, S. J., & Cheater, F. M. (1999). Evidence for nursing practice: A clarification of the issues. *Journal of Advanced Nursing, 30*(1), 10–17.

McSweeney, M., Spies, M., & Cann, C. J. (2001). Finding and evaluating clinical practice guidelines. *Nurse Practitioner, 26*(9), 30–49.

Evidence-based Health Care: A Guide to the Resources

Available online at : *http//ublib.buffalo.edu/hsl/resources/guides/EBHC.html*

University at Buffalo, Health Science Library, Resources, Selected Nursing Web Sites, Evidence-Based Nursing and Health Care Resources

Available online at: *http://ublib.buffalo.edu/libraries/units/hsl/internet/ebn.html*

CHAPTER TWENTY-FOUR

Succession Planning As a Strategy to Prepare Future Leaders

Helen Green
Lesley Downes

There is frequently anxiety that practitioners in key positions will leave an organization and that there will be a gap in appropriate leadership while somebody is recruited, appointed, inducted, and acclimated to that position. One strategy for preventing that is setting up a succession planning program to develop the leadership skills of future senior managers. This proactive approach can ensure that when key positions do become available there are other personnel within the organization who have the skills and abilities to fill the gap. Although succession planning is fairly unusual within the United Kingdom, it was determined that this would be the best way forward for the University Hospital of North Staffordshire NHS Trust (UHNST). This chapter describes how the UHNST went about developing its succession planning strategy, which was necessary because there were few suitable internal candidates to fill key nursing and midwifery positions at senior levels. The strategy was also needed because at the same time, prospective external candidates had no shortage of positions from which to choose.

THE SUCCESSION PLANNING STRATEGY

Succession planning is used by best practice organizations to develop and maintain strong leadership (Butler & Roche-Tarry, 2002). The succession planning program at UHNST was intended to be more of a process than a course that would enable participants to look at their own leadership skills, learn more about the strategic perspective of the organization they worked for, and compare this perspective with other organizations. Tyler (2002) suggests that one common mistake of succession planning programs is that they are seen as an event rather than a process. The formal part of the succession planning program at UHNST was to last a year. It was anticipated that informally the process would continue past the point that the formal input had stopped and that participants would then continue to find opportunities for self-development.

The program was well supported by senior managers within the organization. The deputy chief executive/chief nurse took a personal interest in the program and underlined the value the organization put on ensuring that the opportunity was there for participants to develop to a level where they would be suitable candidates for senior positions. The support of the senior management team was seen as essential to the success of a succession planning program (McElwain, 1991).

The focus of the formal part of the program was based around the concepts of mentorship, networking, and facilitation (Bower, 2000; Tahan, 2002). The program commenced with candidates undertaking psychometric testing and group exercises to enable them to understand their own leadership styles and the strengths and weaknesses in their personalities in relation to their work. External consultants were employed to help this process and all candidates were asked to undertake a residential experience so that they could focus completely on where they were and what they wanted to achieve in their future career without being called back to deal with issues in the workplace.

Visioning was undertaken throughout the formal part of the program. The senior nursing team had agreed about the vision concerning the future requirement for senior nurses in the organization, as well as the objectives they would need to achieve in order to be effective nurse or midwifery managers. The mentors who participated were aware of the organizational vision and helped to ensure that the nurses who participated, or protégés, had this awareness.

Mentoring was undertaken between candidates and members of the senior nursing and midwifery teams. The choice of mentor was made from a list of appropriately qualified senior nurses and midwives but was left up to the candidate to a great extent, although participants were asked not to utilize somebody from their own area of the organization. The mentor's role was to suggest opportunities that the candidates might access within the organization in order to broaden their experience. They also offered an opportunity to go with candidates to meetings to act as "second seat" (Woodhouse, 2002) in order to provide support and critical comments on the candidates' performance when undertaking a new activity, such as chairing a meeting or presenting to senior committees such as the trust board. In addition, protégés were able to discuss career aspirations in an environment where what they said did not have any bearing on their next position, because the mentor did not work within that environment and could give advice and support without any bias.

Networking opportunities were offered via activities suggested by mentors and through formal classroom activities where senior managers such as the chief executive discussed the direction in which the organization was heading, how it was achieving its goals, and the contributions that the senior management team could make to achieve those goals. Senior nurses and midwives discussed their roles as they saw them. This enabled candidates to experience a more strategic understanding of the organization they worked for. External networking visits were organized to the nursing and midwifery regulatory body and other commercial industries in order to examine the management styles adopted by those organizations. Suggestions were also made to the candidates about where they might undertake further individual visits, but the final decision was left to them as to whether the visit would be useful or not and to make arrangements for the visit.

A designated program leader served as facilitator to organize the formal sessions, coordinate the linking up of candidates with mentors, and arrange external group visits. An external management consultant met with candidates on at least seven occasions to facilitate the formal program of leadership development. Action learning sets were also organized so that candidates could be encouraged to learn from each other and identify what new knowledge they needed. This was intended to ensure that candidates realized that they had to take some responsibility for their own development.

THE PRACTITIONER POOL

UHNST employs over 2,000 nurses and midwives in five clinical divisions. Within the divisions, the nursing and midwifery management structure is relatively flat. In some divisions, the ward manager, for example, reports directly to the senior nurse manager for the division. Senior nurses and the midwife of the clinical divisions recommended candidates for the program. Managers recommended candidates who they felt had the potential to take advantage of the program, and in the future would be capable of achieving senior management positions. Although it was anticipated that there would be 10 candidates for the first succession planning program, eight candidates were recommended; one of these withdrew for personal reasons soon after the program commenced. The remaining seven individuals completed the formal part of the program. A second cohort consisted of 10 participants and this group had a slightly different focus in that participants tended to be senior clinical rather than junior managerial staff, as with the first cohort.

Although succession planning has not been common in the UK, health care organizations in the United States have undertaken these programs in order to prepare nurses for administrative vacancies (Abrams, 2002; Greene, 1992). This approach has enabled organizations to make a smooth transition when replacing personnel. In some organizations in the United States, this approach has extended to identifying a specific person to move into somebody else's shoes prior to that person's leaving the organization (Tyler, 2002). This approach was not what was anticipated within our organization. We wanted to increase the pool from which more senior nurses and midwives might be promoted, but were quite clear that we were going to comply with employment legislation around the fair recruitment of personnel and that anybody applying for any position would still have to be successful at an assessment center and interview. It was hoped that the succession planning program would help candidates take the recruitment process in their stride, as they would have a broader perspective of the organization and their own leadership skills. If some participants ultimately gained more senior positions outside the organization, this would not be seen as negative. Rather, having a sufficient recruitment pool would mean that applicants would be available when senior nursing and midwifery positions became available, serving the community as a whole.

For succession planning programs to be successful, it is imperative that senior managers are seen as being committed to the process (McElwain, 1991). This was the case at UHNST, in that the deputy chief executive/chief nurse took a personal interest in what was being planned for candidates. The senior nursing and midwifery team also became heavily involved in both mentoring candidates and providing formal input in relation to their roles within the organization. McElwain recommends that line managers do not identify candidates for succession planning, as this can lead to bias in their selection. For example, managers may select the more extroverted individuals who are politically astute and well known to their line manager, while the quieter, but perhaps more competent employee may be overlooked (McConnell, 1996). Also, there are issues about managers trying to mold successors in their own image or putting forward weak individuals so as not to threaten their own jobs in the future (Kaminsky, 1997). Unfortunately, UHNST does not have a central skills assessment process for employees, as may be typical of some human resources departments (McElwain). It was felt, however, that the senior nurses and midwives would know all potential candidates in their areas and generally be responsible for their personal development plans. Senior nurses and midwives also expressed a commitment to the succession planning process so it was deemed unlikely that they would undermine it.

Part of the succession planning process was to assess the individual leadership skills of candidates and to develop them further. The method of ensuring that candidates were not molded exactly in the image of their present nursing or midwifery manager was to expose them to other parts of the organization and to other organizations. It was recognized, however, that present nursing and midwifery managers did have attributes worthy of role modeling. Because of this, a wider variety of mentors were utilized on the second succession planning program, including some of the prior senior nursing and midwifery team members. Senior general managers were also used as mentors, as well as those from nursing and midwifery professions.

Most candidates would have attended some formal leadership experience that would enable them to consider different leadership styles. What the leadership programs may not do, however, is allow candidates to assess what their natural leadership style is and where they could usefully develop further skills. They also do not always allow candidates to experience other parts of the organization in which they presently work with a view to that next position within the organization.

The model of visioning, mentoring, and networking (Bower, 2000; Tahan, 2002) was seen as a useful method to provide for the individual needs of candidates while enabling a group process of information and action learning. Bower (p. 13) suggests that the success of succession planning can be determined by asking the following questions:

- Has a pool of talented persons who could assume leadership positions been identified?
- Do these persons have the qualifications necessary to chart the future direction of the organization, division, unit, or department?
- Have the CEO, vice presidents, or directors taken responsibility for mentoring the succession talent?
- Are the persons being mentored satisfied with the mentoring experience?
- Are the mentors satisfied with the protégés' success?
- Have contingency plans been developed if mentored persons move onto other positions or places?
- Have the mentored persons who were hired been satisfactory?

OUTCOMES

Although still early in the succession planning process for UHNST, it would appear that the questions posed by Bower (2000) have been amply addressed. The first set of evaluations has yielded positive information from the participants, who indicated that one of the most beneficial parts of the program was the mentoring process. Participants also found that the ability to meet with a group of like minded individuals was very useful, particularly as those individuals came from across the organization and were people that they did not normally have contact with.

In terms of promotions, two members of the original succession planning team have become senior nurses within the organization and one obtained a deputy senior nurse position. Another member has achieved a senior clinical nurse position and two others have taken developmental positions. It is too early to say whether these appointments have been successful but the early signs have been favorable.

Although there is no doubt that nurses and midwives have been supported to move into new positions, most of the evidence around outcomes has not shown a direct relationship between the course and the ability of staff to advance to higher roles. Instinctively, data support that the two are related based on course evaluation data and promotion outcomes. It was determined, however, that more data related directly to program success were needed. To that end, candidates in the second group will undertake further psychometric testing at the end of their program to see if there are any differences from program entry. This should enable a direct link to be made between participation in the program and the development of leadership skills.

There are other potential questions to be resolved in the future. For example, after two succession planning programs, is there a sufficient pool of candidates available to be prepared for senior roles, or have all potential candidates already participated in the program? Can appropriate personnel be recruited to future succession planning programs? Perhaps a review of development activities at all levels across the trust is needed to understand what opportunities exist and to ensure appropriate preparation for all grades. It may also be that a succession planning program for senior nurses and midwives is only viable if offered every 2 years. This would reduce the problem of candidates having expectations of moving into senior roles within the organization, since these roles do not become available every year. Though succession planning programs are thought to enhance the desire to stay working with an organization (Smith, 2002), if candidates do not see the potential to move into more senior positions they may choose to leave so that they can have a place to use their new leadership and management skills.

CONCLUSION

Girvin (1996) and Pulcini (1997) have suggested that nurses have not been well supported to become leaders of the future. To address this concern, there has been much focus on developing leadership skills, including succession planning within the National Health Service (Department of Health, 2000). To address this issue, one acute care trust within the UK invested in both time and financial resources to provide a succession planning program for nurses and midwives who were identified as having the potential to move into senior nurse positions. The strategy has been successful thus far, but additional data collection and analysis will enable direct linkages to be made between the succession planning program and the candidate's development of leadership and management skills. In the meantime, organizational investment in the succession planning program will continue in an effort to avoid having leadership gaps in the future.

REFERENCES

Abrams, M. (2002) Succeeding at succession planning. *Health Forum Journal*, 45(1), 27–28.

Bower, F. (2000) Succession planning: A strategy for taking charge. *Nursing Leadership Forum, 4,* 110–114.

Butler, K., & Roche-Tarry, D. (2002, November) Drawing a blueprint for succession. *Provider,* pp. 51–53.

Department of Health. (2000). *The NHS plan: A plan for reform. A plan for success.* London: Department of Health.

Girvin, J. (1996) Leadership and nursing: Part three: Traditional attitudes and socialisation. *Nursing Management, 3*(3), 20–22.

Greene, J. (1992) Hospitals struggle with the changing of the guard. *Modern Healthcare, 22*(22), 20–22.

Kaminsky, R. (1997) Succession planning: A long-overlooked need. *Caring, 16*(4), 76–77.

McConnell, C. (1996) Succeeding with succession planning. *Health Care Supervisor, 15*(2), 69–78.

McElwain, J. (1991) Succession plans designed to manage change. *HR Magazine, 36*(2), 67, 69, 71.

Pulcini, J. (1997) Succession planning: From leaders to mentors: An open letter to experienced nurse practitioners' leaders. *Clinical Excellence for Nurse Practitioners, 1,* 405.

Smith, E. (2002) Leadership development: The heart of succession planning. *Seminars for Nurse Managers, 10,* 234–239.

Tahan, H. (2002) Relationship management: A key strategy for effective succession planning. *Seminars for Nurse Managers, 10,* 254–264.

Tyler, L. (2002) Succession planning: Charting a course for the future. *Trustee, 55*(6), 24–28.

Woodhouse, B. (2002) Succession planning: Lessons from the legal field. *Seminars for Nurse Managers, 10,* 269–273.

CHAPTER TWENTY-FIVE

Developing Leadership Through Shadowing a Leader in Health Care

Sheila Grossman

Student nurses at Fairfield University are assigned preceptors in most clinical rotations to guide them through specific patient assignments, be it for a day, 1 day a week for 6 weeks, or perhaps as with seniors, over an entire semester. Clinical rotations for the Nursing Management and Leadership course focus on the important leadership skills of problem solving or trouble-shooting problems, collaboration, and teamwork. In the past, students may have had the opportunity to shadow a team leader or charge nurse for a couple of hours before being assigned as the team leader for a day. Others may have been lucky enough to have the team leader shadow students and give then feedback on how they were managing the team or unit. For the most part, however, the assigned faculty member observed students in this role while the actual team leader or charge nurse really led the team or unit. This greatly diminished their ability to develop as leaders because everyone knew they were not actually leading anything but instead practicing some management skills with the instructor. Nurses need to view themselves as leaders, develop their leadership abilities, and embrace the challenges that leaders face in health care today (Grossman & Valiga, 2000). This chapter describes a student experience designed to provide hands-on opportunities to develop management and leadership skills.

THE SHADOWING EXPERIENCE

Self-confidence can be achieved when nurses become competent with clinical as well as leadership skills, such as negotiation, creative thinking, communication, and collaboration. To accomplish this, nurses need to be mentored by experienced nurses who can provide clinical knowledge along with the skills for leading a unit and team of patients. If one believes that leaders are not born but made, and mostly self-made, it becomes clear that nurses can be nurtured and taught leadership. By shadowing a leader, students can develop their talents and prepare for the many opportunities they will have to lead as professional nurses.

The shadowing strategy benefits the traditional undergraduate student and second-degree adult student. Students who participated felt their mentor leader was committed to the rotation, gave frequent, constructive feedback, collaborated with them to make the rotation most effective for growth, perceived their input as valuable, and assisted in empowering them to be more confident in communication and to have a more global vision. Most added that their mentor leader demonstrated good conflict management skills, creative problem solving ability, and a balanced professional and personal life, and they advocated for change in their setting.

The shadowing program strategy described in this chapter is a rotation that was set up as a 42-hour clinical experience to be completed in one semester. It is connected to a senior course, Professional Nursing: Leadership and Management. After interviewing students to determine their interests, faculty connected students to leaders in one of five areas: health care policy and legislation; entrepreneurship; research/quality improvement/protocol development; administration in home care, acute care agency, or community health care agency; or patient advocacy.

Willingness to use a nurse to mentor a student is ascertained through personal or phone contact by a faculty member and by sharing the course description, including purpose and objectives for the shadowing experience. A contract between the school and the agency is made. Students are required to contact the leader and arrange the first meeting based on activities deemed important for the student to accomplish the rotation's objectives. The objectives of the mentoring experience are as follows:

1. Develop an appreciation for the theoretical foundation of leadership from multiple perspectives.
2. Describe the dynamic relationship between leaders, followers, and situations.
3. Identify how leaders use goals, roles, and organizational structures to manage business units effectively.
4. Analyze methods by which leaders use and apply concepts in team building, motivation, and group dynamics.
5. Assess the political aspect of leadership, experimenting with the use of power, influence, and negotiation strategies.
6. Investigate how leaders develop and articulate vision, analyze organizational culture, and become transformational leaders in managing change in turbulent environments.
7. Prepare individual self-assessments of leadership development that identify strengths, areas for improvement, and a personal agenda for continued development.

Students participate in several different supervised leadership-practice activities that include negotiating conflicts, writing a grant, preparing a new care protocol, participating in multidisciplinary clinical rounds and case management conferences, assisting in health policy development, advocating for the public regarding a health-related issue, preparing staff for accreditation, and collaborating with a multidisciplinary team of health care providers. This gives students an opportunity for firsthand experiences in the daily activities of a health care leader and enhances knowledge of the health care system, increases their scope of thinking, and further develops communication and collaboration skills. The need for a mentored leadership experience came from faculty planning for a new curriculum, alumni and employer feedback, and a review of the literature on mentoring, coaching, and role modeling. It is essential that nursing education provide opportunities in the following:

- Negotiation—Nurses must become competent in creating new strategies to provide health care using scarce resources wisely, participating in the discussions of health policy development, and partnering with others.
- Broad thinking—Nurse must focus not only on the competent provision of direct patient care, but also on the broader issues surrounding delivery of care.

- Communication and collaboration—Nurses need to learn to network with representatives from all health care disciplines and community agencies, and share expertise and resources to assist in establishing health policy.

Students are asked to review the mentor and student evaluation tools with the leader at the first meeting, along with their objectives (Figures 25.1, 25.2, 25.3.) It is advantageous to pair mentors with students to shadow in the student's requested clinical area if at all possible.

Students are responsible for analyzing a project that they participate in during the rotation, providing an opportunity to use the theory and skills presented in the course through the development, implementation, and evaluation of a project that exemplifies leadership. Students must receive approval for the project topic from the faculty and obtain necessary approval from the leader's agency before proceeding. In some cases a student may not be involved in the entire project; that is, the project may already be in progress. In other situations, a student may not have the opportunity to complete the project. It is important that students follow the project guidelines even though they may not be involved in all parts of the project. Mentors are asked to assist students to describe what transpired prior to their involvement and to hypothesize about what is anticipated after the student's rotation. General guidelines for this paper are in Figure 25.4.

Students are asked to share in class experiences with their leaders that are germane to the classroom topic so the rest of the class can be informed. They also present their project in a 15- to 20-minute format that includes a 5- to 10-minute question-and-answer period, and students write three logs throughout the semester (Table 25.1). The clinical rotation and concurrent course help to empower students to be more autonomous and accountable. Students evaluate the course and shadowing experience very highly.

SHADOWING AS A STRATEGY TO INCREASE LEADERSHIP SKILLS

Mentoring can be defined as an extended relationship between an experienced person and a novice that promotes the novice's professional, and sometimes personal, growth. It is controversial whether a true mentoring experience can involve an evaluation component. Shadowing a leader in health care is a one-to-one relationship between a student and a nursing leader/mentor, yet it differs from a formal relationship between an experienced person and novice for the purpose of training the novice.

Vance and Olson (1998) describe the benefits of mentoring as including career advancement, professional growth, increased self-esteem and confidence, and preparation for leadership roles and success. They further describe mentoring as a developmental and caring relationship that occurs over time. In historical times mentoring was based on human living, teaching and learning, giving and receiving wisdom in all relationships, leadership, and succession (Huang & Lynch, 1995). Mentoring involves mutual sharing, learning, and growth that occur in an environment of respect (Bower, 2000). It stands to reason, therefore, that a mentor is a role model who can facilitate a person's growth through coaching, teaching, and counseling. Role modeling and experiential learning have been used in nursing pedagogy to teach not only clinical but also interpersonal skills, and to affect change (Kolb, 1984). Important prerequisites to learning that have been cited are personal involvement, immersion in the situation, learning by doing, and practicing in the clinical setting with an experienced nurse (Burnard, 1992).

In the situation described above, there were multiple advantages to the shadowing experience. Advantages for students included personal growth and development, meaningful connections with the leader and his or her network for gaining access to future career possibilities, emotional support, increased awareness of the reality of the workplace, a bridge to professional role, increased political astuteness, opportunity to observe and practice leadership skills, increased leadership skills, gained learning from the experience of others, increased knowledge in specialized field of nursing/health care, and increased awareness of the role of nurses other than bedside clinical nurses.

Advantages for leaders included the possibility of attracting a student to work at the agency after graduation; a chance to work with a person from a different generation soon to be entering the nursing profession; the chance to excite someone to enter one's specialized area; an opportunity to link with the future nurse leaders; an opportunity to role model one's best behavior and demonstrate productivity; internal rewards for assisting another's growth; potential payback for having been mentored oneself; the opportunity to see things differently and be more idealistic; and the chance to receive positive reinforcement.

Disadvantages for students were that time commitments for other courses sometimes impacted what could be done with the leader and they feared possibly disappointing their mentors. The only disadvantage for the mentor was providing alternative activities for students when the unexpected occurred that interfered with the shadowing experience.

Bennetts (2000) reported several benefits to a mentoring relationship where a student is paired with a leader, including increased self-esteem and mental health. Likewise, there is the potential for problems to occur, such as power plays between the student and the leader; however, the literature supports more benefits than disadvantages (Andrews & Wallis, 1999; Bell, 1998; Murdaugh, 1998; Vance & Olson, 1998). Certainly one known benefit is that mentors can assist in connecting students with the "right" person for career success (Peluchette & Jeanquart, 2000).

LEARNING OUTCOMES OF SHADOWING WITH A LEADER

Outcomes based on 143 students who had a shadow with a leader experience include the following:

- All students met their clinical objectives.
- Students' scores on the Grossman and Valiga Leadership Assessment Tool (Grossman & Valiga, 2000) were statistically significantly higher for students who participated in the shadowing experience than those that did not.
- Students' oral and written evaluations of the course were more positive than those completed prior to the shadowing experience.
- Nurse recruiters at agencies that have had students shadow a leader were very positive about graduates' interviewing skills.
- Ninety-two percent of leaders were extremely satisfied with the shadowing experience and expressed a willingness to participate again.

- Just 8 percent of leaders would like to have had more contact with faculty and felt their role was not conducive to having a student shadow them, or felt the student was not adequately prepared for the experience.
- Students found that initial contact and first encounter with the leader were very difficult, but the majority (91%) stated that the experience was definitely far better than they had expected.

SERENDIPITOUS OUTCOMES OF THE ROTATION

Unexpected outcomes of the shadowing experience included the fact that student projects were at a higher level than without the experience and that they were able to deal with issues pertinent to leading and managing a unit or organization. Faculty in concurrent courses, for example, medical/surgical and pediatric nursing, noted that, "students have increased ability to assert themselves with the team," "seem stronger with their delegating skills," "are more able to participate independently with the case manager regarding their patients," and "appear more flexible regarding changes that occur during their clinical rotations." Students developed the first draft of their résumés in a more business-like format and seemed to be more at ease with oral presentations to staff. Business plans were far more realistic since students ask for feedback from their clinical leaders. Also, examination grades were higher when students began having shadowing experiences. Nurse leaders in the community and acute care agencies have volunteered to participate in the shadowing experience, and faculty added two questions to the alumni survey, inquiring about the impact of the shadowing experience on graduates' careers. Last, oral feedback from graduates who participated has been very positive.

CONCLUSION

The shadowing strategy proved to be an enriching experience for undergraduate students at Fairfield University. Students evaluated the experience highly and felt they gained added insight in many areas that will influence their careers. The most significant area of growth identified was communication skills. They gained confidence and knowledge because a leader in health care oriented them to the multiple challenges commonly confronted by nurses that were over and above those encountered in direct patient care. Leaders felt they were privileged to participate in the project. They were able to better understand what the new generation brings to the profession and they felt proud to be able to influence these future nurse leaders.

REFERENCES

Andrews, M., & Wallis, M. (1999). Mentorship in nursing: A literature review. *Journal of Advanced Nursing, 29,* 201–207.

Bell, C. R. (1998). *Managers as mentors: Building partnerships for learning.* San Francisco: Berrett-Koehler.

Bennetts, C. (2000). The traditional mentor relationship and the well being of creative individuals in school and work. *International Journal of Health Promotion & Education, 38*(1), 22–27.

Bower, F. (2000). *Nurses taking the lead: Personal qualities of effective leadership.* Philadelphia: Saunders.

Burnard, P. (1992). Student nurses' perceptions of experiential learning. *Nursing Education Today, 12,* 163–173.

Grossman, S., & Valiga, T. (2000). *The new leadership challenge: Creating the future of nursing.* Philadelphia: Davis

Huang, C. A., & Lynch, J. (1995). *Mentoring: The tao of giving and receiving wisdom.* New York: Harper.

Kolb, D. (1984). *Experiential learning.* Englewood Cliffs, NJ: Prentice Hall.

Murdaugh, C. (1998). The value of mentors and facilitators in the pursuit of excellence. *Journal of Cardiovascular Nursing, 12*(2), 65–72.

Peluchette, J.V., & Jeanquart, S. (2000). Professionals' use of different mentor sources at various career stages: Implications for career success. *Journal of Social Psychology, 140,* 549–564.

Vance, C., & Olson, R. (Eds.) (1998). *The mentor connection in nursing.* New York: Springer.

ACKNOWLEDGMENT

The author expresses appreciation to the Helene Fuld Health Trust for Leadership Development as well as to Lydia Greiner, RN, BS, Manager of Community Services for the Fairfield University School of Nursing Health Promotion Center.

FIGURE 25.1. Student evaluation of mentor (same form used for midterm and final)

Complete this evaluation of your mentor midterm and at the end of your rotation experience. Check 1 for lowest ability and 5 for highest ability to perform the stated behavior. Additional comments can be written on the back of the paper. Review the evaluation with your mentor and have him or her sign that they have read this at the midway and final evaluations. The course coordinator will collect it at the end of the course.

	Statement	1	2	3	4	5
a.	Displays commitment to the mentor-student relationship					
b.	Offers frequent feedback in a constructive manner to the student					
c.	Collaboratively plans/revises goals with the student as the rotation evolves					
d.	Perceives the student's input as relevant					
e.	Displays respect and acceptance of other's opinions					
f.	Provides experiences to meet the rotation and student's objectives					
g.	Empowers others including the student					
h.	Demonstrates creative problem-solving ability					
i.	Advocates for change and is flexible					
j.	Balances professional responsibilities and personal life during time spent with student					
k.	Demonstrates leadership skills that have influenced the student					

Signature_____**Date**_____

FIGURE 25.2. Mentor evaluation of student—midterm.

Complete this evaluation of your mentee midway through the mentorship experience. Check 1 for lowest ability and 5 for highest ability to perform the stated behavior. Review the evaluation with your mentee and have him or her sign that they have read. The student will submit this completed form to the course coordinator by_____.

	Statement	1	2	3	4	5
a.	Initiates a professional relationship with the mentor prior to_____					
b.	Plans and revises goals for each experience and for the general mentorship					
c.	Contributes to the mentor-mentee relationship building upon mutually collaborated goals for the experience					
d.	Maintains professionalism at all experiences					
e.	Articulates the philosophy, mission, and organizational culture of the agency					
f.	Demonstrates accountability regarding all activities and assignments during the mentorship					
g.	Demonstrates ability to empower self and others operating within the agency's organizational structure					
h.	Participates in vision development and goal setting for the implementation of the agency's mission					
i.	Participates actively in at least two of the following experiences: accreditation process, grant writing, fund-raising, agency-wide outcome evaluation, protocol development, a measurable change process, planning a new initiative project, or some other specifically defined project					
j.	Collects pertinent data to analyze the mentor's general leadership style and effectiveness in implementing the vision and carrying out the agency goals					
k.	Collaborates with staff and members of other professional disciplines in an ongoing nature					
l.	Reports an increase in self-confidence regarding ability to be assertive, communicate interpersonally, articulate goals, demonstrate commitment, conduct weekly self-evaluations of strength and areas to improve					

Comments:

Signature_____**Date**_____

FIGURE 25.3. Mentor evaluation of student—final.

Complete this evaluation of your mentee at the end of the mentorship experience. Check 1 for lowest ability and 5 for highest ability to perform the stated behavior. Review the evaluation with your mentee and have him or her sign that they have read. The student will submit this completed form to the course coordinator by _____.

	Statement	1	2	3	4	5
a.	Plans and revises goals for each experience and for the general mentorship					
b.	Contributes to the mentor-mentee relationship building upon mutually collaborated goals for the experience					
c.	Maintains professionalism at all experiences					
d.	Articulates the philosophy, mission, and organizational culture of the agency					
e.	Demonstrates accountability regarding all activities and assignments during the mentorship					
f.	Demonstrates ability to empower self and others operating within the agency's organizational structure					
g.	Participates in vision development and goal setting for the implementation of the agency's mission					
h.	Participates actively in at least three of the following experiences: accreditation process, grant writing, fund-raising, agency-wide outcome evaluation, protocol development, a measurable change process, planning a new initiative project, or some other specifically defined project					
i.	Collects pertinent data to analyze the mentor's general leadership style and effectiveness in implementing the vision and carrying out the agency goals					
j.	Collaborates with staff and members of other professional disciplines in an ongoing nature					
k.	Reports an increase in self-confidence regarding ability to be assertive, communicate interpersonally, articulate goals, demonstrate commitment, conduct weekly self-evaluations of strength and areas to improve					

Comments:

Signature_____**Date**_____

FIGURE 25.4. Guidelines for analysis of project accomplished in leadership rotation.

Project objectives: development of outcome objectives in measurable terms

Purpose: description of problems in agency that triggered this project with a brief rationale

Project description: identification of health issue with documentation of the importance; description of entire project; and explanation of any part the student was not able to participate

Significance to nursing: discussion of how the project was operationalized and exemplified professional nursing leadership

Application of leadership and organizational theory: analysis of the process of developing, implementing and evaluating the project in terms of leadership, organizational structure, power, conflict management, and change theories

Analysis of implementation: analysis of the implementation process in terms of decision making and problem solving processes, and assertiveness and communication skills; analysis of the leader's leadership style and effectiveness in implementing the agency's goals

Evaluation: evaluation of the outcome objectives of the project

TABLE 25.1. Organization of the Log

Log #1	Log #2	Log #3
5 leadership strengths with rationale = 2 points	5 leadership growth areas identified from Log #1 with evaluation of progress = 2 points	Comparison of 5 original identified areas of growth from Log #1 and actual perceived growth = 3 points
5 areas of improvement in leadership with rationale = 2 points	Provide a plan to work on these same 5 leadership growth areas = 2 points	Identification of plan for continued and future growth = 1 point
Writing style (clarity, grammar, APA format) and completed by due date = 1 point	Writing style as with Log #1 = 1 point	Writing style as with Log #1 = 1 point

CHAPTER TWENTY-SIX

Practicing Delegation Skills

Janice M. Jones

The expectation that graduates of baccalaureate nursing programs possess selected management competencies in a variety of clinical practice settings has been reiterated for many years (Joyce-Nagata, Reeb, & Burch, 1989, National League for Nursing [NLN], 1983; Primm, 1986). Furthermore, the American Association of Colleges of Nursing (AACN)(1998) identifies three competencies directly related to the leadership role of the baccalaureate nurse. These include provider of care, designer/manager/coordinator of care, and member of a profession. The junior-senior delegation experience was designed to incorporate these three constructs from the AACN document.

Delegation is a function of professional registered nursing that has been increasingly under scrutiny with the advent of unlicensed assistive personnel (UAP) and their job descriptions. The goals of delegation are to improve others' skills, assign new tasks, build teams, and complete tasks the nurse does not have time to accomplish. Very often, undergraduate nursing students are not able to delegate to other hospital personnel because they are not employees of the institution in which they are having their clinical experience, and union contracts may prohibit students from delegating to an unlicensed assistive person. The experience described in this chapter provided senior nursing students the opportunity to practice the skill of delegation to a novice nursing student in an acute care setting the first semester of their senior year in a nonthreatening environment. The experience also encompassed the principles of peer leadership or coaching and peer teaching and learning as an active learning strategy in the clinical setting.

STRATEGY

The University at Buffalo School of Nursing currently has three leadership/management courses that coincide with selected clinical courses over the last three semesters of the nursing program. The principles of delegation are taught during the student's second management course in the first semester of their senior year. At the same time, first semester junior students are teamed with a senior nursing student for a 1-day experience in a hospital acute-care facility. The senior student, as peer leader and mentor, has several responsibilities prior to, during, and after the delegation experience. We are currently using this strategy with generic undergraduate senior nursing students but the strategy could also be applied with RN students in a management/leadership course who are in a clinical setting with these same students. Faculty who share clinical units with differing levels of students could also utilize this strategy.

Prior to the Delegation Experience

The junior nursing student is assigned to a senior clinical hospital rotation early in the semester. The senior nursing student must contact the junior student 1 or 2 days prior to the clinical experience. This may be done via e-mail or phone. The senior student must brief the junior with regard to the patient's history, diagnosis, condition, nursing care, and medications. The senior also provides direction about where to park, how to get to the institution, where to meet, and other logistical data.

The Day of the Delegation Experience

The senior student gives a report to the junior student. The senior student then delegates selective nursing skills to the junior. This may consist of vital signs, personal care, range of motion, mobility, or medical asepsis. The senior student continually evaluates these skills and the knowledge level of the junior student in relation to them as well as therapeutic communication and universal precautions. The two students work together to provide care for the patient in a safe, competent manner. Patient consent to have two students care for them is sought where appropriate.

Responsibilities of the peer leader include continuous monitoring of the patient throughout the day, assisting the junior student with patient care, informing the junior of any special learning opportunities that may become available on the clinical unit, assisting the junior with documentation, and giving report to the RN who is also responsible for the patient.

The Post-Delegation Experience

The senior student provides a written evaluation of the junior student's performance according to the guidelines set by faculty. The junior student provides a written self-evaluation of performance according to the same criteria. The junior student also provides a written evaluation of the senior's delegation skills using a form developed by faculty in accordance with the National Council of State Boards of Nursing (NCSBN) (1997a, 1997b) guidelines.

RATIONALE AND THEORY

This experience is based on the theory of peer leadership. Peer leadership encompasses the concepts of peer teaching or coaching and peer supervision, and provides intrinsic motivation to the student to develop the skills of clinical judgment and supervision in a nonthreatening environment. Loving's (1993) model of competence validation also provides some support for the peer leadership model. Competence validation is defined as "the process by which the student's identity as a competent beginning nurse is established" (p. 417).

Bos (1998) identified five benefits resulting from a peer leadership experience of junior baccalaureate nursing students. These include (a) practice in prioritizing; (b) enhancement of critical-thinking skills; (c) enhancement of technical skills; (d) realization of peers as resources; and (c) development of managerial skills. Several authors have identified additional benefits to peer leadership, such as a heightened sense of responsibility, an increase in confidence level, growth in interpersonal relationships, and insight into personal leadership styles (Ammon & Schroll, 1988; Broscious & Saunders, 2001).

One of the most difficult tasks for nursing students is prioritizing the care that must be given to patients. Although critical incidents are easy to prioritize, it is the more subtle nuances of care that must be addressed in a prioritized manner. In delegating to a novice student nurse, the senior must formulate a plan of care using critical-thinking skills in explaining the care to the junior student and in selecting aspects of care to be delegated in a somewhat sequential order. The accomplishment of the technical skill is a joint effort between the junior and senior student. The junior student in this instance has just completed testing of basic skills, such as personal hygiene, range of motion, mobility, and medication administration. The senior student at this time may have forgotten the best sites to administer intramuscular injections. The junior student may thus assist the senior in finding the best site for injection. The junior student, therefore, can also serve as a resource person or can assist the senior in giving the medication safely and competently to the patient.

Delegation is the process by which responsibility and authority are transferred to another individual (Zimmermann, 1996). Each state's Nurse Practice Act determines the legal definition of delegation. General delegation principles that apply to the student delegation experience include the following (Boucher, 1998; Parkman, 1996; Sheehan, 2001, Zimmerman, 1996):

1. Assess yourself and your team member(s) in terms of competence and ability to perform the delegated task.
2. Assess your own strengths and weaknesses and that of your team member(s).
3. Know the job requirements or job descriptions of those to whom you are going to delegate.
4. Communicate clearly the objectives and expected outcome of the delegated activity.
5. Evaluate the outcome of the delegated activity.

Prior to the delegation experience, senior students are taught these delegation concepts in the classroom setting during their management/leadership course. Principles related to delegation are conveyed by lecture, discussion, and role playing, as well as through assigned readings from a nursing management text and selected articles on delegation.

The concepts of authority, responsibility, and accountability are initially discussed in relation to delegation. Obstacles to delegation are explored as well as the definition of delegation in relation to New York State requirements. Students also complete a delegation self-assessment questionnaire (Hansten & Washburn, 1992) to assess their readiness and ability to delegate and are instructed in the use of the delegation decision-making tree and delegation decision-making grid (NCSBN, 1997a, 1997b) that may be used during the delegation experience. Clinical cues (Boucher, 1998) for the UAP related to delegation are also discussed. A recurrent theme in the class is that the nurse who delegates a task is still accountable for the completion of the task as well as its outcome. It is impressed upon the seniors that they are still responsible for the primary care of the patient even if the care was delegated partially or fully to the junior nursing student. The class concludes with students completing a small group project, identifying tasks they would or would not delegate and the rationale for their answers.

After completion of the clinical delegation experience, senior students write a self-evaluation of their experience and are evaluated by the junior nursing student in relation to specific criteria. The delegation evaluation tool was fashioned based on the following "five rights of delegation" (Hansten & Washburn, 1992): right task, right circumstances, right person, right direction/communication, and right supervision/evaluation. The evaluation tools were evaluated by the faculty coordinator for the juniors, by the faculty coordinator for the seniors, and by the faculty that teach the management/leadership course where delegation is taught.

PROS AND CONS OF THE STRATEGY

The benefits of the peer leadership delegation experience were reflected in the comments of the students. Senior students' comments were categorized as "an increase in confidence level," "a heightened sense of responsibility and accountability," "growth in time management," "insight into personal leadership style." Junior level comments and faculty responses are also provided below.

An increase in confidence level:

"It was a huge confidence booster and also a great learning tool—we really had to know our stuff in order to be able to explain it to them [junior student]."

"It made me feel extremely confident and knowledgeable while caring for my patient. I have come *very* far since last year!"

A heightened sense of responsibility and accountability:

"[The experience] made me realize how much more I need to learn, as teaching something and have questions asked makes you realize how much you know and do not know about something."

Growth in time management:

"I had to have my act together so that I could explain things to the junior."

Insight into personal leadership style:

"I had to make sure the junior knew what they were doing and give them a chance to do things on their own. But it was hard sometimes because I just wanted to do it myself."

"I had a hard time telling someone else what to do . . . I never want to be a nurse manager."

Comments from junior nursing students included:

"It was an awesome experience!"

"I wish we could have more of these experiences."

"My senior was so professional and knew so much. I hope I can be like her."

Both junior and senior students along with their respective faculty have voiced great satisfaction with this experience. It is difficult to separate the delegation piece from the entire peer approach to clinical, as the two are entwined in clinical practice. The benefits to all students, however, have become readily apparent to faculty.

Faculty responses indicated that the senior students seemed well prepared to delegate. Some of the poorer performing students rose to the occasion in taking the junior student under their wing. Senior students were coached in class about how to approach the junior student, which skills could be delegated, and which skills the junior student may not have, for example, intravenous therapy or sterile dressing changes. The senior student must come well prepared for their clinical experience in order to delegate to another. If the senior is poorly prepared or feels overwhelmed with the kind and amount of work that needs to be done for the patient, the experience can quickly fall apart. Senior students need to know what is expected of them in this experience. Knowing the juniors are evaluating them has added a measure of success to this experience.

The anxiety associated with student clinical experiences has been well documented in the literature (Admi, 1997; Beck & Srivastava, 1991; Kleehammer, Hart & Keck, 1990; Meisenhelder, 1993; Neill et al., 1998; Williams, 1993). By combining the clinical experience of juniors and seniors with differing levels of expertise, anxiety is decreased for both groups of students. Seniors are able to serve as role models and provide a teamwork approach in collaboration with the junior student. Seniors also apply principles of team building, delegation, and mentoring or coaching for performance. Yoder-Wise (2003) describes coaching as communication of the desired performance in a way to allow others to learn, think critically, and grow. The coaching relationship is thus based upon mutual agreement. Juniors benefit from the informal teaching and interaction with the senior, while seniors serve as role models and resource persons.

OUTCOMES

Peer learning is an active learning strategy that has been documented in the literature using a variety of clinical sites (Duchscher, 2001; Iwasiw & Goldenberg, 1993). Senior nursing students have come to practice the delegation process, realizing their own strengths and weaknesses in the process. They have few opportunities to actually practice select management or leadership skills and to correlate didactic management theory to the clinical setting. The senior students' confidence is increased because they know *how* to delegate as well as *what* to delegate. They also know they are responsible for the outcome of the delegated activity and are accountable to make sure the skill is carried out properly. This increased sense of responsibility and confidence along with improved organizational skills served as positive outcomes for the senior student. Functioning as peer mentors, senior students were expected to model professional nursing clinical behavior and attitudes in their interactions with patients, nurses, support staff, physicians, and other health team members. The leadership/management role was validated for the senior students in recognizing their ability to delegate and manage the care of their patients in an interdisciplinary health-care environment.

Junior students generally experienced anticipatory anxiety prior to their initial clinical experience in an acute-care hospital setting. Anxiety for the junior was lessened by being prepared for the clinical experience and by the bonding between the novice junior student and the senior student who has 1 year of clinical knowledge and experience. Reider and Riley-Giomariso (1993) identified select positive outcomes, such as feeling like a real nurse, providing good nursing care, and making a difference with the patient. Juniors were able to enhance their critical-thinking skills in a clinical setting to foster sound clinical judgment in a nonthreatening manner. The development of their technical skills that had been, up to this point, only practiced on other students and mannequins, were refined and adapted to the clinical setting.

All participants in the delegation experience were changed in some way. Seniors expressed more self-confidence and confidence in their ability to provide patient care. Juniors became exposed to the clinical practice of nursing and socialization into the profession. A positive interdependence and cooperative learning is fostered by the active exchange of technical, clinical, and organizational knowledge to stimulate critical-thinking processes for both groups of students. Delegation becomes a leadership skill that comes alive in its implementation for senior nursing students, while simultaneously having benefits related to selected skills of junior nursing students.

REFERENCES

Admi, H. (1997). Nursing students' stress during the initial clinical experience. *Journal of Nursing Education, 36*, 323–327.

American Association of Colleges of Nursing. (1998). *Essentials of baccalaureate education for professional nursing practice.* Washington, DC: Author.

Ammon, K. J., & Schroll, N. M. (1988). The junior student as peer leader. *Nursing Outlook, 36*(2), 85–86.

Beck, D. L., & Srivastava, R. (1991). Perceived level and sources of stress in baccalaureate nursing students. *Journal of Nursing Education, 30*(3), 127–133.

Bos, S. (1998). Perceived benefits of peer leadership as described by junior baccalaureate nursing students. *Journal of Nursing Education, 37*(4), 189–191.

Boucher, M. A. (1998). Delegation alert! *American Journal of Nursing, 98*(2), 26–32.

Broscious, S. K., & Saunders, D. J. (2001). Peer coaching. *Nurse Educator, 26,* 212–214.

Duchscher, J. E. B. (2001). Peer learning: A clinical teaching strategy to promote active learning. *Nurse Educator, 26*(2), 59–60.

Hansten, R., & Washburn, M. (1992). Delegation: How to deliver care through others. *American Journal of Nursing, 92*(3), 87–90.

Iwasiw, C. L., & Goldenberg, D. (1993). Peer teaching among nursing students in the clinical area: Effects on student learning. *Journal of Advanced Nursing, 18,* 659–668.

Joyce-Nagata, B., Reeb, R., & Burch, S. (1989). Comparison of expected and evidenced baccalaureate degree competencies. *Journal of Nursing Education, 28,* 314–321.

Kleehammer, K., Hart, A. L., & Keck, J. F. (1990). Nursing students' perceptions of anxiety-producing situations in the clinical setting. *Journal of Nursing Education, 29*(4), 183–187.

Loving, G. L. (1993). Competence validation and cognitive flexibility: A theoretical model grounded in nursing education. *Journal of Nursing Education, 32,* 415–421.

Meisenhelder, J. B. (1993). Anxiety: A block to clinical learning. *Nursing Education, 12*(6), 27–30.

National Council of State Boards of Nursing. (1997a). *Delegation decision-making-grid.* Retrieved November 24, 2003, from http://www.ncsbn.org/files/uap/delegationdocs.asp

National Council of State Boards of Nursing. (1997b). *Delegation decision-making tree.* Retrieved November 24, 2003, from http://www.ncsbn.org/files/uap/delegationdocs.asp

National League for Nursing. (1983). *Criteria for the evaluation of baccalaureate and higher degree programs in nursing.* New York: Author.

Neill, K. M., McCoy, A. K., Parry, C. B., Cochran, J., Curtis, J. C., & Ransom, R. B. (1998). The clinical experience of novice students in nursing. *Nurse Educator, 23*(4), 16–21.

Parkman, C. A. (1996). Delegation: Are you doing it right? *American Journal of Nursing, 96*(9), 43–48.

Primm, P. L. (1986). Entry into practice: Competency statements for BSNs and ADNs. *Nursing Outlook, 34*(3), 135–137.

Reider, J. A., & Riley-Giomariso, O. (1993). Baccalaureate nursing students' perspectives of their clinical nursing leadership experience. *Journal of Nursing Education, 32*(3), 127–132.

Sheehan, J. P. (2001). Delegating to UAPs A practical guide. *RN, 64*(11), 65–66.

Williams, R. P. (1993). The concerns of beginning nursing students. *Nursing and Health Care, 14*(4), 178–184.

Yoder-Wise, P. S. (2003). *Leading and managing in nursing.* St. Louis, MO: Mosby.

Zimmermann, P. G. (1996). Delegating to assistive personnel. *Journal of Emergency Nursing, 22,* 206–212.

CHAPTER TWENTY-SEVEN

A Capstone Leadership Course Via Distance Education

Deborah A. Rastinehad
Patricia A. Edwards

Technological advances coupled with the rapid and fluid nature of change have altered the landscape of health care organizations and those who work there, including their nurse leaders. Today's nurse leaders are challenged to operate in a dynamic environment in which control and direction are amorphous. This challenge, coupled with the demands of the information age, has precipitated the need to rethink and reengineer educational models for nursing leadership, including the way graduate programs in nursing administration and management organize, frame, and deliver curriculum. Curriculum design and delivery must include course work and experiences that reflect the nature and complexities faced by nurse leaders in the new millennium. This chapter focuses on a capstone experience within a distance education master's program.

EDUCATIONAL LEADERSHIP STRATEGY

Excelsior College in Albany, New York, a leader in distance education for many years, has developed a successful strategy that provides learning experiences that allow students to build their body of knowledge and assess their learning in a variety of modalities. The Master of Science in Nursing program with a major in clinical systems management and a strong health care informatics focus was created to prepare graduates for advanced roles as leaders and managers of health care and information systems. The graduate program was created for the adult learner who wants to study at a distance.

The distance-based program is premised on principles inherent in a social constructive model where a learner-centered approach and a collaborative environment provide a forum for active engagement of all members. The program creates a virtual learning community by connecting students to faculty, peers, and a wide range of resources via computer. The faculty facilitate and guide the learning process, and peer interaction and feedback are essential components of the program. The culmination of the program is the Capstone experience, which combines online discussion, face-to-face interaction, and a precepted administrative practicum.

LEADERSHIP PROGRAM

The curriculum includes graduate core and specialty courses that reflect a problem-centered approach and a real world context. Nursing core courses contain content that is foundational to the development of specialty knowledge. The core covers content areas such as health care economics, role development as a clinical systems leader and manager, policy development and implementation, research utilization, community building, and human diversity. Informatics courses focus on content that is supportive of the role of the clinical systems manager, including information management systems for health care, database design, and the ethical, political, social, and legal implications of information systems management. The specialty component of the curriculum focuses on the knowledge and skills required to work with and integrate systems and build dynamic organizational environments.

Upon entry into the program, students provide information about their motivation, learning style, use of technology, and support systems. They complete an orientation to the online learning platform, and their computer skills are assessed to determine areas where there is a need for additional support and education. Within the courses, faculty-student and student-student interactions serve to build a sense of community where peer support and encouragement are part of the norm.

Numerous group activities and assignments help students to develop and implement the roles of leader and manager, including change management, financial and resource allocation, workforce management, role development, organizational culture, and strategic initiatives. Students engage in a variety of critical-thinking activities to address multidimensional problems. They also use sophisticated written and oral communication processes to assist them to develop the skills required for leadership roles in health care. Their actions are directed toward the achievement of organizational outcomes.

CAPSTONE EXPERIENCE

The capstone experience at the completion of the program provides students with the opportunity to integrate and apply the knowledge and skills acquired in the core and specialty courses to the real world of practice in the form of actual and simulated leadership situations. The capstone is multidimensional and consists of a precepted administrative practicum, online discussion, and leadership retreat. Performance assessment of the student's attainment of program competencies is built into the three components.

During the capstone experience, students are required to develop and implement a management project within a health care enterprise based on needs assessment and organizational data and information. Faculty guide students in the endeavor by providing detailed written instructions as well as multiple opportunities to communicate directly with them regarding the selection of the organization, project, and preceptor. Faculty continue to guide and facilitate student learning through interaction with students during the online seminar component and at the on-site leadership retreat.

The administrative practicum is designed to provide students with the opportunity to experience organizational leadership and management directly and to observe and participate on a management team in a health care organization under the guidance of a preceptor. Students are able to assess the role of the nurse leader and team members within the selected organization and to analyze the structure, culture, and dynamics of the organization, including power, communication channels and information systems, decision making, and problem solving.

The online discussion is designed to allow students to synthesize program content by engaging in structured dialogue about ethical, legal, financial, and sociopolitical issues as they relate to clinical systems management. They critically examine the nurse leader's role and evaluate the role elements of leader, manager, communicator, decision maker, and systems thinker. This component provides students with the support and guidance of faculty and peers while they are completing the administrative practicum, and is a modeling experience in professional networking.

The leadership retreat, a 2-day on-site component, allows students to interact with faculty and colleagues and demonstrate synthesis of their graduate program coursework. The retreat is designed to provide students with an opportunity to participate in active learning and evaluation strategies with faculty and their peer group, and to demonstrate role elements of the leader, including communication and presentation skills. Students conduct a self-assessment of leadership skills and the use of power and influence in order to formulate a plan for self-improvement and career development. They interact in a dynamic manner, receiving feedback to round out the larger learning experience.

PROS AND CONS OF USING ONLINE LEARNING

The capstone experience is a blend of online, on-site, and clinical learning strategies. The paradigm shift from traditional to online learning has inherent controversy. This strategy may be perceived positively by some, while others may perceive it negatively. For example, learning style preferences may or may not be compatible with the online approach to learning. Also, because individuals are unique in many ways, including the way they learn, the problem-oriented, self-directed, learner-centered approach used in nontraditional program learning may not be suitable for learners who enjoy the pedagogical approach of a teacher-directed, subject-centered environment.

Another area of controversy involves the use of the technology necessary for online learning. On the one hand, technology can enhance interactive participation, foster the building of a diverse online community, expand networking opportunities, and serve as a source for program materials and global resources. On the other, technical difficulties such as hardware or software problems can disrupt and cripple learning, frustrate learners, and in some cases actually serve as a barrier to learning. In addition, the cost and need for technical support is sometimes prohibitive.

Finally, although online learning may create a sense of isolation for some, few would argue about the convenience associated with online learning. The flexibility and convenience of online learning eliminates travel issues and the other constraints associated with campus-based programs such as on-site attendance for classes that are held during specified periods of time. Being able to deliver anyplace, anytime educational opportunities leading to a graduate degree has been very important for students who are dispersed across the country. Though some experience problems with time zone differences when trying to schedule synchronous discussions, students are overwhelmingly positive about the online experience. To date we have had graduates from as far away as Alaska and a number from rural areas in the western part of the country who were unable to attend campus-based programs because of time or travel constraints.

OUTCOMES

It was expected that students would achieve the stated program outcomes (see Box) by the completion of the capstone experience and that its three components would provide opportunities for critical discussions and a synthesis of content from the core and specialty courses in the curriculum. Evaluations from the three cohorts of students that have completed the program thus far indicated that these expectations were met or exceeded in all areas. Projects undertaken in the practicum made a significant contribution to the student's organization, and presentations during the retreat provided opportunity to share the information orally and receive feedback. The following is a sample of projects undertaken during the capstone experience:

- Creating and reengineering care processes within an orthopedic unit
- Acuity validation and computerization
- HIPAA training project
- Self-management of diabetes
- Demystifying NIC and NOC: A documentation tool for patient care plans on medical-surgical units
- Patient/family education project

At the onset of the program, faculty developed mechanisms for students to get to know each other and hopefully come together as a virtual class. These included "home pages" for students and faculty profiles and the expectation that at the beginning of the course each participant would provide an introduction, giving some background information and their expectations related to the course and content. Most of the courses had team assignments and, through their synchronous and asynchronous discussions and communication, came together in ways very different from what might happen in the traditional classroom. By the end of the capstone experience, students commented that they felt very close as a group, even though most had never met face to face. Students reported that the relationships built during the program would be lifelong and that the networking opportunities with both expert faculty and students from across the country were a wonderful, unexpected result.

CONCLUSION

Organizations need to operate efficiently and effectively within the parameters of a changing and challenging health care environment, while the demand for knowledgeable and skilled nursing leaders at all levels of management and administration continues to rise. The changing health care environment mandates that these nurse leaders be credible, self-assured, business oriented, and possess the traits of a nontraditional learner. "Visionary, transforming nurse leaders are needed to respond to institutional challenges and speak for the profession and for the public it serves" (Horton-Deutsch & Mohr, 2001, p. 124). Nurse leaders must be aware of and implement elements that create an environment that supports professional nursing practice.

The economic challenges facing educational and health care organizations require a creative approach to designing strategies to develop nurses who will be successful managers and leaders, prepared to meet current and future health care system demands. Innovations in the delivery of educational programs must be explored and carefully evaluated to ensure high standards of academic performance and the successful preparation of students for the demands of nursing management practice. The distance education model described has successfully graduated a number of nurses who have been selected for leadership positions in their health care organizations. These nurse leaders are well prepared to apply the knowledge and skills developed during the program to improve outcomes for health care delivery systems and create partnerships and collaborations within nursing and across disciplines.

Program outcomes.

- [ ] Articulates the role of the master's prepared nurse within the philosophical and theoretical framework of nursing science and links it to the role of the clinical systems manager across systems

- [ ] Uses critical thinking and decision-making skills to identify problems and seek interventions that improve outcomes for health care delivery systems

- [ ] Applies knowledge and skills needed in the use and management of information systems related to client care, organizational operations and policy

- [ ] Implements team building strategies that create partnerships and collaboration within nursing and across disciplines

- [ ] Uses data to make decisions in determining effective utilization and distribution of fiscal and human resources

- [ ] Applies the principles and theories of performance improvement, systems thinking, health policy, and knowledge-based practice to manage the health care enterprise

- [ ] Communicates effectively with multiple stakeholders about professional and health care systems issues using a variety of strategies

- [ ] Develops organizational strategies that address the ethical, legal, and socio-political needs of diverse client populations around the issues of health and access to health care delivery systems

- [ ] Implements the advanced role of the nurse as clinical systems manager according to the scope and standards of professional practice

- [ ] Develops research-based practice using the research process to enhance cost-effective quality

REFERENCES

Horton-Deutsch, S., & Mohr, W. (2001). The fading of nursing leadership, *Nursing Outlook, 49*, 121–126.

CHAPTER TWENTY-EIGHT

Developing a Change Project to Practice Leadership Skills

Lucy B. Trice
Laura D'Alisera
John W. Frank

A change project was the capstone experience for a Helene Fuld Health Trust–sponsored leadership project at the University of North Florida (UNF). Two entities at the UNF, the School of Nursing (SON) and the Institute of Government (IOG), joined forces to develop the leadership project. The IOG provides training programs for a variety of organizations within the UNF service area. The SON and IOG collaborated on the curriculum for the leadership project, with staff from IOG coordinating plans for the workshops and retreat that formed an integral part of the project. The title of the project was E.K.G. Education, Knowledge and Growth: The Heart of Nursing Leadership—Project EKG for short. This chapter describes this capstone experience.

Project EKG was designed to increase leadership competencies in baccalaureate nursing students by first increasing leadership competencies in nursing instructors. Both academic faculty and nurses from clinical sites who work closely with nursing students were targeted. The premise was that as these instructors become more skilled in leadership themselves, they are more likely to model appropriate leadership behaviors in their teaching and interacting with students, and thus provide students with greater opportunities to interpret the principles and dynamics of leadership in their own professional lives.

PROJECT EKG

Project EKG was built around a series of monthly workshops, beginning with a 2-day opening retreat that served to introduce participants to the goals of the project and facilitate self- and other-awareness through use of the Myers Briggs Type Inventory (MBTI) and the Fundamental Interpersonal Relations Orientation-Behavior (FIRO-B) instruments, along with analysis and discussion of the results. Leadership skills such as principles of change, creativity, and collaboration were also explored during this initial retreat. The retreat was followed by a series of workshops at approximately 4-week intervals that dealt with various topics related to leadership competencies, including emotional intelligence, conflict management, public speaking, assertiveness, professional image/business etiquette, and lobbying and issues development. It also included a fieldtrip to the state capitol during the legislative session to meet with legislators, lobbyists, and other governmental leaders, and view legislators in session.

The capstone experience of Project EKG provided an opportunity to practice leadership skills through the selection, development, and implementation of a change project. Adult learners are ideally suited to the use of a change project as a learning tool, which provides relevance for the material to be learned by directly connecting it to the real world. In our experience, change projects can and have been used effectively with nursing students and also with nurses already in the workforce. The literature also supports the importance of experiential learning in general and the use of change projects in particular for incorporation of skills, both management/leadership and other types of skills (Allan & Cornes, 1998; Carlson-Catalano, 1992; Francke, Garssen, & Abu-Saad, 1995; Kaplan, 1990).

EKG participants selected individual projects designed to increase their creativity, leadership, assertiveness, image, and public speaking by practicing these leadership skills. Projects involved a change in some aspect related to the participants' respective workplaces. Participants were expected to develop, implement, and evaluate the effectiveness of their projects. At the final session, participants presented their projects and their analysis of outcomes. Group discussions focused on identifying what actually was being changed in the project, the outcomes, principles of leadership that were exhibited, and potential impact on students and the wider organization. Additionally, ideas were exchanged regarding strategies that might improve success in the instance where the outcome was not positive.

Projects from both academic faculty and from the service industry were ambitious and clearly demonstrated leadership skills. An example of one project from service and one from academia will be presented to illustrate the efficacy of the change project assignment as a strategy for teaching and developing leadership.

EXAMPLE #1: DEVELOPING A NURSING RESOURCE LIBRARY ON A CRITICAL CARE UNIT

Description

Ms. Smith was a staff nurse in a critical care unit. Her project was to take a storage room on the unit and turn it into a nursing resource "library." She envisioned the room as a quiet area to serve as a credentialing station to do annual tests/competencies, a reference library with appropriate nursing journals, and a place to post clinical literature reviews written by nurses who participate in the hospital's clinical ladder program. She successfully implemented this change.

What the Project Sought to Change

The purpose of the project was to inspire and motivate nurses to value continued learning by creating an environment that promotes education in the context of bedside research.

Outcomes

Ms. Smith saw the outcomes of the project as very positive. She had involved the staff in planning the room and its contents; they were using this resource as intended, and had expressed appreciation to her for what she had done.

Principles of Leadership

The principles of leadership exhibited in this project and identified by the other participants included strategic vision with clear goals and capacity to structure a change process to implement those goals; ability to inspire and motivate others; willingness to take a risk; creativity and imagination; collaboration/networking with others on the unit and in the institution to build support for the initiative through multiple layers of the organization, including management, staff, and students; and political awareness as demonstrated by having the unit director announce the project, showing wider ownership. The inclusion of "required annual updates" demonstrated an awareness of the need to stay current and responsiveness to staff interests and needs. She anticipated that this approach would in effect guarantee that everyone on the unit would continue to use the room and thus be exposed to other items in it, in addition to the annual updates. So Ms. Smith effectively planned and moved the change process along.

Potential Impact on Students and New Grads

The project modeled for students how leaders get "buy-in" from others and provided some space for staff to do research themselves, demonstrating a commitment to lifelong learning.

Potential Impact on the Wider Organization

The success of this project provides encouragement for other units to establish similar resource space; the project actively reinforces an organizational culture that values continued education and lifelong learning.

Six-month Follow-up

The library is still in existence and being used, although Ms. Smith has to be vigilant to eliminate extraneous equipment that still finds its way into the room on occasion. Further, more nurses on this unit have joined the local chapter of the critical care nurses association than prior to the project. Although Ms. Smith is reluctant to attribute this happening solely to implementation of the library, she does feel that it has raised awareness on the unit of the need for on-going education.

EXAMPLE #2: MOVING FROM TEACHING TO LEARNING

Description

In this example, Ms. Jones redesigned a health assessment course from a lecture approach with supervised laboratory design to a module-based curriculum grounded in self-directed learning with minimal lecture time. In the modified course, the laboratory portion consists of specific times for individual assistance and check-off of validation rather than a time for structured teaching.

What the Project Sought to Change

The project targeted resistance to self-directed learning from students who prefer to be spoon fed, and sought to motivate students to participate in an open learning environment where faculty and students pursue mutual goals that emphasize critical thinking, integration of past experience, education, and problem solving.

Outcomes

Ms. Jones completed the modularization and the course was implemented in the summer term immediately following Project EKG, with successful results; students were positively motivated and did well from a grade performance standpoint.

Principles of Leadership

The principles of leadership exhibited in this project and identified by the other participants included strategic vision with a clear eye on the future in terms of educational principles; a willingness to take a risk (students not happy with the new way of doing things could have given Ms. Jones poor evaluations, which may have adversely impacted her teaching position); effective communication, collaboration, and networking with peers and administration to achieve buy-in; effective planning and moving the change process along, implementing the revised course with the very next group of students; and revision of the course in this manner, which showed creativity and imagination.

Potential Impact on Students and New Grads

The project has a very direct application to students, in that implementation was in their hands. The by-product of self-direction is to help students recognize their own potential. The project should also boost an "I can do" attitude, and likewise empower leadership in the students.

Potential Impact on the Wider Organization

Other faculty may elect to redesign their courses or portions of their courses to allow for more self-directed learning.

Six-month Follow-up

Ms. Jones indicated there was some initial grumbling from the first group of students, but their scores on tests and their final grades were basically comparable to students who completed the course with the previous format. The second offering of the course was near completion at the time of this writing, and this group of students is actually performing better than students did with the previous format. Other faculty are showing more evidence of thinking outside the box and are indeed incorporating more self-directed learning into other courses. For example, one skills course has also been modularized, using the assessment course as the model.

THE CAPSTONE CHANGE PROJECT

Designing and implementing a change project is an ideal method for allowing learners to practice leadership skills. Identifying areas for change and potential barriers and facilitators requires the use of high-level assessment and critical analysis skills. The areas for change must be targeted, but equally important for success of the project is the analysis of the political and social climate of the unit or workplace in which the change will be implemented. Strategic vision also comes into play, as the concept of planned change is based on the assumption that the future will be altered for the better because of the change being implemented in the present. Communication, collaboration, and risk taking are necessary to develop and implement the plan for change. Following implementation, assessing the outcome of the project again requires critical thinking and analysis.

Important to the success of the change project as a learning tool is creation of a "safe learning environment." It is essential that learners feel safe—for example, that their grade will not depend on the outcome of the change project—so that they are willing to practice the risk taking inherent in implementing change. To create a safe environment, success is defined as completion of the assignment, measured by the thoroughness of the implemented planned change process and the depth of analysis of project outcomes, rather than whether or not the change itself was successful. The learner's analysis should include conclusions about the outcome of the change project implemented. For example, was the change successfully implemented, why or why not, and what could have been done differently to enhance an already positive outcome or facilitate a positive outcome if one was not achieved.

The final step in using the change project as a tool for teaching leadership is the learners' presentation of the projects to peers. Individual learning takes place through work on the project, but overall learning of the group is greatly enhanced through hearing how each learner went through the process, including the analysis of outcomes. Presentations allow for group processing of the projects themselves, including a sharing of ideas about what to do next time for those whose projects did not have positive outcomes. Discussion of the presentations can be a forum for analyzing the leadership skills demonstrated in each project. Additionally, the act of preparing and delivering the presentation allows for practice in thought organization and public speaking, both of which are important leadership skills.

There are two added bonuses or serendipitous outcomes in using a change project as a learning tool for leadership skills. The underlying purpose of using the project is to allow learners to practice leadership skills. At the same time, however, they are practicing the steps of planned change. The opportunity to cement both sets of skills is invaluable in developing leadership. Additionally, completing a change project with a positive outcome is empowering for the individual, by enhancing self-image and "making a difference" in one's workplace, both of which are important to developing leadership. Even a project with a negative outcome affords a measure of empowerment through the analysis of what went wrong and the identification of future strategies to achieve positive outcomes. Often, learning takes place as much from mistakes as from successes. Another advantage of sharing through presentations is that each project with a positive outcome will have an empowering effect on the entire group.

There are also drawbacks to using the change project as a learning strategy. Completing the steps of change takes time. It cannot be done overnight or even in a week or two. To use this strategy effectively, the learning program must be sufficient in length. Also, there is risk of loss of self-image in those whose projects do not have positive outcomes. This particular drawback should be kept in mind when structuring assignments and when facilitating discussion during presentations. Every effort should be made to assist participants to see that an unsuccessful change project is not a failure, but an opportunity to learn what will be of assistance in future projects.

In summary, there are several clear advantages to using a change project as a method for teaching leadership skills. First and perhaps foremost is the opportunity to practice one's skills in a real-world setting, rather than in a contrived classroom setting. This experience affords an opportunity not only to practice the skills, but also to learn on the spot, as well as in reflection on the process, both individually and through peer interaction. Structuring the assignment so that the environment is safe is a win-win situation, because students take on the assignment with greater commitment and freedom, not focusing so much on having their grades be based on the positive outcomes of their projects. Presentation of the completed projects provides for further practice of leadership skills. Last, individual learners derive a sense of empowerment through completion of the project. On the other hand, a disadvantage of this strategy is that students may be disappointed when their projects do not have positive outcomes. To avoid this, care must be taken to emphasize the value of the learning that has been accomplished even when projects have negative outcomes.

OUTCOMES

In addition to practicing leadership skills through planning and implementing a change project, learners also gain experience in working through the steps of planned change. Further, while successful implementation of change is empowering for the individual learner, coming together to discuss and analyze each other's projects has the added effect of empowering the entire group. The best-case scenario is that the workplaces where these change projects were completed become more open to change. Other areas within the institution may see the change as valuable and choose to emulate the project or develop another. Also, there may be a spillover effect of empowerment of workplace peers as they see their peers achieving.

CONCLUSION

Today's increasingly complex health care system poses a unique challenge for nurses in terms of leadership. Nurses at every level, from top-ranked management to the newest nurse in the trenches, need to be equipped with the knowledge and skills to lead and manage effectively. To move forward on nursing's agenda for autonomous practice and improved patient care that focuses on health promotion and maintenance as well as illness care, leadership will need to become a part of every nurses' repertoire of skills.

The foundation for leadership skills often begins in the classroom, whether in the basic nursing curriculum or, following graduation, in various continuing education programs. This classroom experience is necessary in order to lay the groundwork for acquiring skills in self-knowledge, critical thinking, communication, collaboration, risk taking, creativity, inspiring and leading change, strategic vision, and other characteristics associated with leadership. To cement these skills in order to translate them from rhetoric to action, however, experiential learning that allows for actual practice of these skills is essential. Two examples of change projects exemplify the use of a capstone change project to teach leadership skills to adult learners, one related to a nursing student population and the other to practicing nurses. Positive aspects of this strategy for developing leaders far outweigh any negative aspects that were identified during the capstone project experience.

REFERENCES

Allan, D., & Cornes, D. (1998). The impact of management of change projects on practice: A description of the contribution that one educational programme made to the quality of health care. *Journal of Advanced Nursing, 27,* 865–869.

Carlson-Catalano, J. (1992). Empowering nurses for professional practice. *Nursing Outlook, 40*(3), 139–142.

Francke, A. L., Garssen, B., & Abu-Saad, H. H. (1995). Determinants of changes in nurses' behaviour after continuing education: A literature review. *Journal of Advanced Nursing, 21,* 371–377.

Kaplan, S. M. (1990). The nurse as change agent. *Pediatric Nursing, 16,* 603–605, 618.

CHAPTER TWENTY-NINE

Growing Leaders in Developing Nations

Sharon M. Weinstein

With the transition from the Soviet Union in the 1990s, a plethora of new independent nations evolved, and at the same time, something ended. Members of the health care community, once linked by a common country, were no longer able to communicate with their former colleagues through international conferences and symposia. This chapter describes an initiative to develop leaders across continents.

The American International Health Alliance (AIHA), founded in 1992 through a cooperative agreement with the United States Agency for International Development (USAID), facilitated communications and partnerships between US health care providers and their foreign counterparts, but more important, across country lines. Previously considered midlevel personnel, nurses have benefited from these changes more than any other group by becoming part of an ongoing community of nurse leaders and scholars. Initial efforts by US health care providers focused on building a base of knowledge related to clinical practice, nursing curriculum, and the creation of nursing associations. Building on the success of these programs, I worked with colleagues to create the International Nursing Leadership Institute

(INLI), a unique yearlong three-session learning experience designed for nurse leaders.

Using adult learning principles and an interactive approach to learning resulted in the creation of a cadre of developing leaders for developing nations. The strategy could be implemented in any emerging country but was targeted to the Newly Independent States (NIS) of the former Soviet Union and Central Eastern European countries. Nurses in the NIS and Central and Eastern Europe (CEE) faced numerous challenges following the dissolution of the Soviet Union (see Figure 29.1). Unlike their colleagues in the United States and western Europe, the role of the nurse in these regions was viewed as an extension of the physician's role—a middle level worker rather than an independent professional. Lack of professional standards, the absence of nurses in positions of power and influence, low status, insufficient pay, high turnover, and low morale all presented an opportunity for significant change. Thus evolved the partnership model, creating the first nursing initiative in 1992 (Weinstein & Brooks, 2003).

FIGURE 29.1 Participant Countries, INLI Program.

New Independent States (NIS)	*West NIS*
Russian Federation	Belarus
	Moldva
Caucasus	Latvia
Armenia	Ukraine
Azerbaijan	
Georgia	*Central/Eastern Europe*
	Albania
Central Asian Republics	Croatia
Kazakhstan	Latvia
Kyrgyzstan	Romania
Tajikistan	
Turkmenistan	
Uzbekistan	

THE STRATEGY

Early in 1992, nursing emerged as a key issue throughout NIS and CEE countries. Cognizant of the need to tackle nursing issues within the context of a partnership model, US nurse leaders developed nursing task forces to meet the challenges of nurses at an institutional level and to provide a forum for the exchange of ideas and lessons learned. The task forces were the driving force behind the nursing agenda with a focus on three areas: education, practice, and leadership.

Education

A series of in-country conferences focused on education and curriculum reform. Local nursing resource centers (NRCs) provided nursing faculty, students, and practitioners with alternative forms of learning. Each site was equipped with computers, textbooks, videotapes, anatomical models, and educational posters that addressed clinical, managerial, and psychosocial aspects of health care. The centers have encouraged independent learning and enhanced traditional teaching methodologies. Nurses attest to the impact of the nursing initiative and the NRC on their profession.

Basic nursing education in the NIS/CEE has traditionally been viewed as vocational training rather than university-based. Comprised primarily of physician educators to teach nurses, a move toward development of a cadre of nursing faculty evolved. The natural starting point was the creation of a baccalaureate-level model. Traditionally, baccalaureate and advanced practice nursing were not available in all countries. Nursing education has now expanded from a 2-year program to advance clinical and management training. Four-year baccalaureate nursing programs and continuous learning have become commonplace, including skills laboratories, postgraduate training, and the extensive use of the NRCs. International nursing conferences have extended the learning process and NIS/CEE nurses attended the International Council of Nurses meetings in London and Copenhagen.

Clinical Practice

Changes in clinical practice occurred with the introduction of clinical practice guidelines, nursing standards, and policies and procedures. Process workshops introduced practice patterns that have transformed nursing's role and image. Countries such as Kyrgyzstan and Russia have seen the development of new nursing roles for clinical nurse educators, clinical managers, and nurse teachers.

Leadership

The first nursing association in Russia was founded in 1992 to serve as a voice for the nursing profession before the government, other nongovernmental organizations, and the public at large. Although delegates from 44 regions of the Russian Federation emerged as fledgling leaders, they lacked the experience and advocacy skills necessary to enter into a policy dialogue with local officials. Training in organizational development and strategy formulation to influence policy change that was supportive of the nursing profession contributed to the success of these associations, which now exist in all countries of the former NIS/CEE. The All Russian Nursing Association, which follows the *federation* model, has applied for membership in the International Council of Nurses (ICN).

RATIONALE

Leaders have historically helped others to integrate their personal values with the values of the workplace—and to explain the paradoxes when values collided. Because senior nurses in NIS/CEE countries have always taken a back seat to physician administrators within their respective institutions, it was essential that they develop the skills associated with senior leadership roles. Many participants in the first INLI class had traveled at some point to the United States and had seen their counterparts in the work environments in which they practiced. The partnership model set the stage for early development and helped to identify emerging nurse leaders in each country and region. Over a 3-year period, these early leaders became presidents and executive directors of local nursing associations and chief nurses of their respective health ministries. The INLI format satisfied the next phase of the leadership model—the ability to sustain the successes and disseminate them to a larger pool of nurses.

Faculty members were chosen from US nurse leaders with experience in the NIS/CEE countries. We used adult learning methods to create an integrated curriculum, graduating the learner into an ongoing community of colleagues and peers. Instruction was active, student-centered, and based on the learner's goals. We created an environment that had real-life application for the material being learned, built on previous life experiences and promoting positive self-esteem and self-worth (Training Post, 2003).

TABLE 29.1 Core Subjects Covered in the Yearlong INLI Curriculum

Session One	Session Two	Session Three
Leadership competencies	SWOT analysis	Ethics
Adult learning principles	Time, change, and barrier management	Critical thinking
Expectations of INLI participants/faculty	Performance appraisals/ human resource management	Customer service
Group norms and group dynamics	Systems thinking	Professional development
Introduction of the theme	Continuous quality improvement	Mentoring and coaching
Project development, management, and monitoring	Meeting planning	Developing strategic partnerships
Computer skills	Influencing policy development	Quality management
Teamwork	Negotiation/conflict resolution	
Publishing/dissemination strategies		
Communicating with diverse audiences		
Evaluation methodologies		

Faculty used a series of leading management books to generate the curriculum (Table 29.1). Students and faculty, in full costume, acted out the stories. For example, the parable of *Who Moved My Cheese* (Johnson, 1998) encouraged students to have contingency plans and to expect change. A maze was created and students moved through the maze to reach their destinations, facing multiple stumbling blocks along the way, including a shortage of cheese (supplies). *The Oz Principle* (Connors, Smith, & Hickman, 1998) told students that they could be or do whatever they wanted . . . if they wanted it badly enough! The author contended that like Dorothy and her companions in *The Wizard of Oz,* most people in the corporate world possess the power within themselves to get the results they need. Instead, they behave as though they were victims of circumstance. The authors demonstrated how anyone can move beyond making excuses to obtaining the results they want, an important leadership tool. Faculty played the role of the characters, and led students through the story, ending in Dorothy's ability to return home as a result of the power within. *Goldilocks on Management* (Mayer & Mayer, 1999) featured a series of revisionist fairy tales for serious managers. A message from the author's story of "Chicken Little" reminded students that they could control rumors with timely, accurate, and effective communication. Costumes, props, and teamwork enriched course content.

Critical thinking is an imperative for the professional nurse. A number of quantitative researchers have studied and measured the associated skills for critical thinking (Andrews, 1999; Cammuso, 2003). The Neuman systems model was used to explore application to foreign nurse leaders by building on the concept of intervention to strengthen the line of defense or deal with interpersonal and extrapersonal environmental stressors. To gain these skill sets and apply interventions, INLI students participated in thought-provoking exercises in the classroom, worked collaboratively in small cross-country groups, and completed reflection journal entries. Students were also required to develop a project, with local ministry and institutional approval. Assignments and presentations were critiqued for evidence of critical thinking, such as identifying, defining, collaborating, prioritizing, choosing options, clarifying, and summarizing.

Lessons on systems enabled learners to understand big-picture thinking and the impact of change in complex systems. Once we embrace the idea that systems thinking can improve individual learning by inducing people to focus on the whole system, and by providing individuals with the skills and tools to enable them to derive observable patterns of behavior from the systems they see at work, the next step is to justify why this process is so important to organizations of people (Larsen, 1996).

Lessons on the use of cause-and-effect thinking helped students understand organizational issues. Participants learned about 360-degree performance appraisals and the importance of feedback from multiple sources. Guest faculty from global nursing organizations, such as Sigma Theta Tau International Honor Society (STTI), the American Organization of Nurse Executives (AONE), the World Health Organization (WHO), and the ICN enhanced the quality of the education. For example, Patricia Thompson (STTI) taught the students a scholarly approach to leadership, and Kirsten Stallkneckt (ICN) addressed the students on the ICN mission and her role as president.

Based on faculty input, classroom content, and project development, participants were asked to rate the teaching team's effectiveness in using resources, time, materials, group activities, and interpreters. Following graduation, participants were encouraged to continue to work with INLI graduates in their respective countries of the NIS and CEE. Armed with the talent and tools needed to advance in their nursing careers, the first class graduated in June 2000. Four graduates were selected to serve as faculty for the next round of training workshops. Subsequent classes achieved similar results, and 34 of the 60 graduates have been granted international membership in AONE or been inducted as community leaders in STTI.

PROS AND CONS OF THE PROGRAM

INLI has served as the primary vehicle for the development of sustained nursing leadership for the region. As a result of the partner-to-partner program and participation in INLI, former staff nurses and nurse managers have achieved recognition as presidents of local and national nursing associations, faculty in colleges and schools of nursing and ministry chief nurses. The partnership model has empowered them to be more resourceful and independent; be critical thinkers; plan for nursing's future; educate colleagues, patients, and the community; manage departments, nursing units, and organizations; represent their organization and profession to the public; and speak with one collective voice.

OUTCOMES

Through the exceptional leadership of nurse leaders, educators, and clinicians in the developing nations of the NIS and CEE, the discipline and practice of nursing has advanced in a multitude of ways that serve the people from all regions and have produced cross-country linkages. No longer considered a middle-level health job, nurses now view nursing as a career that focuses on personal vision, career, and succession planning. They view themselves as role models, coaches, and mentors, and have emerged as advocates for the profession with a focus on continuous learning. For example, Ruzanna Ginosyan, chief nursing officer at Emergency Scientific Medical Center in Armenia, whose responsibility included serving lunch to foreign guests in 1993, told the author, "I can now eat lunch with you, but I cannot serve you because I am a professional."

Graduates are aware of the need to share knowledge with colleagues, to respect the wisdom of long-term employees, and to encourage creativity (National Health Service, 2002). The newly developed leaders in these still developing nations collaborate with others, have developed a global network of colleagues, and are respected as innovators in their countries and beyond. The impact of the leadership development model over the past decade is impressive. Accomplishments are the direct result of an intense voluntary effort on the part of US nurse leaders and the determined passion of the newly developed nurse leaders. Nursing education reform is a global concern. There is a remarkable similarity in the issues being tackled, including new program development (Salvage, 1995). The INLI program has tackled the challenge of developing the next generation of nurse leaders for developing nations in the NIS/CEE regions.

REFERENCES

Andrews M. (1999). *Transcultural concepts in nursing care* (3rd ed., p. 535). Philadelphia: Lippincott Williams & Williams.

Cammuso, B. (2003). *The Implementation of strategies to develop critical thinking skills in freshmen nursing students.* Retrieved November 20, 2003, from the Ninth Biennial International Neuman Systems Model Symposia Web site: http://www.neumansystemsmodel.com/news/page1.htm#NeumanBook

Connors, R., Smith T., & Hickman, C. R. (1998). *The Oz principle.* Paramus, NJ: Prentice-Hall.

Johnson, S. (1998). *Who moved my cheese?* New York: Putnam.

Larsen, K. (1996) *Systems thinking.* Retrieved November 15, 2003, from Learning Organizations Web site: http://home.nycap.rr.com/klarsen/learningorg/

Mayer, G. G., & Mayer T. (1999) *Goldilocks on management.* New York: Amacom (American Management Association).

National Health Service. (2002) *The national nurse leadership project.* Retrieved November 15, 2003, from the National Health Service Web site: http://www.nursingleadership.co.uk/resourc/r_tools.htm#culture

Salvage, J. (1995) Global trends in nursing education. In D. M. Modly et al (Eds.), *Advancing nursing education worldwide.* New York: Springer.

Training Post. (2003). *How to apply adult learning principles.* Retrieved November 20, 2003, from the training post web site: http://www.trainingpost.org/alpover.htm

Weinstein S., & Brooks, A. M. (2003). *Nursing in the NIS/CEE region: Its changing face. Reflections on Nursing Leadership, Fourth Quarter,* pp. 16–19, 44.

ANNOTATED BIBLIOGRAPHY

Prepared by Angela Northrup Wantroba

Aroian, J. (2002). Leader as visionary. *Nursing Leadership Forum, 7,* 53–56.

Developing nurse leaders for today and tomorrow is a priority, considering the powerful relationship between leadership strength and the influence of the nursing profession on the future of health care. This article addresses leadership theories and research as they relate to visionary leadership. Education for visionary leadership is also addressed, including the competencies and skill sets for effective visionary leaders. Visioning is a powerful force for change in shaping organizations and building teams for the future.

Bos, S. (1998, Apr.). Perceived benefits of peer leadership as described by junior baccalaureate nursing students. *Journal of Nursing Education, 37*(4), 189–191.

This article describes student perceptions of a peer leadership experience that were incorporated into their clinical experiences. Using self-evaluations, student responses were placed into six categories: benefits, practice in prioritizing, enhancement of critical-thinking skills, enhancement of technical skills, realization of peers as resources, and development of management skills. Peer leadership experiences need to be assessed for their value in teaching leadership to nursing students.

Cook, M. (2001). The attributes of effective clinical nurse leaders. *Nursing Standard, 15*(35), 33–36.

The focus of this article is identifying the attributes of effective clinical nurse leaders. A cross-section of nurses and nursing students were asked to choose study participants who exhibited effective leadership qualities. From these participants five attributes were identified: highlighting, respecting, influencing, creativity, and supporting. They went on to distinguish five typologies of effective clinical nurse leaders, that is, discoverer, valuer, enabler, shaper, and modifier. The author suggests that leadership preparation is needed during initial nurse preparation so that nursing leadership can be secured for the longer term.

Copp, S. (2002). Using cooperative learning strategies to teach implications of the Nurse Practice Act. *Nurse Educator, 27*(5), 236–241.

This article describes cooperative learning strategies as promoting greater student involvement, greater retention of material, and transfer of learning. Following a 1-hour lecture on the topic, senior nursing students in a leadership course were given a group assignment to present the Nurse Practice Act. They were divided into five heterogeneous groups as determined by their cumulative grade point average. Results from student evaluations were positive. The purpose of collaborative learning was to provide active learning opportunities for the students, which helps students develop problem-solving skills.

Cox, L. (2003). Enhancing student leadership development in community Settings. *Nurse Educator, 28*(3), 127–31.

The authors describe a leadership module for senior nursing students that focuses on systems theory and partnership with communities. Nursing students attended a 3-hour orientation seminar that focused on six parts to the module. The experience allowed students to gain critical knowledge of the interrelationships, patterns, and structures that provide key information for problem solving in issues of community health.

Cronewett, L., & Redman, R. (2003). Partners in action, nursing education and nursing practice. *Journal of Nursing Administration, 33*(3), 131–133.

There are many health care settings that are sites for the clinical education of nursing students. The authors challenge clinical sites to evaluate their affiliations with nursing schools. Emphasis is on the idea that the partnerships between nursing education and nursing practice should be encouraged to grow and be mutually beneficial for both.

DeSimone, B. (1999). Perceptions of leadership competence between interns and mentors in a cooperative nurse internship. *Nurse Educator, 24*(4), 21–25.

This article describes a nurse internship that brought together new graduates with nurse managers and nursing faculty for a 1-year period. During the year graduates worked with a mentor (nurse manager) and were taught leadership skills. The interns and the mentors measured their leadership competence at the second and last weeks of the program. These competencies consisted of communication, association, sanction, delegation, initiation, and external legitimacy. At the end of the program, perceptions of leadership competence improved in every category.

Dienemann, J. (2002). Leader as achiever. *Nursing Leadership Forum, 7,* 63–68.

The outcome of leadership· productive achievement is explored in this article. Without achievement one is judged to not be a leader. Thus, the ideal leader must be a visionary, critical thinker, expert, communicator, mentor, and achiever of organizational goals. This article explores the organizational context that supports achievement, measures of quality nursing care, fiscal accountability, leadership development, and rewards and punishments. The educational content and teaching strategies to prepare graduates to be achievers are discussed.

Fonville, A., Killian, F., & Tranbarger, R. (1998). Developing new nurse leaders. *Nursing Economics, 16*(2), 83–88.

The authors describe the development of an associate clinical nurse manager (ACNM) role in a rural hospital to train aspiring clinical nurse managers. The development of the ACNM role allowed staff nurses the opportunity to work in a leadership role that was time limited (1 year) and designed to identify potential future nurse leaders. Over the course of the year, all participants experienced day-to-day unit management, scheduling, payroll, budgeting, productivity reporting, interviewing, and performance appraisal. The program's success was far-reaching in that several leaders were identified and promoted and a new sense of appreciation was granted to the clinical nurse managers.

Frank, B. (2002). Leader as expert. *Nursing Leadership Forum, 7,* 57–62.

A rapidly changing and uncertain health care delivery system requires well-educated nurse leaders who can work to achieve organizational missions that are appropriate for the needs of all who seek health care. Educators in undergraduate and graduate programs can use the four ways of knowing as outlined by Carper (1978) to design curricula that will prepare nursing leaders as experts.

George, V., Burke, L., Rodgers, B., Duthie, N., Hoffmann, M., et al. (2002). Developing staff nurse shared leadership behavior in professional nursing practice. *Nursing Administration Quarterly, 26*(3), 44–59.

This article describes the conceptual model shared leadership and the results from three studies that were conducted to demonstrate implementation of a shared leadership concepts program in an organized delivery system. Findings demonstrated increased staff leadership behaviors, autonomy, and improved patient outcomes. The authors assumed that shared leadership training builds skills and, when utilized by staff, would lead to increased professional nursing autonomous behavior. Study results revealed that leadership behaviors and autonomy increased after the training and continued for at least 6 months.

Greenwood, J., & Parsons, M. (2002). The evaluation of a clinical development unit leadership preparation program by focus group interviews—P. 1: Positive aspects. *Nurse Education Today, 22,* 527–533.

This article provides details of the first clinical development units (CDU) leadership preparation course, focusing on the positive data that were brought to light. A second paper focuses on the negative aspects. CDUs are clinical units where nurses strive to develop nursing practice. They attempt to promote excellence in nursing through three strategies: by providing consumer-centered care, by developing nurses who are creative and autonomous, and by improving the quality of care by reorganizing nursing work and implementing evidence-based practice. Evaluative data demonstrated that the leadership preparation course was successful in providing leaders with the skills they sought to acquire but did not allow leaders to assimilate this new knowledge.

Greenwood, J., & Parsons, M. (2002). The evaluation of a clinical development unit leadership preparation program by focus group interviews—P. 2: Negative aspects. *Nurse Education Today, 22,* 534–541.

This is the second of two papers that reports on the evaluative data of the first clinical development unit (CDU) leadership preparation program. This course was conducted over a 6-month period and consisted of six 2-day workshops. A negative aspect that caused the leadership preparation program to be changed is the high attrition rate of leaders from CDUs. After CDU training, two thirds of the leaders were "poached" by private hospitals, promoted, or left their jobs to go to school. It is now required that two leaders per clinical unit attend the course.

Haynor, P. (2002). Leader as communicator. *Nursing Leadership Forum, 7,* 77–82.

This article examines common communication factors that have an impact on leader effectiveness (language, listening, mode of delivery, and feedback) and the role of the organization, organizational culture, and group dynamics in the development of the leader as communicator. Communication, as with any skill, is a learned behavior that is honed over time. Communication is a two-way process with stimulus-response shaping future behavior. But it is even more complex when used in an organizational setting because there are multilevel communications and multiple messages, senders, and receivers, as well as competing agendas. Leaders in today's complex health care organizations must be skilled communicators to earn trust and respect. Once earned, others are willing to support the leader's vision to help make it a reality.

Hambridge, P. (1997). Learning practical leadership. *Paediatric Nursing, 9*(10), 6–7.

In this innovative nursing leadership project, participants were given the opportunity for professional development with practical content. The project attempted to explore the relationship that senior nurses and ward leaders have with their colleagues and patients. The project comprised seven main components: action learning, personal development plans, reflective diary, having a mentor, workshops, observation of care, and storytelling. The results of the project showed that ward leaders could influence the care of patients through their ability to transfer techniques, skills, and talents to other members of the team.

Hayes, L. (2002–2003). A primary care leadership programme. *Primary Health Care, 12*(10), 22–25.

The author describes a leadership program that was designed to improve health and health care. The focus was on developing strategic influencing skills in those working in health care and integrating the values and knowledge needed to function well at clinical and political levels. A person-centered approach is utilized on the assumption that learning must be experiential. Effective communication skills are vital, build meaningful relationships, and have a more positive effect.

Kenner, C., Androwich, I., & Edwards, P. (2003). Innovative educational strategies to prepare nurse executives for new leadership roles. *Nursing Administration Quarterly, 27*(2), 172–179.

The authors evaluate distance learning for nurse leaders at Excelsior College. The issue of economic costs of institutions and the economic advantages of the program are addressed. Leadership characteristics are identified and discussed with the new health-care-delivery environment in mind.

Krejci, J., & Malin, S. (1997). Impact of leadership development on competencies. *Nursing Economics, 15*(5), 235–242.

The article focuses on a study of a 3-day leadership development program. Participants, mostly nurses, had associate degrees, diplomas, master's degrees, or doctorates. The study examined the effects of leadership development on participants' perceptions of their leadership competencies and if the effects would persevere after 3 months. Participants were asked to rate their understanding and skills for each of 12 competencies. Those with a master's or higher degree rated themselves higher at the beginning of the program than the participants with associate degrees or diplomas. After 3 days of training the ratings were similar. At the 3-month follow-up, results (with a return rate of 29%) were similar to the ratings posttraining.

Krichbaum, K. (1997). Preparing students for leadership in practice. *Creative Nursing, 3*(2), 12–14.

The author describes nursing students' eagerness to learn clinical skills and view leadership education as being unnecessary. A leadership course was developed with the goal of equipping students with the skills necessary to participate in their social and political environments. The long-term goal is to empower nurses to act to improve the quality of care for their patients. The course that was developed was a combination of didactic teaching and small-group problem-solving sessions. In addition to lectures in small-group activities, the students observed leadership in action in various acute and long-term-care settings.

Krugman, M. & Smith, V. (2003). Charge nurse leadership development and evaluation. *Journal of Nursing Administration, 33*(5), 284–92.

The authors describe the development and evaluation of a permanent charge nurse role and report the outcomes of a leadership model over 4 years. The charge nurse role was developed using Kouzes and Posner's Leadership model as the theoretical framework. There were four main objectives of the developing the charge nurse role: improve charge nurse leadership, improve unit functioning, maintain patient satisfaction, and attain nurse job satisfaction. Two instruments were used to measure data, which were collected at baseline, post-implementation, and at additional time periods. Selection of charge nurses was a competitive process and viewed as a promotion.

Lemire, J. A. (2002). Leader as critical thinker. *Nursing Leadership Forum, 7,* 69–76.

A leader possesses the critical-thinking knowledge and skills that provide the framework from which complex problem solving evolves. This article explores the leader as critical thinker, including a progressive plan for integrating critical-thinking concepts and associated teaching strategies into RN to BSN and graduate curricula. To improve the critical thinking of nurses, educators must emphasize the cognitive and disposition aspects of critical thinking, promote active and sequential learning, role model critical thinking, design practica that focus on leadership and critical thinking, and conduct valid and consistent evaluations. The acquisition and application of critical thinking and problem-solving skills are progressive and refined through lifelong learning and experience.

Lemire, J. A. (2002). Preparing nurse leaders, A leadership education model. *Nursing Leadership Forum, 7*(2), 47–52.

The nursing profession continues to struggle with defining the leadership role for nursing and developing the knowledge and skills to effectively influence a tumultuous health care environment. This study describes the leadership education model (LEM). Leadership knowledge, skills, and principles that evolved from a literature search were validated through a descriptive study with responses from over 500 nursing administrators, educators, and students. Statistical analyses showed a high level of agreement on the importance of the 31 items on the tool as well as a high level of consistency for agreement between groups. The leadership profile provided the foundation for developing the LEM with six major components of a leader: visionary, expert, achiever, critical thinker, communicator, and mentor. The goal is to encourage integration of the LEM into RN to BSN and graduate curricula on a progressive learning continuum.

Lipley, N. (2003). Research shows benefit of nurse leadership training. *Nursing Management, 10*(2), 4.

The author cites research to confirm the value of nurse leadership training for both patients and staff. Data suggest that nurses who feel they have good leaders are more satisfied with their jobs. Leadership was perceived as being positive if there was teamwork and the manager had a good relationship with the staff.

Lockwood-Rayermann, S. (2003). Preceptor leadership style and the nursing practicum. *Journal of Professional Nursing, 19*(1), 32–37.

The author describes the preceptor role and how it can influence the work experience of a new nurse or student nurse. An examination and discussion of the potential preceptor's leadership style should be conducted in order to make the experience positive for the preceptor, student, and faculty. Situational leadership and the four different leadership styles identified by Hersey and Blanchard provide a useful model for faculty to identify leadership traits in preceptors. Although preceptorships are time consuming and stressful, spending time matching students to preceptors can contribute to a more positive outcome for everyone.

Mathena, K. (2002). Nursing manager leadership skills. *Journal of Nursing Administration, 32*(3), 136–42.

The author used the situational leadership model (SLT) for this research. The SLT is characterized by five component technologies that include personal mastery, mental models, building shared vision, team learning, and systems thinking. The following skills were identified as critical to the success of the nurse executive: visioning; interdisciplinary team-building workload-complexity analysis; work process analysis; stakeholder analysis; and interactive planning. The nurse managers who returned the surveys identified these five variables as being most important to the success of their role: communication, negotiation, critical thinking, conflict management, and the balance between work and home.

Mellon, S., & Nelson, P. (1998). Leadership experiences in the community for Nursing students: Redesigning education for the 21st century. *Nursing and Health Care Perspectives*, 19(2), 120–124.

The authors describe a nursing school project that took place in an alternative high school for pregnant or parenting teenage women. The nursing students' leadership project consisted of addressing health concerns and screening this population of 400 women and their 200 children who attended the nursery at the school. They planned a health fair with eight interactive workstations where various skills and topics were taught. The stations focused on the women and gave them guidance on how to care for their children. Nursing students also developed school nurse protocols and produced a teen parent handbook on health and parenting issues.

Nelson, M., Howell, J., Larson, J., & Karpiuk, K. (2001). Student outcomes of the healing web: Evaluation of a transformative model for nursing education. *Journal of Nursing Education, 40*(9), 404–12.1

The Healing Web is a transformative nursing model that would hypothetically influence specific student competencies, for example, caring abilities, leadership skills, assertiveness, and professional nursing behaviors. Students participating in the Healing Web program scored higher in caring knowing, caring courage, leadership, and assertiveness than their counterparts who participated in traditional clinical experiences. Mean leadership scores were greater for BSN students participating in the Healing Web than traditional group scores.

Pullen, M. (2003) Developing clinical leadership skills in student nurses. *Nurse Education Today, 23,* 34–39.

The author analyzes the way leadership skills are developed in the nursing curriculum. The four skills that are identified for discussion are self-knowledge, communication skills, risk taking, and keeping informed. Self-knowledge is characterized by developing interpersonal skills and reflective practice. Communication skills are developed through discussions and presentations. Risk taking involves promoting advocacy and encouraging students to think laterally. Keeping informed is important because the person with the newest and best information often prevails. It is important to minimize barriers to leadership for student nurses in order to identify potential leaders.

Scheick, D. (2002). Mastering group leadership, an active learning experience. *Journal of Psychosocial Nursing, 40*(9), 30–51.

Learning to lead therapeutic groups is an active learning experience that can be growth enhancing. This article describes the sequencing of

instruction of group theory and skills with examples from a baccalaureate nursing curriculum. Therapeutic groups are a cost-effective treatment to use with patients who are mentally ill. Group leadership ability
complements the management and negotiation skills needed in professional nursing roles. In the first clinical course during the sophomore
year, students participated in an instructor-led experiential learning
group, focusing on values clarification, peer support, and acculturation
to initial nursing roles. In the junior year, students used journal writing
to internally process, self-evaluate, and influence their own practice of
mental health nursing. In the senior year, cooperative and active learning is emphasized.

Spooner, S. H., Keenan, R., & Card, M. (1997). Determining if shared leadership is
being practiced: Evaluation methodology. *Nursing Administration Quarterly,*
22(1), 47–57.

The authors described a study that determines shared leadership
behaviors in RNs who are working in staff positions in a critical care
hospital setting. Scenarios based on clinical situations were used to
measure three shared leadership concepts: empowerment, accountability, and partnership in decision making. Many hospitals have responded to the need for management change by adopting a shared management philosophy, that is, shared governance that builds on the concepts
of participation and shared vision. The purpose of the study was to
describe the mental models of nurses after implementation of a shared
leadership model and to establish a baseline for future research.

Vance, Connie. (2002). Leader as mentor. *Nursing Leadership Forum, 7,* 83–90.

A key component of leadership development for nursing students is
mentorship. Leaders are called upon to develop others and to grow the
next generation of leaders. Through the teaching-learning role and by
serving as active mentors with students, leader-teachers can promote
leadership skill development and leadership succession in the profession.
Teaching the mentor concept as part of leadership occurs through student-teacher relationships in the classroom and in practicum experiences. Research and anecdotal studies are needed that illustrate curricular, course, and programmatic inclusion of mentorship and the benefits
and outcomes of this educational approach to leadership development.

Wissmann, J., Hauck, B., & Clawson, J. (2002). Assessing nurse graduate leadership outcomes, the "typical day" format. *Nurse Educator, 27*(1), 32–36.

This article presents the development and implementation of a leadership outcome assessment model. Leadership outcome assessment consists

of five phases: identification of nursing graduate leadership outcomes; curricular enhancement for development of nursing graduate leadership outcomes; development of leadership outcome assessment activities and assessment tools; selection and training of external assessors and student orientation; and a culminating leadership outcome assessment day. Analysis of assessment tools that were completed by the external assessors and self-assessment tools completed by students provided assurance that participants could demonstrate the leadership capabilities needed for practice.

Wolf, M. S. (1996). Changes in leadership styles as a function of a four-day leadership training institute for nurse managers: A perspective on continuing education program evaluation. *Journal of Continuing Education in Nursing, 27,* 245–52.

This study measured changes in knowledge and application of the Hersey and Blanchard model of leadership styles and leadership style adaptability after a 4-day management training session. Leadership styles refer to four patterns of communication the leader may use: telling, selling, participating, and delegating. After the training, participants were able to obtain short-term changes in their primary leadership styles that are responsive to the subordinates' level of readiness. The dominant leadership style of 50% of participants prior to the training was "selling." Only a small number of participants (4) identified delegating as their primary style before the training; 20 (out of 144) identified delegating after the training.

Index